Brand Hollywood

From the growth in merchandising and product placement to the rise of the movie franchise, branding has become central to the modern blockbuster economy. In a wide-ranging analysis focusing on companies such as Disney, Dolby, Paramount, New Line and, in particular, Warner Bros., *Brand Hollywood* provides the first sustained examination of the will-to-brand in the contemporary movie business. Outlining changes in the marketing and media environment during the 1990s and 2000s, Paul Grainge explores how the logic of branding has propelled specific kinds of approaches to the status and selling of film. Analysing the practice of branding, the poetics of corporate logos, and the industrial politics surrounding the development of branded texts, properties and spaces – including franchises ranging from *Looney Tunes* to *Lord of the Rings* and *Harry Potter* to *The Matrix* – Grainge considers the relation of branding to the emergent principle of 'total entertainment'.

Employing an interdisciplinary method drawn from film studies, cultural studies and advertising and media studies, *Brand Hollywood* demonstrates the complexities of selling entertainment in the global media moment, providing a fresh and engaging perspective on branding's significance for commercial film and the industrial culture from which it is produced.

Paul Grainge is Associate Professor of Film Studies at the University of Nottingham. He is the author of *Monochrome Memories: Nostalgia and Style in Retro America* (2002), the editor of *Memory and Popular Film* (2003), and co-author of *Film Histories: An Introduction and Reader* (2007).

Brand Hollywood

Selling entertainment in a global media age

Paul Grainge

Routledge
Taylor & Francis Group

LONDON AND NEW YORK

First published 2008
by Routledge
2 Park Square, Milton Park, Abingdon, Oxon, OX14 4RN

Simultaneously published in the USA and Canada
by Routledge
270 Madison Ave, New York, NY 10016

Routledge is an imprint of the Taylor & Francis Group, an informa business

© 2008 Paul Grainge

Typeset in Baskerville by Bookcraft Ltd, Stroud, Gloucestershire
Printed and bound in Great Britain by Antony Rowe Ltd,
Chippenham, Wiltshire

British Library Cataloguing in Publication Data
A catalogue record for this book is available
from the British Library

Library of Congress Cataloging in Publication Data
Grainge, Paul, 1972–
Brand Hollywood : selling entertainment in a global media age / Paul
Grainge.
  p. cm.
  Includes bibliographical references and index.
  1. Motion pictures–United States–Marketing. 2. Corporate image.
  3. Brand name products. I. Title.
PN1995.9.M29G73 2008
384'.830973–dc22   2007016784

ISBN10: 0-415-35404-8 (hbk)
ISBN10: 0-415-35405-6 (pbk)

ISBN13: 978-0-415-35404-2 (hbk)
ISBN13: 978-0-415-35405-9 (pbk)

To Claire,
and in loving memory of my Mum

Contents

Illustrations

I am indebted to the companies and archives below for permission to reproduce the following images. In particular, I appreciate the time that Dolby Laboratories spent capturing stills from their promotional trailers on my behalf. Dolby Trailers are copyrighted by Dolby Laboratories, Inc; Dolby and the double-D logo are registered trademarks of Dolby Laboratories.

Acknowledgements

I began this book in 2002 and would like to thank, from the outset, the University of Nottingham for a generous research grant that helped kick-start the project and for two well-timed sabbaticals at the beginning and the end of the writing process. In helping the book to completion, I am very grateful to the Arts and Humanities Research Council for a matching leave award that proved crucial.

In writing this book, I have been helped by a number of people. Colleagues within the Institute of Film and Television Studies at the University of Nottingham (and within the School of American and Canadian Studies) continue to provide a blessedly convivial working environment. Of those who shared thoughts on branding, and matters arising, I'd like to thank Roberta Pearson, Gianluca Sergi, Julian Stringer, Sharon Monteith, Peter Urquhart, Mark Gallagher and Jake Smith, as well as Mark Jancovich, Eithne Quinn and Rebecca Feasey. I also wish to express my thanks to James Lyons, Steve Neale, Robert Burgoyne, Geoff Smith, Richard Maltby, and a couple of anonymous readers, who all read drafts of key, or otherwise troublesome, chapters and helped me refine my thoughts at an early stage. Within the entertainment industry, I am particularly grateful to Ioan Allen for taking the time to read my chapter on Dolby and to his assistant Julie Morgan for providing Dolby trailer stills. At Warner Bros., Nils Montan and Barbara Brogliatti were kind enough to reply to my, sometimes begging, e-mails. In shepherding the book throughout, I owe much to my editors, Rebecca Barden and Natalie Foster, and to the excellent team at Routledge. Early versions of two chapters have appeared previously. Chapter 3 appeared as 'Branding Hollywood: Studio Logos and the Aesthetics of Memory and Hype' in *Screen* vol. 45, no. 4, 2004: 344–62, and chapter 4 appeared in a different guise as 'Selling Spectacular Sound: Dolby and the Unheard History of Technical Trademarks' in Jay Beck and Tony Grajeda (eds), *Lowering the Boom: New Essays on the History and Theory of Film Sound*. My thanks go to Oxford University Press and the University of Illinois Press, respectively, for permission to reprint.

This book could not have been written without the support of family in both Nottingham and Portsmouth. Mike and June Morris, together with Joanna Morris and Mark Kirton, have been a constant source of help and merriment, while Catherine, Andy and Thomas Redmond have been endlessly hospitable on the

South Coast. I know that Andy and Mark will be particularly pleased to find out what I have been doing on those sabbaticals. As ever, the love and support of my parents, David and Jane Grainge, form the bedrock of where I am today. Very sadly, my Mum passed away, aged 56, towards the end of my writing *Brand Holly-wood*. As a person, she was someone of exceptional warmth, devoted to her family. While Mum would have no doubt preferred me to use simpler words in this book, she would also have continued, on a regular basis, to beat me and Dad at Scrabble. I miss her greatly but feel comforted that she had opportunity to know my son, Daniel, who was born in 2005. Cheeky and determined, Daniel is a source of constant joy and I never tire of him racing into my office to bash the computer keyboard. It is, in fact, my favourite part of the day. For Daniel, and for everything else in my life, I owe the greatest debt to my wife Claire who, with everlasting patience, lets me know when it is time to stop working. She is the love of my life and it is for this reason that I dedicate this book to her, and to the memory of my wonderful Mum.

Introduction

Entertainment economies

In 1978, Hugh Hefner held a fundraising party at the Playboy mansion to help rebuild the famous 'HOLLYWOOD' sign. While declared a cultural historic monument five years before, the sign was nevertheless ravaged by termites and prone to collapsing. Since the sign first appeared, put up in 1923 to advertise a new housing development, the white fifty-foot letters of 'HOLLYWOODLAND' had been slowly crumbling. While the end of the sign quickly disintegrated, never to be replaced, the wind and damp had taken its toll on various other letters. In 1949 the wind blew over the H causing the sign to tilt precariously. Over the years the D also fell down, the first O disintegrated, the third O tumbled down Mount Lee and someone set fire to the second L. Although bestowing the sign with landmark status in 1973 gave it legal protection from those who would destroy or cinder its frame, the letters remained in a state of disrepair. As the quintessential symbol of Los Angeles and the American film industry, Hefner's party was part of a drive by entertainment industry celebrities and the Hollywood Chamber of Commerce to restore the sign.[1] As a result of fundraising activity the flimsy sign, made initially from canvas, plywood and telephone poles, was replaced with 194 tonnes of concrete, sunk with steel beams and sheet metal (Lelyveld 2002). Unveiled at a diamond jubilee gala in 1978, a year after *Star Wars* (1977) had inaugurated the effects-laden era of the merchandised blockbuster, much excitement focused on the techno-display of outdoor lasers that were made to bounce, dance and explode across the renovated letters. As a form of brand spectacle, the new Hollywood landmark was, in more ways than one, a sign of the times.

From its state of dilapidation in the 1970s the Hollywood sign swiftly became a trademarked property. With the extension of intellectual property provisions in the United States during the 1980s, the Hollywood Chamber of Commerce trademarked the image of the sign in order to generate revenue from the licensing of merchandise, advertising and film rights. These funds were used in part to help pay for the maintenance of the sign. They were also linked to a wider impulse within the city of Los Angeles to appropriate images from Hollywood's past in the name of urban renewal. This included billion-dollar ventures such as the Hollywood Redevelopment Project launched in 1986 under the auspices of Los Angeles City Council and Universal CityWalk, a controlled leisure space opened in 1993 by

Universal's parent company, MCA. Each served to create spectacular commercial landscapes based on Hollywood mythology and the malling of popular entertainment. If these projects made concrete 'the triangular relationship between LA, Hollywood, and hegemonic consumerism' (Stenger 2001: 70), the Hollywood sign became an integral part of the city's brand economy in this context.

Accordingly, the sign was fenced off and protected to maintain its signifying lustre and an elaborate security system installed in 1994 to warn off trespassers (Pool 1994). As with any trademark, commercial signs can acquire new meanings when appropriated and recoded for particular ends. The Hollywood sign had been transformed on a number of occasions since receiving landmark status, formally rented to companies such as Fox, Pepsi and Paramount who adjusted letters to advertise specific films and products, and unofficially altered in other cases – made to read 'HOLLYWEED' in recognition of a new state marijuana law, 'HOLYWOOD' during a papal visit and 'OLLYWOOD' in the midst of the Iran-Contra scandal. If these instances make literal what Rosemary Coombe terms the 'struggles that take place on the terrain of the sign' (Coombe 1998: 86) – describing the means by which social groups and corporate actors seek to adapt signs, texts and images to their own agendas – new forms of surveillance, together with tighter rules about commercial renting, limited the possibilities for symbolic appropriation. From a rickety advertisement in the 1920s to a national landmark in the 1970s, the contemporary history of the Hollywood sign is suggestive of the means by which logos and trademarks have become forms of guarded property. While the iconicity of the sign is long established, it has been used more deliberately since the 1980s to 'brand' the cultural geography of Los Angeles and the entertainment industry; it has become part of the city's landscape of fantasy, an architectural monument to the history of movie making that at once obscures the fact that film production has largely dispersed from Hollywood to a range of locations and factories around the world.

The last point is significant in connecting the practice of branding in the film industry, the focus of this book, to the central questions that occupy contemporary brand critique. Within the growing critical literature on brands, the cultural work of logos, signs and trademarks has often been read symptomatically, an aspect of the thickening hegemony of global capitalism and of the social disjunction represented in the production and promotion of goods. For Naomi Klein the pervasive trend across manufacturing industries to exploit cheap labour markets, often using overseas sweatshops and otherwise casualized workforces, has been wilfully occluded by massive increases in advertising expenditure by companies seeking to produce not 'things' but 'brands', which Klein associates with 'a profound shift in corporate priorities' (Klein 2000: 25). This relates more broadly to issues concerning the restructuring of capitalism, the enhanced power of multinational corporations and to neo-liberal ideologies which, as well as burnishing policy frameworks of deregulation and free trade, have contributed to fundamental shifts in the constitutive relationship of production to consumption. Jean and John Comaroff write: 'Neo-liberalism aspires, in its ideology and practice, to intensify the abstractions inherent in capitalism itself: to separate labor power from its human context, to replace society with the market, to build a universe out of aggregated transactions' (Comaroff and Comaroff 2001: 15). In a cultural moment where, it is feared, the power of the market is overcoming the very basis of democracy and citizenship, and where the productive labour of real people and the objective materiality of actual commodities have less significance than the 'intangible value' created through marketing, branding has been read as a symbolic locus of capitalist abstraction, rendering more opaque, or spectral, 'the workings of power, the distribution of wealth, the meaning of politics and national belonging' (ibid.).

Within anti-capitalist manifestos such as Klein's *No Logo*, a resulting political impetus has been to re-embed brand signifiers within contexts of power. While Klein's focus on corporate awareness campaigns, consumer boycotts, street protests and culture jamming has been criticized for assuming the style radicalism of the culture which it ultimately berates (Heath and Potter 2005), a baseline of contemporary critical activism has been to subvert and demystify the symbolic economy of branding. This leads to wider debates about the nature of commodity culture and more generally to leftist politics. While some lament the commercially-saturated atmosphere of contemporary culture, seeing it as a fundamental threat to the critical conditions of civil society (McChesney 1999), others reject the fallacy of a mythic public domain tainted by commercial speech, instead focusing on the struggles of meaning and identity that take place through, and in relation to, commodification and its discourses and practices (Coombe 1998; Jenkins 2006). It is not my intention to trace these debates in full. They provide a context, however, for situating the critical primacy given to brands, specifically the relation of branding to portraits of social transformation associated with shifts in the organization of consumption during the 1980s and 1990s.

Branding has been linked to structural changes, or intensifications, in the basis of consumer culture, which is especially associated with the move from Fordism to post-Fordism in the last third of the twentieth century. As a critical label, Fordism describes a mode of production based around the factory, the rationalization of labour and the standardization of goods. With the exhaustion of mass production systems in the post-World War II period, brought to a head by the crisis that hit advanced capitalist states in the 1970s, it is argued that more flexible models of industrial operation emerged, characterized by the increasing geographic mobility of financial capital and production processes. This is associated with a contiguous move towards niche marketing, the establishment of global production and distribution networks enabling businesses to respond more effectively to rapid transitions in consumer fashion and taste. According to Michael Curtin, a 'dialectical relationship between processes of globalization and fragmentation' has been duly created within cultural and consumer industries, marketing organizing its approach to audiences in terms of mass markets *and* specialized taste segments (Curtin 1996). While 'global branding' has become a means through which advertisers seek to construct international consumption communities for products and commodities, this is cross-cut by the need to respond flexibly to cultural preferences and local differences. Whatever the dynamics of homogenization and diversity involved, the driving seat of capitalism in the post-Fordist system, so it is argued, 'is no longer occupied by the heavy engineers and production managers but rather by the marketing directors and design consultants, the retailers and the producers of "concepts"' (Slater 1997: 174). Across retail, service, manufacturing and media industries in the 1980s and 1990s, branding assumed new currency in the attempt both to manage the relationship between products and consumers and to structure and stabilize global markets.

The film industry can be situated in this context. Indeed, it has been seen as an exemplary model of capitalist restructuring in its move from a studio system to a flexibly specialized part of a global image business (Storper 1989; Aksoy and Robins 1992).[2] Aida Hozic suggests that between the 1960s and the 1990s Hollywood's importance as a locus of film manufacturing declined, linked to what she calls the 'hollowing out' of studios as production centres and the transferral of power to those in corporate hierarchies with responsibility for distribution, financing and marketing (Hozic 2001). If Hollywood's contemporary history is underlined by the restructuring of global media industries – studios now part of consolidated media empires where profits are derived in large part from the control of royalties, licensing fees and the rights to brand names and characters – the phenomenon of 'runaway' film production has been matched by investment in decontextualized media signifiers that erase and obscure the traces of labour, especially that of offshore 'below-the-line' screen work. Rosemary Coombe put this well: 'As production moves elsewhere and the industrial landscape fades from public view ... the power of the corporation in the imaginary space of post-industriality is most evident in the exchange value of the brand name, the corporate logo, the advertising lingo – the "distinction" these signifiers assume in the market' (Coombe 1998: 144).

While Coombe speaks in general terms about the increased flow of commercial signification within postmodern culture, her comment is relevant to Hollywood and its place in a burgeoning global entertainment complex. Of course, studios have long used the exchange value of brand names as a basis of corporate power, principally the names of stars which can 'open' a film and thereby reduce market risk. Competitive distinction has also been established, however, through a rich interplay of logos and trademarks, especially significant in a blockbuster economy where licensing and cross-promotional tie-ins establish mega-budget movies as cultural and commercial events. Just as they establish market buzz, brand signifiers operate in residual ways, sustaining the industrial aura of Hollywood in more general terms. While the studio logos that initiate credit sequences continue to associate the Hollywood majors with the 'guarantee' of superior production values, the Hollywood sign might also be seen as a small but suggestive facet of the 'place myth' of the entertainment industry, territorializing the image of an industry that is reproduced and regulated across global manufacturing and export zones. It is here that we return to issues of abstraction. If the screen industry is defined by what Toby Miller *et al.* call the 'new international division of cultural labour'

(Miller *et al.* 2001), describing Hollywood's control of international labour markets, co-productions and other globally dispersed operations, the apparatus of brand promotion used by Hollywood (from product-specific stars and marketing to industry-specific logos, ceremonies and hillside landmarks) consecrates a point of industrial origin even as the meaning of 'Hollywood' has become more opaque in terms of its material and symbolic geography.

Within brand critique, it is the abstractions and power asymmetries inherent within contemporary economic systems – specifically the *obfuscations* of production that come from outsourcing and the *enchantments* of promotion that are driven by the growth in advertising, marketing and product design – that give corporate logos, trademarks and brand names their political potency. According to Jim McGuigan, 'There could hardly be anything more significant than the ubiquitous and exploitative brands if we are interested in the ruses of culture and power' (McGuigan 2004: 29). This understands branding as a defining feature of 'neo-liberal globalization'. While this framework of analysis can be applied to the film business, underpinning questions of hegemony as they relate to the increasingly borderless industrial and textual economies of 'American' film (Miller *et al.* 2001; Keil 2001), my approach in this book is different. Rather than establish branding as a metaphor for the injuries of global capitalism, as for McGuigan, or examine particular kinds of media property or corporation in the name of such critique, my aims are more modest and more situated; I explore how the contemporary film business has sought to adjust itself to changes in the entertainment environment during the 1990s and 2000s. Examining the circumstances in which branding has been taken up, articulated and implemented by the motion picture industry, the questions that emerge from this book are less obviously concerned with the machinations and cynicism of brand marketing (without denying that such exist) than with the scope and nuances of Hollywood's *promotional culture of production*. To be more specific: in what respect has the discourse of branding coalesced within formations of industrial talk, sense and behaviour, and with what implications for the status and selling of film? What modalities does branding assume in cinematic culture and what do these modes reveal or imply about the patterning of film experience? To what degree is branding a mark of corporate power and authority, or suggestive of uncertainties and contradictions in the attempt to manage the relationship between products and consumers? In all of the respects mentioned above, to what degree is the will-to-brand historically new or particular in industrial-aesthetic terms?

Following Charles Acland's call for a 'bid for precision' in contemporary cultural analysis (Acland 2003: 37), I seek to move away from the generalizing impulse, marked within strains of political economy and popular critique, to equate brand marketing with the impoverishment of cultural and political life. Whether in aesthetic laments about product placement (Crispin Miller 1990) or in activist critiques of multinational logos (Klein 2000), the polemical force of anti-brand positions often depends on rather arbitrary divisions being drawn between 'art' and 'commerce', 'citizen' and 'consumer'. In short, they are inclined, in the words of Rosemary Coombe, towards a 'seductive but ultimately untenable nostalgia' for a world set apart from the commodity-driven culture in which we live (Coombe 1998: 271).[3] Rather than condemn or be unduly fatalistic about the commodified relations that shape contemporary social life, it is necessary, instead, to examine the historically specific conjunctures in which interests and meanings are brought into being and actively negotiated. Within cultural studies, this often concentrates upon the diversity of attitudes and practices that exist among consumers, audiences and subordinate social groups. However, we must also consider with equal sensitivity to context and complexity the interests and meanings worked out within the field of cultural production. With respect to my interests, this means better understanding the *contingencies* of branding as a discursive and material practice.

Critically, *Brand Hollywood* seeks to widen and deepen the analysis of branding in the contemporary motion picture business, moving beyond default cries about the commercial debasement of film and the routine, if understandable, preoccupation with Disney, to examine the import and inscriptions of branding across a range of institutional sites – within trade discussion, corporate strategy, logo design, trademark licensing, and the management of film libraries, blockbuster properties and multiplex exhibition. Drawing specific attention to the gestalt of 'total entertainment' that emerged in the 1990s, I analyse the *practice, poetics* and *politics* of branding as a multivalent feature of the diversified and franchised entertainment economy in which films circulate. These issues ultimately focus on Hollywood's position in a global media market that has seen seismic shifts in corporate organization and 'convergence' transforming the landscape of media in which dominant definitions of cinematic entertainment take shape.

Branding matters: marketing, synergy, rights

Branding is hardly new to the film industry. Historically, it can be traced back to the use of company trademarks in the early 1900s and the formalization of product branding around stars and serials in the 1910s (Bakker 2005; Desser and Jowett 2000). Ever since branding techniques emerged in the late nineteenth century as a means of differentiating products within an expanding consumer marketplace, the film industry has sought to adapt modern selling techniques for its own needs (Staiger 1990). While branding has a history, its current cultural visibility is closely tied to the growing role that multinational entertainment corporations have assumed in contemporary life. When it was reported in May 2005 that revenue from the *Star Wars* franchise had reached $20 billion – a figure that exceeded the gross domestic product of Bulgaria, Libya, Lebanon and the large majority of African states – the paradigmatic status of Hollywood within the global economy was never more apparent (Smith 2005). If the consolidated entertainment business can be seen as a flagship for the organization of global capitalism – entertainment becoming the second largest US export sector after aerospace in the 1990s – branding has become linked to key transformations and developments within contemporary cultural industries.

This is especially marked in a period where changes in the entertainment economy, proceeding along the axes of globalization and media consolidation, have levelled effects on the way that the commodity of film has been conceived. As Richard Maltby suggests, the expansion of ancillary markets such as television, videotape, DVD and pay-per-view has required 'that movie production be seen as the creation of entertainment software that can be viewed through several different windows and transported to several different platforms maintained by the other divisions of tightly diversified media corporations' (Maltby 1998: 24). The migration of film texts across media has been matched by accelerated traffic of commodities across geographic borders, intensifying since 1993 when Hollywood's international revenue exceeded domestic rental figures for the first time. According to Charles Acland, increasing reliance on revenue from both international audiences and ancillary markets has cultivated an understanding of the film commodity as a 'mutating global product' (Acland 2003). Branding has assumed new strategic import in this context, holding media mutations in place while extending a film's mobile commercial afterlife.

In accounting for change, there have emerged three major critical approaches to the discussion of branding and film. These might be summarized as the treatment of *marketing*, *synergy* and *rights*. While these are interlaid with more particular concerns, from the role of stardom to the function of movie trailers, branding has become an especial point of analysis for treatments of cinema and the cultural industries in the 1980s and 1990s, a period widely regarded as heralding key transformations in the organization of media. Issues of film marketing are, of course, as long as the history of the medium itself. However, the systematic expansion of marketing research since the late 1970s, co-linked to the conglomeration of the movie business, the increased power of marketing departments within film companies and the precipitous increase in marketing budgets in the last few decades, has given marketing acute industrial as well as critical significance. If, as Tiu Lukk comments, a modern 'marketing campaign is tackled with the same zeal and methodical planning as a general preparing for an invasion' (Lukk 1997: ix), it has brought to focus its assault strategies. As theorists of film marketing have shown, this is not simply a case of instigating a brand barrage. Although event movies are generally associated with saturation advertising and co-ordinated promotional tie-ins and merchandise, the 'dialectic of globalization and fragmentation' has given rise to flexible marketing strategies that involve the adaptation of global blockbuster campaigns to local marketing contexts, as well as specific initiatives in niche marketing (Danan 1995). In the latter case, companies such as Miramax have used media controversy and other publicity techniques to carve out profitable crossover markets for 'quality indie' film, amongst other specialized products (Wyatt 1998; Perren 2001). As these issues suggest, a key strain of brand analysis has been to consider how films (and film companies) are variably *positioned*, relating to particular, institutionally produced, conceptions of the domestic and international audience.

Marketing does not simply occur after a movie has been made in this context; it can shape the aesthetic identity of film from its conception. This has formed another strain of marketing analysis, critics examining the way that marketing considerations impact on movie style and meaning. In a multidimensional analysis of Hollywood film in the 1990s, Thomas Austin describes the 'industrially motivated hybridity' of commercial cinema, examining the different 'invitations to view' that coalesce around a text and the 'discursive formulations' that bear upon a film's generic identity (Austin 2002). Branding, here, relates to expressions of cinematic 'hype' and to the purposefully fluid means by which films address different kinds of audience at once. This argument differs from the critique of 'high concept' film offered by Justin Wyatt, stressing the singularity of 'bold, marketable images [that] are designed to target a specific audience and to convey a strong image carrying film through all the release windows' (Wyatt 1994: 108). Although Wyatt is concerned like Austin with the plurality of textual meaning in contemporary film culture – marketable film content flowing into other texts and commercial venues such as soundtracks and music videos – branding is linked in Wyatt's argument to the modular intrusion of 'marketing aesthetics' within film narrative. While Austin demonstrates how production, marketing and reception inform one another as processes, Wyatt establishes marketing as a key determinant of movie style, an expression of cinematic excess reflecting the 'corporate authorship' of Hollywood film in the 1980s and 1990s.

Within marketing approaches, branding is an important, but also often implicit, feature of discussion. The term comes more forcibly to surface in the related consideration of synergy. As in Wyatt's analysis, this connects developments in film style with broad transformations in the entertainment industry, specifically the consolidation and streamlining of media behemoths such as Time Warner (at the time of writing, owner of Warner Bros. and New Line), Viacom (Paramount, DreamWorks), Disney (Walt Disney Pictures, Touchstone Pictures, Miramax), the News Corporation (Twentieth Century Fox), Sony (Columbia-TriStar, MGM/UA) and NBC Universal. As a concept, synergy is best described as a principle of cross-promotion whereby companies seek to integrate and disseminate their products through a variety of media and consumer channels, enabling 'brands' to travel through an integrated corporate structure. Extending the borders of film to other platforms and commodities, either managed by commercial partners or by other corporate divisions, branding creates the reproducible iconography that can help extend the 'experience' of consumable entertainment, transforming film into a 'branded media property'. As Naomi Klein suggests, 'The rush to branding has been most dramatic in the film industry … Newly merged entertainment conglomerates are always looking for threads to sew together their disparate holdings in cross-promotional webs and, for the most part, that thread is the celebrity generated by Hollywood blockbusters' (Klein 2000: 44).

While much discussed, synergy has practical difficulties that are often ignored in brand criticism. The decentralized nature of companies like Time Warner, for example, has often set different corporate divisions against each other rather than unify them for co-ordinated brand attacks. As Henry Jenkins points out, 'Collaborations, even with the same companies, are harder to achieve than we might imagine looking at top-down charts mapping media ownership. The closer to the ground you get, the more media companies look like dysfunctional families' (Jenkins 2004: 37). In a related vein, licensing and merchandising partners such as toy manufacturers Hasbro and Mattel have periodically cooled towards the promise of 'toyetic' blockbusters, unsettled by the high premiums and overproduction of stock accompanying event movies such as *Batman Returns* (1992) and *Star Wars: Episode 1: The Phantom Menace* (1999). Nevertheless, market synergy became a powerful concept for media operations in the 1990s, Disney becoming its arch corporate practitioner (Wasko 2001). If contemporary cinema is defined by the migration of texts across media, branding has become central to the analysis of films' extended commercial environment, as well as to the spaces created through, and in relation to, the cultural lexicon of film. From the translation of Hollywood blockbusters into video games and theme park rides (King 2000) to the creation of spatial fantasies such as studio stores (Simensky 1998), megaplex developments (Acland 2003), restaurant chains such as Planet Hollywood (Stenger 1997), and company-built towns like Disney's Celebration (Ross 1999), synergy has become a basis for examining the particularities of contemporary entertainment spectacle. Raising issues of corporate ideology and power, the concept is also linked to questions of media textuality and consumption, in particular the immersive and interactive experience of film and the possibility that (movie) brands are, in some way, inhabitable.

Ultimately, the status of any brand is secured by its legal recognition as intellectual property. Regimes of law have become a different point of departure for brand critique in this regard. Celia Lury, for instance, connects legal infrastructures of copyright and trademark to particular models of cultural reproduction, suggesting that branding is linked to the exploitation of new technologies of replication and an accordant shift in emphasis from a regime of rights based around copyright (emphasizing originality and authorship) towards that of trademark (focusing more centrally on reproducibility and 'exhibition value'). Branding, she suggests, emerges as an increasingly significant production strategy in a market where the basis of commercial, legal and cultural authority has changed (Lury 1993, 2004). This not only affects the production of cultural work, witnessing the increase, for example, of titles and characters designed to be licensed across other products, but also shapes rights of ownership in other areas, such as the legal protections given to star image (Gaines 1991). It is in this climate that members of the Hollywood and global sporting elite can lay claim to themselves as brands (public personae figured as an exclusive property right) and that animated characters such as Mickey Mouse and Bugs Bunny represent more secure forms of image property for studios who no longer 'own' stars in a strict or contractual sense.

The legal affirmation of cultural rights should not be seen to foreclose the signifi-cance given to any particular image, logo, slogan or brand name. As Rosemary Coombe suggests, commodified texts remain discursive properties and are subject to 'multiple social authorings' (Coombe 1998: 38). If intellectual property has a cultural life, the meaning of a brand is not simply determined by those who circu-late and co-ordinate mass media representations but is also forged in cultural instances where texts, symbols and images are used by social agents, interpreted by audiences and taken up by fan groups in potentially unforeseen ways. This has wider resonance for the analysis of marketing and synergy, raising questions about the modes of resistance, appropriation and recoding that attach themselves to commodified forms. While it is important to recognize monopolies of power in the field of representation, brand signification remains a source for the construction and contestation of meaning; it does not position goods or sustain commercial mutations in ways that are ever straightforward or uncomplicated. Brands are instead a locus of rich symbolic activity, 'simultaneously participating in a poetics and politics driven by social groups with differential abilities to influence the complexes of signifying forms within which they have agency' (ibid.: 26).

My point in briefly summarizing these approaches to branding and film is not to claim any one as my own. While concerned with questions of marketing, synergy and rights, *Brand Hollywood* is situated in and between these critical vectors and the respective concentration they bring to the promotion, permeability and protection of media content. Following the work of Charles Acland, I adopt a model of cultural critique that is concerned with analysing shifts in the understanding and experience of cinematic entertainment, one that seeks to build up 'an inventory of contexts, sites, dispositions, and knowledge that make up the everyday life of popular film culture in our historical situation' (Acland 2003: 17). This extends the discussion of branding beyond specific films and their marketing campaigns, beyond strict business histories, and beyond critical accounts anxious to decide whether branding represents the domination of commercial signification or contains within it possibilities for consumer resistance. Instead, it takes stock of the specific forms of discourse that have become productive within industry common sense and have propelled changes in the selling of filmed entertainment. Acland suggests that if 'we are to begin to understand our cultural environment we need an accounting of the kind of intellectual production that occurs within industrial ranks' (ibid.: 32). This includes ideas about culture that, he argues, circulate among industrial contexts but are also acted upon and form the basis of decisions about what films are made and the parameters of when, how and where they are consumed.

Acland's wider project is to expose what he calls 'some recent historical traces that have formed an *episteme* of popular entertainment and the global audience' (ibid.: 14). Crucially, he argues that a new understanding of movies and moviegoing emerged in the mid-1980s, mobilizing a set of discourses about film's intermedia and international tendencies that have been subsequently worked out in relation to specific sites such as the motion picture theatre. Indeed, Acland's analysis of the megaplex in the 1990s provides a means of examining the circulation of ideas about public film consumption and the desire to shape and stabilize global audiences. He writes: 'Around talk of national culture, global culture, new media, the entertainment business and leisure pursuits are layers of sedimented images, sounds, ideas and metaphors. These are not only a list of artifacts but also practices appended to those artifacts' (ibid.: 14). If this speaks of the elements of language and logic that assemble around popular film culture – Acland draws attention, for example, to 'theming' within commercial entertainment venues, a mode of organizing space in ways that help reconnect cinemagoing with other kinds of leisure practice – the logic of branding has become a powerful 'sedimented trace' in media cultural thought and practice; it has become an artifact of market(ing) knowledge lodged within current understanding of cinema *as event*. The branding of filmed entertainment is shaped by ideas of the global audience in this respect, but also by the concept of the 'new consumer', industrial assumptions of passive mass consumption giving way to paradigms of audience (inter)activity in media time and space. In a series of ways, branding has become a more deliberate means through which film is both discussed within corporate reports, trade journals and entertainment news, and encountered through the media 'interface' of logos, trademarks and brand signifiers (Lury 2004).

In a fundamental sense, branding underwrites what Acland calls the 'permanent marketing campaign' in contemporary cinematic culture, an enduring promotional mode that can be seen as an expression of Hollywood's industrial prowess, in one sense, but also potentially of its paranoia. If, as Tom Shone suggests, the fortunes of the motion picture business since the 1980s have come to resonate 'somewhere in the vague ballpark between sparkling good health and imminent demise' (Shone 2004: 151), the concept of industrial crisis has never been far away from the giddiest celebrations of Hollywood's market success. In the 1980s, the perception of crisis was especially parsed in relation to anxieties about the practice of cinemagoing, brought home (quite literally) by the expansion of video and the perceived inadequacy of dingy theatre screens. In the 1990s, any satisfaction about the resurgence in movie attendance, sparked by the return of distributors to the exhibition business in 1986, was matched by renewed concern about the steep escalation of production and marketing costs, the average movie budget rising from $38.75 million in 1990 to $75.6 million in 1997, reaching $96 million by 2005 (Bart 1999; Holson 2006). As a percentage figure, Hollywood budgets rose by 60 per cent in real terms during the 1990s, marketing budgets doubling. Unease about these sharp investment hikes was exacerbated by industry-wide overproduction, too many films competing for screen space in a market where success was precariously tied to a film's performance in the all-important opening weekend (Connor 2000; Shone 2004). As ever, Jack Valenti was a reliable barometer of crisis perception. In 1998, it seemed palpable to the President of the Motion Picture Association of America (MPAA) that while cinemagoing had not been affected by the 'intrusions' of alternative media – what he summarized as 'VCR, laser discs, VCDs, CD-ROMs, cable and TV stations, sporting events, satellite home delivery, optic fiber, digital magic, the World Wide Web' – it remained the case that 'costs remain a great shaggy beast prowling the movie forest, a fiscal Godzilla slouching towards our future' (Valenti 1998). To Valenti, the film industry was distinguished in the 1990s by 'a terrible confluence of hope and terror', the powerful resurgence of the movie business tempered by escalating budgetary costs and the profit-dinting spectre of digital piracy.

The permanent marketing campaign emerged within this broad picture of uncertainty about the cultural and fiscal stability of the film commodity. As a term, it suggests how marketing, and the rationale of branding, became intrinsic to the activities of studios, technology companies, theatrical exhibitors, entertainment journalists, commercial retailers and consumer industry partners in serving to instil 'the promotion of a general interest and involvement with the newness of cinematic texts as an expression of contemporary living' (Acland 2003: 79). In this context, brand marketing was no longer aligned with the promotion of discrete motion pictures; it became linked to the reformulation of public and domestic film culture at large, heralding a new gestalt of 'total entertainment'. Acland suggests that 'we are in the era of a permanent marketing campaign, where the selling of an entertainment environment is ongoing, an activity punctuated by commodity texts. The extension of film marketing is also a function of the widening life cycle of film texts, drumming up audiences as works pass from one territory to another, from one medium to another' (ibid.: 77). If movie production is now largely about the creation of entertainment software, the permanent marketing campaign can be seen as a platform for the patterning of activity within contemporary film culture; in Acland's terminology, it 'becomes a mode of experiencing and understanding a wider environment of entertainment, and a world of new images, sounds, and specially fabricated sites' (ibid.: 79).

This book is specifically concerned with cinematic 'images, sounds and sites' as they have become a locus of brand activity. It looks at how branding has come to 'make sense' to corporate actors within the entertainment industry and how this has propelled specific kinds of approach to the status and selling of film. My analysis is roughly bracketed by the years 1995 and 2003, a period associated with proclamations about a 'new economy' (and its discontents) and to which the gospel of branding became closely identified. For much of this period, at least until the dot-com crash in 2001, the US economy witnessed an unprecedented boom. Rapid growth in gross domestic product, labour productivity and investment, matched with sky-rocketing equity prices and personal/corporate debt, fuelled an explosion of consumption. In this context, branding moved to the heart of marketing as a discipline, organizing the exchange between producers and consumers through its co-ordination of information, image and media. For Thomas Frank, the idea of 'the brand' formed part of the intellectual basis of neoliberalism at the end of the 1990s, a discursive symptom of 'the general belief among opinion-makers that there is something natural, something divine, something inherently democratic about markets' (Frank 2000: 15). What I have loosely termed the 'global media age' relates to a series of shifts in the general understanding of economics, markets, and of the relation between production and consumption at the turn of the twenty-first century. However, it is also defined more precisely by mergers and acquisitions in the cultural industries, driven by the emergent logic of 'convergence'. For my purpose, this is emblematized by the merger between Time Warner and Turner Broadcasting in 1996, and the context and fallout of the marriage between Time Warner and America Online (AOL) in 2000. While I am sensitive to earlier and later developments in the history of entertainment branding, I concentrate on a period where branding became an organizing principle – what some would call an orthodoxy – within the (new) media economy of Hollywood.

Beyond Disney

Critically, *Brand Hollywood* responds to Aida Hozic's call that film studies should remember that movies are, and always have been, 'commodities among other commodities inextricably entwined with the world of consumption' (Hozic 2000: 207). As a means of focus, I concentrate on the complexities of cultural production rather than those of use and reception. This does not forgo the latter, but seeks to build a sustained picture of the dominant definition of cinematic entertainment as it has shaped, and been shaped by, the concept of branding. In so doing, I believe it is important to avoid making casual assumptions about the present or overdramatizing the epochal significance of what may be called, with deliberate doubleness of meaning, the commercial Logos of contemporary culture. Branding can be used to reveal intriguing new perspectives on fundamental transformations and developments in contemporary cultural industries, but this should always acknowledge what David Hesmondhalgh calls the 'complexity, ambivalence and contestedness of culture' (Hesmondhalgh 2002: 265). While this requires 'an open-minded attitude towards the kinds of uses and pleasures that people take from texts', including the pleasures that may be taken from logos, ad movies, merchandised blockbusters and other brand media, it also means considering what Hesmondhalgh terms the 'very real complexities involved in making capital out of culture'. This points towards a much less certain, or ideologically coherent, picture of the way that media oligopolies exercise power, or more specifically, the way that members of their dynastic but 'dysfunctional families' (in this case film studios) negotiate uneasy transitions in corporate ownership, technological infrastructure and media consumption.

Organized in three parts, *Brand Hollywood* makes nested arguments about the relation of branding to industrial strategies, contexts and processes. Part I situates the issue of branding in discursive terms. Examining the relationship of branding to changes in the marketing and media environment, it explores the concept of 'total marketing' and 'total entertainment' within and between consumer and cultural industries. Using management literature, corporate confessionals (annual reports, autobiographies) and trade publications (*Variety*, *Hollywood Reporter*, *Advertising Age*, *Brandweek*) to establish the currency given to ideas of the brand in the

1990s, Part I also considers textual examples of brand-based entertainment. This provides a means of addressing questions of *critical industrial practice*. In developing this term as a form of method, John Caldwell writes: 'it is difficult to explain the current world of conglomeration, deregulation, repurposing, and globalization without fully acknowledging the extent to which textual production – and the analysis of texts by industry – stand simultaneously as corporate strategies, as forms of cultural and economic capital integral to media professional communities, and as the means by which contemporary media industries work to rationalize their operations in an era of great institutional instability' (Caldwell 2006: 102). It is in respect of Caldwell's last point that I draw on two pregnant examples – *Chanel No. 5: The Film* (2004) and *The Matrix* (1999) – to consider how particularized junctures of industrial flux have shaped the contemporary 'articulation' of branding and filmed entertainment.[4]

Having established a framework for analysing the discourse and practice of entertainment/branding, I turn in Part II to specific logo histories in order to examine the aesthetic style of corporate branding within post-classical cinema. Considering the trademarks of two studios majors (Warner Bros. and Paramount) and a pivotal technology company (Dolby), Part II considers the *poetics of branding*. While largely unexamined in film studies criticism, corporate logos remain an enduring narrative and affective threshold within the film experience. Assuming a more pronounced role in the formal, stylistic and thematic unfolding of Hollywood trailers and credit sequences, logos have become especially significant in patterning cinematic appeals to sensory and spectacular experience. As such, Part II examines the industrial and emotive function of logos and their presupposition of an imaginative and somatic relationship with film, one that suggests 'encounter' or that provides invitation to 'enter a world'. Together, these logo histories illuminate what Vivien Sobchack calls 'acts and representations of "ultra-hearing" and "ultra-seeing"' (Sobchack 2005: 3). If, as I argue, logos suggest equivocations of corporate anxiety and prowess in the post-classical period, especially figured around the form of the modern blockbuster, they also demonstrate industrial attempts to affect, or allegorize, the gestalt of total entertainment.

Part III opens out the discussion of branding in terms of its situation within global media industries; it examines the primary avenues through which branding manifests itself in the production, distribution and exhibition of filmed entertainment. To this end, I concentrate specifically on Warner Bros. as set in the context of Time Warner. Analysing the brand dynamics enveloping old studio properties (Looney Tunes animation), new media franchises (*Harry Potter* and *Lord of the Rings*) and urban entertainment space (Warner Village cinemas), Part III provides a detailed examination of the means by which a major studio functions in brand terms. Unlike studies of Disney, which often stress the all-conquering triumph of brand ideology, the context afforded by Time Warner (the largest and arguably most troubled media conglomerate of the 1990s) provides a vantage point more able to draw out the uncertainties and contradictions of the contemporary will-to-brand. Through case studies in the recent history of Warner Bros., I explore the industrial *politics of branding,* raising questions that relate the gestalt of total enter-tainment to issues within global consumer culture, specifically the meaning of commodities, the contraction of markets and the spatial formulation of branding within structures of the global and the everyday.

The three parts of *Brand Hollywood* raise questions that interpenetrate and cross each other. The practice, poetics and politics of branding are not discrete issues but suggest different points of critical emphasis that open out wider, and I hope indica-tive, perspectives on the industrial and affective economy of contemporary cinema. Conveyed throughout the book is an argument about the processes of 'selling entertainment' in the global media moment, an argument with the partic-ular aim of underlining branding's significance for mainstream commercial film and the industrial culture from which it is produced. Examining the relation of branding to transformations in the environment of contemporary film – all the while sensitive to the way that cinematic culture may be lived in ways that depart from industrial hopes and expectations – *Brand Hollywood* demonstrates precisely why any assessment of the currents shaping the contemporary motion picture busi-ness must account for the lustre of its logos.

Part I

Brand culture

Chapter 1

The cultural economy
of branding

In April 2001, US Secretary of State, Colin Powell, announced the appointment of Charlotte Beers to the State Department. As undersecretary of public diplomacy, her remit was to bring the knowledge of marketing to America's wider public relations strategy. As a veteran ad-agency executive, and former Chairman of the J. Walter Thompson Co., Beers was suitably placed to realize Powell's goal of 'branding the department, marketing the department, marketing American values to the world, and not just putting out pamphlets' (cited in Teinowitz 2001: 8).[1] The idea that a nation could be sold through the rationale and apparatus of consumer goods marketing was not specific to the United States. In its vision of renewal for the United Kingdom, brand promotion became an unabashed feature of public-sector discourse under New Labour (itself an exercise of political re-branding), the rejuvenation of British national identity linked to the work of 'new cultural entrepreneurs' who could help establish and secure the country's status as a 'trademark' or 'PLC' (Leadbetter and Oakley 1999). As in the United States, branding offered itself as a distinct cultural strategy, if not solution, to uncertainties facing the nation state in a period of fraught global geopolitics and borderless capital flow.

More interesting than the values or monikers ascribed to British and American culture at this time was the sublimation of branding into the discourse of national identity. By the end of the 1990s, branding was not simply a concept for the marketing of goods and services; it had taken on a promiscuous existence in ranging discussions about the management of identity, and not only those of sneakers and coffee, but of cities, countries, corporations, civic authorities, public institutions and personal life itself. 'Brand thyself' became a clarion call in a period defined by narratives of the marketplace; the rationale of branding was applied not simply to manufacturing and service industries but to museums, universities, charities, government agencies and a myriad of non-commercial bodies anxious to fortify or revitalize their consumer appeal. If, as Andrew Wernick suggests, contemporary culture is defined by the 'extension of promotion through all the circuits of social life', the rhetorical profligacy of branding came to suffuse communicative processes beyond the traditional domain of commercial selling (Wernick 1991). Within critical accounts, the dispersal of branding into everyday sites, activities, locations and media was at once suggestive of the expansion of marketing into non-commercial provinces and of a new dynamic of consumption affecting both the shape of markets and the sociology of everyday life. Before analysing the specific implications of branding in and between the marketing and movie business, it is worth situating in general terms the way that branding has been discussed theoretically.

Concentrating on the 'regime of signification' that branding encapsulates, Wernick relates the evident growth in promotional forms to large-scale transformations in the nature of capitalism, signalling 'not simply a shift to a new mode of producing and circulating signs (cultural commodification), but an alteration in the very relation between culture and economy' (Wernick 1991: 185). This is linked, more specifically, to the promulgation of 'sign value' within the processes of capitalist reproduction. Critically, this picks up a key theme within postmodern social theory. According to Jean Baudrillard, the meaning of goods in postmodern culture is no longer related to practical utility but to the inscribed value of the 'commodity sign' (Baudrillard 1988). To use the example of Nike, the focus of commodity fetishism shifts from the materiality of the sneaker to the fecundity of the Swoosh. In Baudrillard's formulation the apparent disconnection of signs from any material referent has profound implications for concepts of meaning and the real. In a different theorization of the contemporary 'economies of signs and space', Scott Lash and John Urry relate the growth in prominence of cultural industries and cultural goods to a capitalist system where objects are similarly 'dematerialized', but where the velocity of signs generates new forms of social structure and identity (Lash and Urry 1994). Despite differences in theoretical inflection, contemporary life is understood in each case through frameworks of transition and discontinuity; postmodern social theory has furnished a concept of epochal transformation based on the 'breakdown or implosion of difference between representation and reality, sign and material good, culture and economy' (Slater 1997: 174–209).

Liz McFall suggests that underlying such accounts is a view that 'in contemporary industrialized economies, formerly autonomous cultural systems have given way to advertising and other forms of promotion, as the instruments of the economic system, to determine meaning and ultimately culture' (McFall 2002: 152). If signifying practices have become central to contemporary economic life, branding has been linked in critical discourse to the conjoining of aesthetic and commercial practices, and to the more fundamental 'de-differentiation' of cultural and economic domains. As Lash and Urry put it, 'the economy is increasingly culturally inflected and culture is more and more economically inflected. Thus the boundaries between the two become more and more blurred and the economy and culture no longer function in regard to one another as system and environment' (Lash and Urry 1994: 64). In accounting for our current 'promotional culture', branding is often linked to the inexorable rise of marketing and design industries in the 1980s and 1990s, but also, symptomatically, to a new social formation based on the vertiginous expansion of signs.

In itself, branding cannot be defined neatly in 'cultural' or 'economic' terms; it consists inescapably of both elements and has done so from advertising's earliest history. In the late nineteenth century, branding emerged as a practice for differentiating goods. With the rise of mass production, advertising became a means of creating difference between standardized manufactured products. By establishing a brand identity around a given product or service, consumers were made less susceptible to appeal from competitors. Advertising enabled firms in oligopolistic markets to protect market share from attack without threatening overall market revenue through competitive price-cutting (Stole 2001). From its origins in the 1880s, branding has maintained a deliberate economic function easing the flow of goods into the market. This has been achieved by investing commodities with meaning through symbolic processes. Branding is an integral feature of modern consumer capitalism, a specific form of economic *and* cultural activity that has shaped the structure of market relations.[2]

Branding is hardly new. However, its function has arguably changed by the way that regimes of capital knit the relation between production and consumption in historically specific ways. In line with the transformational thrust of social theory, critical accounts of advertising have routinely linked changes in style and institutional practice to the 'logic' of commodity capitalism. Liz McFall goes on to suggest that 'the over-arching tendency in socio-cultural analyses understands advertisements to have attained their current form as a function of gradual, incremental, evolutionary processes unfolding throughout the century'. More specifically, she suggests that changes 'are regarded as the outcome of an ongoing process of evolution in which advertising becomes increasingly persuasive, pervasive and culturally/economically hybridised' (McFall 2004: 90). Seen as a tool of capitalist commodity production, an axiomatic theme is the move from instrumental to emotional advertising, the ubiquity and significance of promotional communication based not on what consumers know about a product but on how they are made to feel and identify *as* consuming subjects.

This has been examined more specifically in production-led accounts that analyse the status of 'commodity aesthetics', concentrating on the way that changes in advertising style have been shaped by institutional developments in advertising's use of media, research techniques, and other working practices (Haug 1986; Leiss *et al.* 1986). If advertising campaigns were largely product-centred before the 1950s, pitching rational buying arguments to undifferentiated audiences in ways that sought to discipline consumers and educate their tastes and desires, it is commonly argued that use-centred messaging came to the fore in the postwar period. This was a result of the new emphasis on targeting, motivational research, product management and sales communication emanating from the 'marketing revolution' of the 1950s and its focus on managing consumer behaviour (Dawson 2003). Adam Arvidsson explains that the marketing techniques which developed in response to new and diversified patterns of consumption in the fifties, figured around the middle-class and booming youth culture of the period, focused centrally upon ideas of the brand. He writes:

> The concept of 'the brand' itself has a long history within marketing thought and practice. Now, however, there was a notable shift in emphasis. Originally brands had referred to producers. They had generally served as a trademark or a 'marker's mark' that worked to guarantee quality or to give the potentially anonymous mass-produced commodity an identity by linking it to an identifiable (if often entirely fictional) producer or inventor or a particular physical place. Now the brand, or the 'brand image', began to refer instead to the significance that commodities acquired in the minds of consumers.
>
> (Arvidsson 2005: 244)

It is this transformation in marketing's 'disciplinary paradigm' that informs the history of branding within the second half of the twentieth century. Herein, 'the brand refers not primarily to the product but to the *context of consumption*. It stands for a specific way of using the object, a propertied form of life to be realized in consumption' (ibid.).

In formal terms, the genealogy of branding is linked to important transitions in advertising approach and production context. Technological changes alone have produced new possibilities for promotional communication, as have key shifts in the profile of consumers and the use of information about their behaviour (Schudson 1986). In particular, the global restructuring of capitalism, specifically the impact of information and communication technologies in the 1980s and 1990s, has led to a striking acceleration in the flow of cultural imagery and, with it, brand signification. However, this promotional conjuncture should not be recouped within teleological schemes or totalized in terms of its social and political significance. Indeed, recent studies of advertising have drawn back from grand portraits of social transformation, recognizing the conceptual limitations of theories that oppose 'culture' and 'economy' to dramatize some epochal convergence between the two.[3] The idea that advertising has become increasingly persuasive, pervasive and hybrid is endemic to theories that witness the colonizing reach of commercial speech in contemporary life. As Liz McFall suggests, however, 'persuasiveness is a contingent experience' (McFall 2002: 149). It is in this respect that we must understand the vicissitudes of advertising and marketing as a practice, including the multiple processes at work in producing concepts and objects such as 'the brand' (du Gay and Pryke 2002; Lury 2004).

Rather than relate branding to a socially transformative shift in the culture/economy dynamic, typical of accounts that witness the insuperable rise of marketing, I want to examine branding as a discourse in this chapter. From this perspective, branding is less significant for what it might reveal about the 'condition' of a given social moment, than for how organizations of meaning coalesce in particular ways, and how this may in turn animate specific kinds of industrial and textual practice. By concentrating on regimes of knowledge that develop within and across industrial sectors one can locate more precisely dynamics of change, as well as continuity, within specific industries, accounting, for my purpose, on the terms by which the advertising and film industries have been drawn closer together within formations of talk, sense and behaviour. Together, both this chapter and the next consider the 'articulation' of branding and entertainment in the 1990s and 2000s; they examine, respectively, the circumstances in which consumer branding has assumed the pose of entertainment in our current historical moment, and how popular entertainment has increasingly assumed the function and status of brand. Taking stock of the contemporary marketing and media environment – and what Henry Jenkins calls the 'affective economics' of our promotional world (Jenkins 2006)[4] – I establish in Part I a context for analysing the place and status of cinematic entertainment at the turn of the twenty-first century, suffused as it has become with the beguilement of the brand.

This chapter will first examine how marketing practitioners took up the idea of the brand in the 1990s. Responding to the perception of change within the advertising industry, to uncertainties about the fragmentation of the mass audience, and to the fear of 'clutter' generated by the pluralization of media channels, branding developed as a strategic means of stabilizing markets, establishing a more proximate relationship with consumers thought to be more 'active' than ever before (Moor 2003). The currency of the term was also defined, however, by accounting systems designed to measure the corporate value of non-tangible assets, and through juridical infrastructures expanding the legal protection given to intellectual property (Hart and Murphy 1998). Establishing broad transitions in the contemporary marketing environment, I go on to examine the relation between consumer goods marketing and the film industry. Although Hollywood has a long history of engagement with commercial culture, business and critical literature has spoken of a seated 'convergence' between the two; Hollywood has become a focal site for developments inferred in the merging of cultural and economic realms. While this has renewed arguments about the commercialization of popular film, my consideration of consumer branding and filmed entertainment treats the precise, and frequently uncertain, institutional relationship between 'Hollywood' and 'Madison Avenue'. To this end, and as a means of focusing on the impetus given to marketing goods through experiential means, I consider the recent history of product placement and 'branded entertainment', studying examples such as BMW's film series *The Hire* (2001) and the blockbusting 'ad movie' *Chanel No.5: The Film* (2004).

Total marketing and the idea of the brand

Concerned with the 'disposability' of feeling in modern cultural life caused by what he calls 'intensifying media onrush', Todd Gitlin describes the necessity of personal coping strategies. Positing an admixture of navigational modes that seek to manage the torrential clamouring of media signals, Gitlin also describes the need for 'stratagems of inattention'. He writes: 'An unavoidable consequence of all the flashes and shouts for attention … is clutter and cacophony. As a result, when we pay attention to any particular signal, we must pay inattention elsewhere. Coping, in other words, demands a willed myopia. Everyone learns not only to see but not to see – to tune out and turn away' (Gitlin 2002: 118). If metaphors of saturation have long been used to characterize the world of mass-produced media images, sounds and symbols in which we live, the escalation of 'clutter' became a renewed source of anxiety for advertising executives in the 1990s, fearful that advertising's capacity to penetrate and be heard had become increasingly difficult in a multimedia environment rich with (commercial) information, and where the abundance of advertising had intensified consumer scepticism towards its most obvious forms. As the CEO of the J. Walter Thompson Co., Chris Jones, remarked in 1999:

> From the consumers' experience, the worlds of entertainment, sports, the Internet, marketing and media are snowballing, building critical mass, overwhelming people with messages that intensify daily life. To reach the consumer, advertising is having to develop new business models that call for lightning fast ways to pierce the galaxy of messages. What we thought was 'clutter' on the TV screen is already looking like cause for nostalgia.
>
> ('21st century chat room', *Advertising Age* 1999: 76)

It was in response to this sense of transition within business models that branding formed the core of a new marketing orthodoxy in the 1990s; the cultivation of 'brand relationships' figured centrally in attempts to reach out to what marketing literature would call the 'soul of the new consumer' (Lewis and Bridger 2001).

In trade discussion, branding was no longer a matter of transmitting the meaning of goods. Instead, it meant identifying the 'core values' of a product or service and managing these as an issue of communicable vision. While the concept of brand management originated with Procter & Gamble in the 1950s, based around the breakdown of stand-alone products and their managed differentiation through mass advertising, this was no longer seen to meet the needs of a complex promotional culture. In presenting a compelling vision of the commodity in global and local markets, evangelical 'brand shepherds' (Winkler 1999) were required to make the values of a company resonate more intimately with particular social experiences, lifestyle values and civic aspirations (Willmott 2001). Rather than connect an image to a product through conventional media advertising, branding sought in purpose to elicit new modes of consumer engagement, turning disposable and potentially distracted feelings into emotional and fully exploitable commercial commitments.[5]

Before outlining these strategies in more detail it is necessary to consider the significance accorded to 'branding' by the contemporary advertising industry. Mica Nava suggests that 'in order to understand the relationship of advertising imagery and campaigns to commodity production and political economy we must have some sense of the assumptions and operations of advertising and publicity as cultural industry' (Nava 1997: 39). Nava suggests that what emerges from industrial accounts of advertising during the 1990s, apparent in both trade magazines and interviews with workers, is a picture of an industry defined by 'far more extensive demoralisation, fragmentation and suspension of disbelief' than is often acknowledged in academic criticism (ibid.: 40). This is to ignore neither the surge in global advertising spending from the mid-1990s nor the enormous consolidation of power that occurred within and across advertising agencies in the period. As in other industrial sectors, advertising was defined by a series of mergers and acquisitions in the 1980s and 1990s, creating an oligopolistic structure dominated by a handful of global advertising conglomerates. The expansion of mega-agencies such as Saatchi & Saatchi, the Omnicom Group, Young & Rubican, and Ogilvy & Mather saw the globalization of major US and European agencies. These transnational advertising conglomerates would swiftly dominate the industry, leveraging the benefits of integrated networks and vast capital and research resources to allocate brand-building globally (Kim 1995; Aaker and Joachimsthaler 1999).

Despite this concentration of industrial power, a profound level of uncertainty distinguished the advertising industry in the 1990s, created not least by the recession of the early nineties, repeated a decade later, that led to widespread questioning of agencies by advertising clients. Obliged to think how best to spend corporate marketing budgets and seeking greater accountability, the commercial value of television and press advertising came under intense scrutiny, conventional advertising methods seen as an unpredictable means of reaching consumers (Nixon 2002). This perception was linked both to renewed doubts about what audiences do with advertisements and, more significantly, to the fragmentation of audiences resulting from the proliferation of media channels. The emergence of new media technologies and delivery systems in the 1990s, specifically the penetration of cable and digital technology, produced a very different marketing and media environment to that of previous decades. Notably, network television advertising became increasingly unsettled in a burgeoning multichannel world (Shergill 1993). This was matched by significant shifts in advertising expenditure moving towards emergent technologies such as the Internet. At stake in these developments was the logic of the cultural niche, generating questions not only about the identification of market segments but of finding the appropriate *mix* of promotion to capture audience attention.

Of course, advertisers do not simply identify or uncover sections of the markets but actively work to produce them. As Anne Cronin suggests, 'markets are a product of the imaginative practices of executives in advertising agencies'. She continues: 'the knowledges generated by the agencies are oriented towards self-promotion, because agencies are forced to compete in order to present themselves to potential clients as experts in knowledge about the consumer' (Cronin 2000: 41). It is in this respect that advertising and marketing occupations function in the capacity of 'cultural intermediaries'. This has been theorized as a growing professional class, associating goods and services with particular cultural meanings and addressing these as values to ever more diverse and discriminating buyers (Lash and Urry 1994: 222). Occupationally concerned with mapping shifts in lifestyle and taste, intermediary knowledge has become central to the constitution of contemporary identity, both in the formulation of individuality – what Cronin calls 'consumer citizenship' – and in the designation of market segments defined by age, gender, ethnicity, income, class and so on. Whether in the buying and selling to children, teenagers or other culturally rendered markets such as the 'Hispanic' niche in the United States (see Langer 2004; Quart 2003; Davilá 2001), the advertising and marketing industries play an integral role 'reconstituting individuals into consumers and populations into markets' (Davilá 2001: 2).

This process does not take place in a discursive or industrial vacuum, however. While advertising is a material device employed in the definition and qualification of markets, it is also shaped by historically precise contexts of production that inflect its practices, tools and techniques and generate rival claims of skill and expertise. Celia Lury and Alan Warde suggest that in appealing to clients, agencies produce complex myths of the market that are increasingly understood in terms of consumer behaviour (Lury and Warde 1997). Significantly, the growth of management and brand consultants during the 1990s put new myths of the market into play, suggesting a key transferral of power to the consumer in a dispersed media environment (Winkler 1999; Kapferer 2001). Generating specialist knowledge claims, marketing theorists refigured paradigms of brand management for a new business era. Rather than simply make and place adverts, brand consultants offered a *total marketing* approach designed to navigate a world made up of niche and networked consumers, communities and groups. It appeared that new forms of knowledge were required for new kinds of consumer. In a treatise on the significance of public relations, Al Ries contends that 'advertising has lost its power to put a brand name into the mind. Advertising has no credibility with consumers, who are increasingly sceptical of its claims and whenever possible are inclined to reject its messages' (Ries and Ries 2002: xvi). Of interest here is the myth of the sceptical consumer. In significant ways, the language of branding developed in accordance with the perception of ineffectiveness on the part of traditional advertising and in line with a view that consumers are today more informed and at the same time more fleeting in their modes of commercial engagement. In a period defined by audience fragmentation and accelerated media flow, branding was taken up within commercial literature as a means of expanding, systemizing and managing the function of contemporary marketing, addressing the consumer in ways that were both proximate and increasingly personal in approach.

Non-traditional advertising media assumed greater significance in this context. Indeed, the function of 'ambient' communication spawned a minor industry of contractors specializing in stunts and promotional messaging that could target niche groups in carefully defined environments (Shankar and Horton 1999). With the surveillance capacities of electronic sales data and product-tracking – the result of innovations such as UPC scanners, loyalty cards, television meters and Internet search engines – companies could learn instantly about the tastes, desires and preferences of their customers, disaggregating information to understand particular market segments and their geographies. Ambient communication was a means of achieving intimacy in this context, inserting brands into an expanded range of everyday spaces. This could include anything from petrol pump advertising and event sponsorship to the use of consumer websites and other kinds of 'viral' marketing campaigns.[6] While stealth advertising was not in itself new, it being part of a long history of commercial stunting, ambient strategies were indicative of attempts in the 1990s to 'experientialize' the encounter with brands (Pine and Gilmore 1999).

At one level, this was an outgrowth of changes in creative priority that had taken place in the advertising industry during the 1980s. With the rise of so-called 'third wave' agencies, advertisements were more assiduously structured around 'emotional' rather than 'unique' selling positions. While the idea of a switch in format from product-based to image-driven advertising should not be overplayed, the creative prioritization of emotion (achieved, for example, by the sensory use of filming, editing and lighting techniques within advertising style) foreshadows the affective brand strategies that would emerge in the 1990s. According to one marketing bestseller, 'emotional branding' is now central to a 'people-driven economy that puts the consumer in the seat of power'. Mark Gobé writes:

> The future of branding is listening carefully to people in order to be able to connect powerfully with them by bringing pleasurable, life-enhancing solutions to their world. In the future, traditional companies will not be able to rely on their brand history or dominance in classical distribution systems, they will have to focus on providing brands with a powerful emotional content.
>
> (Gobé 2001: xxv)

There are, of course, problems with the idea of the sovereign consumer in this account. Not least, Gobé ignores the various limits that are placed on interactions with brands. As Adam Arvidsson observes, brand management recognizes the autonomy of consumers but also pre-structures and anticipates 'the agency of consumers and situates it within a number of more or less precise coordinates' (Arvidsson 2005: 245). Put simply, branding relies on the participation of consumers but on terms that have been forethought. This underlies Naomi Klein's pithy description of a new marketing consensus developing in the early 1990s: 'the products that will flourish in the future will be the ones presented not as "commodities" but as concepts: the brand as experience, as lifestyle' (Klein 2000: 21).

Whatever the lifestyle in question, and the stakes of its determination, the idea of 'brand experience' has become central to the affective economics of cultural life, and the particular desire amongst marketers 'to expand consumers' emotional, social and intellectual investments with the goal of shaping consumer behaviour' (Jenkins 2006: 63). It is in this respect that 'values and beliefs' have continued to assume significance with commercial culture. This extends to organizational relations within companies themselves, the idea of the brand increasingly absorbed across all levels of corporate activity (publications, advertising, signage, uniforms, training) to create encompassing visions of brand *esprit* (Mottram 1998). Rather than market discrete products, the corporate brand (Microsoft, McDonald's,

Virgin, Starbucks, Disney) has moved to the fore, seen as a more reliable means of building 'deep' relationships with both consumers and shareholders. In the latter case, the concept of the brand is linked to estimations and potential fluctuations of corporate value. Celia Lury writes, 'the brand is an example not only of a cultural form but also of a modality of economic power' (Lury 2004: 10). This suggests a more literal, fiscal freighting to the term 'affective *economics*'. As much as a marketing model, branding has become a mark of corporate performance. Accordingly, any delineation of 'the brand' in the 1990s and 2000s must account for its status as a commercial asset.

In August 2001, *Business Week* published its first ranking of the world's most valuable brands; in the top ten were Coca-Cola with a brand value of $69 billion, followed by Microsoft, IBM, GE, Nokia, Intel, Disney, Ford, McDonald's and AT&T.[7] Acknowledging the move from tangible to intangible worth, the list was designed to nudge American accountancy practices towards British principles of financial measurement, the London Stock Exchange endorsing 'brand valuation' in 1989 in response to mergers and acquisitions that saw companies purchased for sums far beyond the total of their material assets (Batchelor 1998). This endorsement was a step towards the rationalization of brand equity, exacerbated in the US by shocks such as 'Marlboro Friday' in 1993. This saw the Philip Morris Co. announce a 20 per cent cut in the price of Marlboro cigarettes as a means of competing with bargain brands. Causing momentary apoplexy for the advertising industry (share prices plunging for ad-reliant consumer goods companies), Naomi Klein suggests that 'Marlboro Friday' also threw into relief the stock market success of corporations driven by marketing such as Microsoft and Nike (Klein 2000: 14). The concept of brand equity developed significant discursive propulsion as a result. Indeed, by the time *Business Week* published its inaugural ranking of global brands, Marlboro had assumed 11th place with a brand value of $22 billion. Also on the list, however, were brands with negligible designations of lifestyle 'attitude', ranging from the news agency Reuters (52nd – $5 billion) to the aerospace manufacturer Boeing (63rd – $4 billion). This reflected the dissemination of brand strategies amongst companies that sold to other businesses rather than to consumers, extending the promotional-cum-fiscal idea of branding across industrial sectors.

As a form of corporate worth, branding was sanctified by new accountancy methods. However, it was also secured by legal regimes that assigned increasing levels of protection to intellectual property. Indeed, juridical discourse represents a co-constitutive site in the formalization of branding's nascent cultural/economic power. According to Rosemary Coombe, unprecedented shifts in trademark law have taken place since the 1970s, its legal basis moving away from any residual notion of consumer protection (bound in safeguarding the public from confusion or deception over competing goods) towards the ratification of corporate power and the capacity of trademark owners to 'fix the signifier' and 'own the sign' (Coombe 1998: 26). Coombe is quick to argue that fixing the meaning of signifiers does not foreclose the counter-hegemonic impulse to disarticulate and rearticulate the meaning of texts; she suggests that the commodity sign is a site of expressive struggle. However, it remains the case that contemporary brand culture has been shaped and enabled by legal regimes especially disposed towards the privatization of signs. Branding is economically valuable to the degree that its signifiers can be legally defined and protected. Accordingly, intellectual property law has in recent decades – loosely coterminous with the economic significance given to service and cultural industries and their traffic in ideas, images and information – reaffirmed the principle of ownership inscribed in logos, trademarks, insignia and other forms of corporately 'authored' text.

The specificity of branding in the 1990s can be measured in relation to various forms of institutional discourse, co-linking ideas of consumer behaviour, corporate equity and intellectual property in ways that have come to yield a particular effectivity within cultural and economic practice. While the idea of branding is of course not exclusive to the nineties, its recent currency can be seen as a specific coalescing of market(ing) knowledge. This can be situated in relation to broad transitions in the restructuring of capital, culture and the law, but also in relation to specific market events (Marlboro Friday) and to emergent transformations in the structure of media. It was the last of these, specifically the fragmentation of media audiences resulting from new information technologies and global communications capabilities, which brought 'entertainment' to the fore within the brand strategies of consumer companies. As media consultant Michael J. Wolf suggests, 'consumer businesses are going to have to be partly about entertainment in order to be noticed in the increasingly crowded marketplace' (Wolf 1999: 17). As an industry based on the selling of experience, Hollywood has been positioned, just as it has sought to position itself, as an unrivalled source of 'ambient' and 'emotional' communication.

It is the relation between consumer branding and the film business that I want to explore next. As a result of financial pressure within the film and television industry during the 1990s, consumer companies sought to exploit and solidify ties with the entertainment industry as a means of extending their cultural reach (Nussenbaum 2003, 2004). With media fragmentation and new digital technologies 'forever changing the paid-media advertising model', *Advertising Age* assessed the situation for brand marketing in the following terms: 'One result of this collective reassessment [about advertising models] is greater engagement with the entertainment industry, with the end game pointing towards a paradigm shift where brand marketers view content providers less as vendors and more as partners' (Kim 2002: 40). While for some this apparent collapse in the boundary between art and commerce represents a deepening of the challenge to ingrained hierarchies of taste and aesthetic value (Seabrook 2000; Collins 2002), for others it heralds the ultimate victory of consumer capitalism (Crispin Miller 1990; Wasko 2003). Rather than celebrate or condemn the present condition of the 'art-culture system' (Lury 1996), I want to examine how one of its visible features – product placement and the contemporary emergence of 'branded entertainment' – can illuminate the practice of branding as a market cultural form. Resisting the tendency to moralize about the intrusions of commerce in cultural life, I want to focus on a conjuncture – what Elizabeth Moor calls 'a certain instability in the realm of culture' – caused by the constant movement 'between consumers who seek "experiences" and producers who seek to brand these experiences' (Moor 2003: 58).

Branded entertainment: Hollywood marries Madison Avenue

In seeking modes of address that reduce the risk of alienation, suspicion or boredom on the part of consumers, Hollywood has long been a bedfellow of advertising in the development of wider consumerist ideologies. As numerous film scholars have shown, Hollywood is deeply implicated in the world of consumption, and has been so from cinema's beginnings (Desser and Jowett 2000). Describing the role of Hollywood in the burgeoning consumer culture of the 1920s, Sara Ross comments: 'As it would in later decades the young film industry regarded other media industries as allies in the effort to posit the popular media as arbiters of all other types of consumption. At the heart of the film industry's participation in the construction of a consumer culture were efforts to develop media consumers, not just film by film, but for the long term as well' (Ross 2000: 57). Mass-circulated images not only promoted standards of behaviour, appearance and lifestyle in this context, Hollywood functioned as a 'show window' for a range of commercial goods, especially geared towards American women's consumer practices, as well as other target groups such as children (Eckert 1978; deCordova 1994). Systemized forms of tie-in merchandising and product placement have their antecedents in the studio era, Hollywood film serving from the outset to 'magnetize other commodities' (Gaines 2000: 105). What remains new, in historical terms, is the expansion and rationalization of these commercial alignments, and the equivocal nature of branding's particular forms of disclosure and excess.

According to Janet Wasko, Hollywood film since the 1980s has become increasingly commercialized, not only in the range and degree of commodities that are produced in conjunction with feature films, but in the more deliberate and co-ordinated placement activities that feature products within screen entertainment. If, as Wasko contends, the 'Hollywood film industry is rapidly becoming a major advertising medium', this has been signalled by the burgeoning number of product placement agencies that survey scripts and seek promotional opportunities for commercial clients (Wasko 1994, 2003). This has been matched by the growing significance of licensing and merchandising deals used to defray the mounting costs of producing and marketing studio movies. Wasko suggests three main implications resulting from these processes of commercialization: firstly, that a marketing or sales agenda has come to impact on creative decision-making, scenes and script development catering to the whims of commercial partners; secondly, that film has become an economic 'multiplier' for other products and businesses, stimulating markets in advertising, toys, games, consumer electronics and fast food; thirdly, and relating to the first two, that a 'disturbing' cultural consequence emanates from '"real world" commodities [being] introduced into the fantasy world of film', serving ideologically to 'enhance the commodification of culture and the intensification of consumer society' (1994: 217).

What interests me here is the sense of collusion that has developed within accounts of the contemporary relation between Hollywood and Madison Avenue. This includes the sense that the cultural commodity of the motion picture has been subsumed by a deeper economic logic. While there are certainly grounds for analysing Hollywood's commercialization in the last three decades – a central proposition of critical political economy – this is quite a different thing, as Don Slater points out, 'from the methodological presumption that culture and economy have ever represented different logics or moments which are now empirically converging' (Slater 2002: 60). This presumption is evident in Wasko's fear that 'real' economic life is seeping into the 'fantasy' world of Hollywood film. Wasko provides an indispensable portrait of the industrial workings of Hollywood in the 'information age'. However, economic and cultural categories are employed in her argument in a largely unproblematic manner, what Slater depicts more broadly as 'an artefact of an intellectual division of labour which has historically separated economy and culture and leaves analysts deeply perturbed when it finds them in close cahoots' (ibid.: 71). In general terms, Wasko is disturbed by the surrender of culture to commercial imperatives. However, as Constance Balides writes, 'treating the incursion of commerce on everyday life, art, and films as the conclusion of the argument ends the argument too soon. It also effects a tautology in which commercial culture is critiqued for being commercial. Measuring experience along a continuum from authenticity to inauthenticity and judging art according to models of creative autonomy or of commercial exploitation are inadequate frameworks for analyzing an everyday life that is so extensively mediated and commercialised' (Balides 2000: 148). Specifically, Balides suggests that such arguments fall short in their tendency to find economic factors determining representation, 'an approach that often involves an impoverished sense of textuality and results in the insufficient conclusion of the encroachment of commerce on the artistic integrity of film' (ibid.: 141). It is with this caution in mind (explored in more detail in chapter 5) that we might think about the industrial and textual phenomenon of branded entertainment.

Undoubtedly, the advertising and entertainment industries have assumed increasing points of overlap. The decision by Coca-Cola in 1994 to launch a new advertising campaign using the expertise of the talent agency Creative Artists Agency (CAA) instead of the advertising agency McCann-Erikson was at once suggestive of Hollywood's place in the promotional nexus of American brand commerce. As anxieties about traditional advertising methods have crystallized, marketers have increasingly looked to the talent, forms and idioms of entertainment to develop markets and consolidate consumer awareness. Carrying significance for client–agency relations, this has also created competition between film studios and network/cable broadcasters as they seek external finance to protect against the escalating costs of moviemaking and the decline of network television advertising, respectively. Hunting commercial partners to help develop or wholly underwrite the production of media content, renewed efforts have been made, in the words of *Daily Variety*, to 'land that brand' (Graser 2002). Despite the perception of difference between Hollywood and Madison Avenue, the two industries have seen a growing interpenetration of clients and concerns, leading to questions of how they might best work together (Fahey 1999).

This institutional cosying has not alleviated practical tensions and uncertainties in the cross-fertilization of their practices, however. The function of product placement is indicative here. Despite the claims made against product placement by critics, the practice remains an inexact strategy for marketers, less controllable than traditional media advertising and sitting askance to the industry's typical buying frameworks. While placements enable brands to be set discreetly (or not) in the environment of popular culture, linked to film and television products that are distributed globally and maintain a commercial life way beyond that of a singular advertising campaign, the continuing predominance of barter arrangements means that placements are not always guaranteed to occur in a film or perhaps in the form and context desired.[8] Samuel Turcotte speaks of the 'cultural gulf' that exists between corporate marketers, studio executives and creative personnel when it comes to product placement. He suggests that 'since the corporate marketers themselves have little control of the message, the audience, nor the timing, product placement is primarily used to expand on what has been done with their real ad dollars' (Turcotte 1995). In the wider marketing context, product placement is a small but indicative feature of contemporary brand practice. The growth and consolidation of the placement industry demonstrates the lure of ambient communication and the attractions of entertainment media to consumer brands. At the same time, product placement reveals a nagging anxiety about when, if and how audiences are actually paying attention.

Product placement has become a popular form of alternative marketing. In advertisers' best hopes, placement creates what Michael Solomon and Basil Englis call 'consumption constellations' within visual media, forging symbolic synergies where products and brands become distinct within memories of the audience (Solomon and Englis 1994). However, the effectiveness of product placement is far from certain. Although the media research company, Nielson, launched a product placement measurement service in 2003 – attempting to recognize the significance of ambient media within the ratings systems used by media planners – this offered little to alleviate qualitative concerns about the degree to which brands are actually recalled by audiences. Of course, it is not the effectiveness of any single product placement that gives placement activity its cultural and ideological power, but what Todd Gitlin would rather call its plenitude (Gitlin 2002). This has become a source of imaginative fantasy within science fiction. When the character John Anderton (Tom Cruise) walks through a futuristic mall in Steven Spielberg's *Minority Report* (2002), billboards literally call out in a personalized promotional bombardment: 'John Anderton, you could use a Guinness now', 'Get Away John

Anderton'. In its envisioned use of data tracking, the film portrays an over-stimulated commercial environment whose time, in many ways, has already come. And yet, the contemporary 'torrent' of promotion, so often used in science fiction to mark the future of our collective present, does not prove the triumph or control of consumer capitalism. Indeed, Elizabeth Moor suggests that affective relations between producers and consumers are highly unpredictable when it comes to the transfer of (brand) meaning and value. 'This unpredictability derives partly from the fact that knowledge of consumers may remain elusive even in terms of a great deal of information about them, but also because marketers themselves do not necessarily know in advance what kinds of work will "work"' (Moor 2003: 58). As the panic-stricken flight of John Anderton may at some level attest, the escalation of commercial surveillance and promotional signification does not solve 'the problems of producers in their attempts to capture consumers who are always on their way somewhere else' (ibid.).

Nor does it predetermine the means by which audiences deal with the presence of commercial signs in their cultural engagement with texts. Indeed, the place and power of brand names in Hollywood film must be understood in relation to widespread changes in contemporary visual entertainment and media literacy. Aida Hozic suggests that in the studio era product placement, merchandising and tie-ins maintained a semblance of invisibility (Hozic 2000). However, following a number of landmark product placement deals in the 1980s – mythologized in the sales leap of Reese's Pieces after the appearance of the confectionery in *E.T.* (1982) – an increasing number of films have displayed products with spectacular obviousness, from the commercial *mise en scène* of *Jurassic Park* (1993) and the self-parodying placements of *Wayne's World* (1992) to the starring role given to the parcel service FedEx in *Cast Away* (2000).[9] Despite the way that placements may be drawn within genre (whether played straight or for comedy), product placement has become more insistently visible, dropping the facade of stealth promotion and drawing attention to itself in overt modes of textual performance. The culmination of this tendency is expressed in the development of major commercial tie-ins that explicitly integrate film and consumer brands, typified by the $20 million that BMW paid for the placement campaign surrounding the launch of its Z3 Roadster, appearing centrally in the marketing and plot sequences of the James Bond movie *GoldenEye* (1995).

As a form of commercial spectacle, the visibility of product placement since the 1980s has responded to the formalization of relations between the film business and global consumer industries. Its cultural significance cannot simply be read from these industrial synergisms, however, telling though they are. One must also account for changes in audience competence, linked to broad transformations in media culture where new information technologies have allowed for greater flow and manipulability of signs and images, what Jim Collins associates with a regime of 'textual hyperconsciousness' (Collins 1995). Rather than shatter the basis of narrative cinema or sully Hollywood's formal purity, as the likes of Mark Crispin Miller (1990) argue, product placement must be seen within a

Figure 1.1 The spectacle of product placement in *Cast Away* (2000). Courtesy of Dreamworks SKG and the Ronald Grant Archive.

cultural terrain marked by exceptional textual density and by new styles of reflexivity vested in the production and consumption of (promotional) signs. For audiences literate in the appeals and subversions of brand commerce, product placement has become commonplace but also potentially risible, leading to critical reading protocols more readily based on parody, irony and scepticism. In one illustrative case, James Lyons notes the investment of Starbucks in its own negative imaging in *Austin Powers: The Spy Who Shagged Me* (1999). Ironically cast as the 'evil empire', Lyons argues that 'the attraction of the film for Starbucks lay in the way in which such a high profile opportunity for self-mockery enabled it to defuse and co-opt recent criticism of its behaviour, re-working the meanings of such criticism within a fictionalised and suitably "witty" representational vehicle' (Lyons 2004: 156). In this case, product placement strikes a complexly visible relation with its target audience in working over brand appeal. *Austin Powers* provides an example of the means by which product placement has become profoundly unbothered by any semblance of invisibility. However, it also belies residual uncertainties about the way that placement strategies must tactically navigate the threat of rile or ridicule on the part of audiences, especially prone in periods of sustained business expansion (the 1920s, the 1950s, the 1990s) to scrutinize advertising, in particular its penetration of cultural media forms (radio, film, television, Internet).

It is in light of consumer scrutiny and potential resistance to the profusion of advertising messages – by the end of the 1990s, businesses in the US spent $250 billion a year on advertising, adults being exposed to an estimated 3,000 ads per day (Stole 2001: 83) – that brands sought to mark their association with entertainment media in more calculated forms. In 2003, a fictional studio executive in *Looney Tunes: Back in Action* responds to the sudden appearance of Wal-Mart in the film, and a rush of crassly verbalized product names, by saying, 'the audience expects it; they don't even notice this kind of thing anymore'. In the same year, Steven Heyer, former CEO of Coca-Cola, addressed a conference of actual studio executives with the following promise:

> We will use a diverse array of entertainment assets to break into people's hearts and minds. In that order ... We're moving to ideas that elicit emotion and create connections. And this speeds the convergence of Madison and Vine. Because the ideas which have always sat at the heart of the stories you've told and the content you've sold ... whether movies or music or television ... are no longer just intellectual property, they're emotional capital.
>
> (Heyer, cited in Jenkins 2006: 69)

Made anxious by the difficulties of cost and control associated with product placement and tie-in deals, and with marketing literature professing the need for businesses to afford consumers 'a memorable sensory experience that ties in with the positioning of the company, product or service' (Schmitt and Simonson 1997), the 'emotional capital' of film and television anchored various initiatives in 'branded entertainment'.

Rather than associate a brand name with an established entertainment vehicle, the consumer brand in this case becomes the motor of media content. Steve Marrs, CEO of Brand Entertainment Studios, a New York consultancy launched in 2002, explained: 'If you can create an environment that is entertaining to your desired consumers and allows them to be entertained in the context of the brand, then you have an ideal form of communication with your consumer that is relevant, original and impactful' (cited in Hays 2003). Significant here is the idea that entertainment can be fashioned in the 'context of the brand'. Advertising has long gathered audiences by trading in entertainment, whether honed through commercial sponsorship of popular shows (for example, soap operas or reality programming) or through its own symbolic creativity in advertising linked to prized events such as the Super Bowl or World Cup. However, the desire to 'embed' brands within the landscape of popular entertainment has led to media content being loosened from the direct or discreet aesthetic of commercial selling associated with 'plugola'. Within the model of new marketing, branded entertainment can be seen as 'one of a range of possible strategic choices in the attempt to insinuate marketing practices more deeply into the lives of consumers' (Moor 2003: 39).

Perhaps the most influential example of its kind was BMW's series of short car-chase films *The Hire* (2001), distributed exclusively via the Internet. Costing $10 million to produce, eight separate films were made, directed by John Woo, Joe Carnahan, Tony Scott, John Frankenheimer, Ang Lee, Wong Kar-Wai, Guy

Ritchie and Alejandro González-Inárritu. While movement between the advertising and film industry can be traced in the careers of numerous movie directors,[10]
The Hire was notable for the way it sought to position itself on the cutting edge of
website video technology. It differed in this respect from the brand campaign that
BMW used in *GoldenEye*. Rather than propel the hype of the mass-market blockbuster, BMW used niche strategies of promotion that relied on word-of-mouth and
active consumer engagement. Cultivating audiences who would seek out the films,
The Hire was an example of the means by which marketers sought to co-link entertainment content with new technological infrastructures to give brands greater
credibility, interactivity, and depth of appeal.

In being viewed an estimated sixty million times on the Internet, and with its
own cross-promotional opportunities (BMW would later reprise the series in the
form of a comic strip), *The Hire*'s cult status set the precedent for other ventures in
branded entertainment.[11] As a marketing initiative, *The Hire* offered a model for
penetrating contemporary placement and tie-in clutter. At the same time, its
importance should not be overstated. One marketing consultant said: 'there's a lot
of talk [about branded entertainment] but there's very little movement …
everyone wants to know about it and be advised, but actually doing it is another
thing' (cited in Graser 2002). Similarly, describing the trend towards 'embedded
commerce' within contemporary US television (including the proliferation of on-
screen banner ads, product placement, single-sponsor infomercials and entertainment programming), William Boddy suggests 'the response of TV viewers to the
increasingly desperate attempts by advertisers and broadcasters to integrate
commercial message and program forms remains largely untested, and crucial to
any outcome' (Boddy 2004: 127). For all the fear or fanfare (depending on your
perspective) ascribed to branded entertainment, there remains hesitancy amongst
studios, networks and advertisers about what fusion of entertainment and branded
content might alienate, or be accepted by, consumers. With the acceleration of
content across media systems, however, ventures such as *The Hire* established a
precedent for the strategies and costs that consumer brands were increasingly
prepared to meet to actualize the 'memorable sensory experience' of Hollywood-
style entertainment. These developments were no better illustrated than in the
production spectacle of *Chanel No 5: The Film*, Baz Luhrmann's 'ad movie' starring
Nicole Kidman.

It is worth briefly examining this commercial as it provides a more focused
means of thinking about the contemporary lines of convergence between Hollywood and Madison Avenue. While more conventional than *The Hire* as a form of
advertising, part of a sub-genre of mega-budget spot commercials, it also draws
attention to the specificity of branded entertainment within contemporary media
culture. In a period where media boundaries have become less circumscribed,
branded entertainment is suggestive of a cultural landscape where cinematic
encounters, and determinants of film art and practice, have become more fluid.[12]
Broadly, the Chanel advertisement demonstrates what John Frow calls a 'convergence of, on the one hand, the commercial branding of aesthetic goods, and, on the

other, the aesthetic valorization of commercial goods' (Frow 2002: 56). In more specific terms, the advert relates to a juncture in contemporary television advertising form where the erosion of network audiences and the uncertain impact of digital video technologies (such as TiVO) had begun to raise questions about the traditional thirty second commercial. Writing in 2002, William Boddy observed that 'the mere threat of the personal video recorder has already encouraged a range of new technological and advertising countermeasures to the digital recorder's ability to evade standard television commercials' (Boddy 2002: 249). *Chanel No. 5: The Film* can be read in this context, seeking to prevent literal and figurative ad-skipping by transforming the brand commercial into a cultural event in itself.

Brand regimes: selling Chanel

Advertisements have long drawn upon the popular language of film and its aura of celebrity. Chanel is a case in point. With a brand value estimated in 2001 at $4.27 billion, Chanel has nurtured associations with film stars ranging from Marilyn Monroe to Catherine Deneuve. Ever since the publicity bonanza that came with Monroe's coy confession that the only thing she wore in bed was 'Chanel No. 5', the fashion brand has sought to renew its connection with female screen icons. While the 1970s saw Deneuve appear in a series of commercials, the use of Nicole Kidman in 2004 reprised a well-established connection between film stars and the fashion industry. This relationship has been forged in a number of ways, encompassing celebrity endorsements, specific couture relationships (such as that between Givenchy and Audrey Hepburn), the launch of individual brand lines and the annual spectacle of the dressed and highly accessorized catwalk of the Oscars. Chanel's ad movie was part of an enduring brand alignment between Hollywood and the fashion business. If, as Peter Bradshaw put it in the *Guardian*, the commercial was 'a celebrity-enriched piece of exquisite corporate art that celebrates luxury goods – as well as flogging them' (Bradshaw 2004: 14), this description could be applied to any number of texts, from *Breakfast at Tiffany's* (1961) to *Sex and the City* (1998–2004).

Ever since the studio era, where fashions were showcased on screen and merchandising techniques glamorized stars in fan magazines and consumer advertising, Hollywood has helped shape modern ideas of beauty, giving lifeblood to the fashion and cosmetics industries and to specific companies such as Chanel which introduced its signature No. 5 scent in 1921. Competing in the global fashion and fragrance market, and seeking to reposition No. 5 as something apart from 'the scent you buy your mistress in the airport or your grandma for her birthday', Chanel's ad movie was designed to 're-ignite an audience's emotional relationship with a square bottle filled with gold liquid' ('Take Five' 2004). Rather than foreground images of the perfume or the stars who endorse it, as in previous advertisements, creative focus turned on the concept of the Chanel brand, translated into a composite of images figured around a female character (Kidman) representing the 'very essence of the woman who wears Chanel No. 5'. To realize the 'emotional relationship' desired by Chanel, the advert took the form of a short film, focusing less on the product than on possibilities of living, feeling and behaviour. Shot at Fox Studios in Sydney at a reported cost of $33 million (US), the commercial would initially run at three minutes and would echo, in a visual and thematic sense, Luhrmann's *Moulin Rouge* (2001). Cast as a tragic romance, Kidman plays 'the most famous woman in the world' who momentarily escapes to a rooftop garret with a bohemian artist played by the Brazilian actor Rodrigo Santoro. Overlooking the night lights of a metropolitan city, they begin a love affair before Kidman, urged by an impresario, reluctantly returns to her life of celebrity. The final scene depicts Kidman stepping onto a red carpet in a blaze of paparazzi flashbulbs, looking wistfully to the rooftops. To an arrangement of Debussy's *Clair de Lune*, the commercial ends with a close-up of a lustrous diamond insignia in the shape of No. 5, worn as a pendant on Kidman's back, accompanied by the voiced memory of the artist recalling 'her kiss, her smile, her perfume'.

Rather than sell a bottled fragrance, the commercial animates 'Chanel' as a brand signifier. The corporate brand is symbolized in a pendant but also in the commercial's *mise en scène*. Most significantly, 'Chanel' appears as a giant electrified hoarding typical of the modernist city. While the ad movie evokes New York, the overall look of the commercial borrows unmistakably from *Moulin Rouge*, a film whose Parisian tableau and visual style depend on elaborate textual syntheses between past and present, high art and popular representation. Appropriately enough for a film that freely 'quotes' other cultural texts, *Moulin Rouge* functions as a cinematic intertext for *Chanel No. 5: The Film*. Much could be said of Kidman's star image and Luhrmann's visual style in the re-fashioning of Chanel's identity. In many ways, their respective combination of porcelain aura and creative flamboyance met the self-image of a fashion house based on the legacy of Coco Chanel and the cult of Karl Lagerfeld. My specific interest in *Chanel No. 5: The Film*, however, is less with Chanel than with the articulation of branding and entertainment within the company's marketing strategies. In the tradition of fashion branding, *Chanel No. 5: The Film* used Hollywood to sell glamorous visions of style. More unusually, however, the commercial was also staged and sold as a quasi-cinematic event. While a half-hour 'making-of' documentary and the publicity hype surrounding the shoot gave some indication of this, the commercial became a virtual microcosm of the global Hollywood blockbuster, marked in its runaway production and technical virtuosity but also in the form of its worldwide distribution and marketing.

Like a major Hollywood blockbuster, the ad movie was given a global release in November 2004, just before the Christmas holiday season. After its world premier in Australia (after the popular television programme *A Current Affair*), the commercial was shown in Hong Kong, France, the UK and the US, followed by wide release in other major markets. Its release in the United Kingdom is suggestive of the commercial's aspirant cinematic status. Targeting an affluent female audience, it was first shown in movie theatres during the release of *Bridget Jones: Edge of Reason*

(2004). This was followed by its television 'premiere' a week later, broadcast as a complete commercial interval within Channel 4's screening of *Moulin Rouge*. Prior to this, a teaser trailer announced the premiere via oblique images of gold liquid and a square perfume bottle. Generating media 'buzz', the commercial was also publicized in television listings and in full-page news advertisements styled in the form of a movie poster. 'Inviting' viewers to the premiere, media observers were 'duly provoked and intrigued by the audacity of this art-commerce crossover' (Bradshaw 2004). Consuming a full block of paid television advertising, the commercial made strenuous efforts to confuse its status as text and event, the premiere including a minute-long credit sequence.[13] While the labour involved in most advertisements could generate end credits of this sort, *Chanel No. 5: The Film* assumed the formal conventions of a major studio movie. In terms of its size, stars, spectacle and cost-to-screen time, this was not without genuine claim.

Of course, the commercial's position within the British terrestrial screening of *Moulin Rouge* was by no means incidental; it enabled the ad movie to 'play' as a parenthetical sequence of the film itself, Kidman reprising Satine (the luminous star) and Santoro assuming the role of Christian (the loving artist). Specifically, the ad movie came after a scene in *Moulin Rouge* where Satine faints during an exuberant performance of 'Diamonds Are a Girl's Best Friend'. Suffering from the disease of consumption and revived through smelling salts, the film would duly cut to the first commercial break. This transition was signalled by the signature of Stella Artois, a brand that has long sought to equate itself with the cultural prestige of art cinema (similar to Channel 4) and whose adverts and film-season sponsorships quote directly from the soundtrack and visual style of *Jean de Florette* (1986). Bookmarked by the taste assurances of 'a reassuringly expensive beer', the ad movie worked to combine the character of Satine with the star image of Kidman. Having faced intense public scrutiny after her separation from Tom Cruise, the concept of the advert was based, for Luhrmann, upon the beautiful tragedy of mythologized women. He reflects, 'it is the yearning to escape this responsibility by way of innocent romance that can best be understood by all women' ('Take Five' 2004). This brand messaging multiplies the possible meanings and levels of interpretation between film and commercial. While 'the most famous woman in the world' wears $30 million of diamonds after Satine sings boldly of their virtue, the courtesan aspires to be 'a real actress, a great actress' after we see Chanel's 'essential' woman trapped and bedazzled by her/Kidman's own actress celebrity. Luhrmann opines: 'This kind of tragic story is what Nicole and I spent a lot of time exploring in *Moulin Rouge* – there's even a connection between Satine and this new character' (ibid.). In promotional terms, Satine becomes Kidman becomes Chanel in a visual narrative designed to accentuate, and alchemize, the cultural iconicity of film, stardom and brand.

My brief textual treatment of *Chanel No. 5: The Film* is not designed to epitomize some new and fundamental accord between consumer branding and the film business; I do not want to claim from this isolated case some wider cultural theory or restrict different types of audience engagement or reading formation surrounding the commercial and its screen life in theatres, on television, YouTube and so on. Instead, I want to think about the specificity of 'branded entertainment' as a contemporary cultural mode. Discussing issues of continuity and change in the everyday life of popular film culture, Charles Acland offers a valuable corrective to synchronic theories that unduly privilege 'the immediate' and 'the moment'. He writes that 'ongoing connections are as central to the formation of contexts as new ones and hence deserve a prominent place in our thinking. In all cultural analysis we might pose the following question: What is the relationship between the emergent and the residual and between the appearance of novelty and of repetition?' (Acland 2003: 17). On these terms, *Chanel No. 5: The Film* demonstrates a residual tendency among consumer/fashion brands to create allure through the auspices of Hollywood stars and stories, using visual techniques that finesse advertising's sometimes blunt and uncomfortable association with commercial selling. However, there is also an emergent tendency at work, the ad movie assuming 'the appearance of novelty' in the way it is framed and financed as cinema. In a fragmented media environment where people increasingly make choices about which channels and which commercials they watch, spot advertising has been called into question and inveighed with new directions: towards faster cutting rates, towards the value of ambient locations (checkouts, computer screens) and towards the promotional mixing of stealth and spectacle. It is in this marketing context that film shorts like *The Hire* and hybrid commercials such as *Chanel No. 5: The Film* emerged in the late 1990s and early 2000s. While, as branded entertainment, they might be seen to express the aesthetic tendencies of a hyper-commercial world, they also, at the same time, reflect new cartographies of taste and consumption emerging in a culture where traditional boundaries between media industries, texts and audiences have grown ever more difficult to maintain. They belong, in short, to what Mica Nava calls the scopic regimes of contemporary life, 'to regimes of representation and regimes of consumption and looking that extend beyond the immediate iconography of capitalism, that are heterogeneous, differentiated, fragmented, yet part of the ubiquity of the visual and new forms of communication and cultural promotion' (Nava 1997: 46).

The 'convergence' of Hollywood and Madison Avenue has been read symptomatically. In the admixture of cultural fascination and anxiety that defines much writing on the culture of contemporary promotion, there rests a diagnosis of advertising's simultaneous proliferation and invisibility, an outgrowth of the contention that culture (the art of Hollywood) and economy (the artfulness of Madison Avenue) have merged irrevocably. Product placement and branded entertainment have been understood as lamentable features of a world succumbing to insatiable commodity logics. Without wishing to relegate issues of corporate power, this chapter has sought to understand brand marketing as a *contingent* practice. In so doing, I have cautioned against theories that associate branding with 'a univocal world of signs controlled by an abstract force demonized simply as Capital' (Coombe 1998: 134). Elisabeth Moor suggests: 'Rather than seeing the work of marketing as an example of the subsumption of society under capital, it may be more accurate to describe it as the attempt to co-create diffuse and largely immaterial affective territories, which may or may not become exchange value, and which may be more or less successful in mapping consumer space' (Moor 2003: 53). This, I feel, provides a more nuanced framework in which to situate consumer industries and their attempt, through entertainment, to 'break into people's hearts and minds'.

Responding to the complex aggregation and fragmentation of audiences, and to the promotional density of media life, increasing currency has been given to entertainment as a means of coalescing affective bonds ('emotional capital') between consumers and brands. Despite the concentration of signifying power that accrues to corporate brands it remains an uncertain process where companies are never fully able to fix the meaning of signs or capture consumers who move between media in increasingly fleeting ways. Having analysed the specificity of branding from the vantage point of consumer marketing, I want to focus in the next chapter on the contiguous means by which cultural industries have shaped the will-to-brand. As we shall see, this carries its own significance and implications for the way that entertainment and branding have been articulated within the 'affective territories' of cultural and media space.

Chapter 2

Media branding and the entertainment complex

The history of modern entertainment branding is inextricably linked with the Disney Company and its transition in the 1950s from a studio specializing in cartoon animation to a company whose activities would take place within, and in many ways herald, the postwar integration of leisure markets, connecting movie production to developments in television, tourism, theme parks and consumer merchandise. The symbol of this transition was of course Disneyland, the first fully designed theme park that, in emulating the educational principle of world fair expositions and in exorcizing the unruly pleasures of urban attractions like Coney Island, signalled a new type of suburban amusement for middle-class American families. Opening in 1955, the park would form the cornerstone of Disney's entertainment empire. It would also consolidate the name of the company and its association with the paternal figure of Walt Disney. This was achieved through dedicated strategies of cross-promotion, 'Disneyland' fashioned both as a theme park and as a television programme running on the ABC network that Walt himself would host. Organized around the same four divisions as the park – Fantasyland, Adventureland, Frontierland and Tomorrowland – the television series was an exercise of brand marketing. While the Disney Company had been associated with the production of safe and wholesome family entertainment since the 1930s, these were parsed as edifying values as the company planned for the diversification of its activities. Christopher Anderson writes: 'In uniting the TV program and the amusement park under a single name, Disney made one of the most influential commercial decisions in postwar American culture. Expanding upon the lucrative character merchandising market that the studio had joined in the early 1930s, Disney now planned to create an all-encompassing consumer environment that [Walt Disney] described as "total merchandising"' (Anderson 1994: 134). It is in this form of proto-synergy – including the rhetoric of 'total' experience associated with the consumption of movies, their products and associated leisure attractions – from which modern principles of entertainment branding would emerge.

To speak of entertainment branding is to recognize, first and foremost, the particular status that cultural products, specifically the pre-eminent mass amusement of motion pictures, have historically assumed as commodities. If, as Jane

Gaines argues, the film industry is a prototype for other cultural industries, being the first to institute a modern star system and to provide opportunities for advertising tie-ins and product placement, she also suggests that film is a strange and atypical commodity on its own terms (Gaines 2000). Film is difficult to define as a commodity because it is, at the same time, both a product and an experience; it is a physical roll of celluloid and object of transaction between producers, distributors and exhibitors, but also a leisure activity based upon the selling of time and attention. Latterly, this relationship has been materialized into purchasable, collectible, and more fully manipulable objects such as video and DVD. However, a core ambiguity lies at the heart of the commodity status of motion pictures. Thomas Elsaesser puts this well when he suggests that Hollywood has long been defined by the struggle to decide what its key business is. He writes: 'The history of Hollywood could be written as the successive moves to install and define the *commodity "film"*, while at the same time extending and refining the *service "cinema"'* (Elsaesser 2002: 14). From its beginnings, film has differed from other commodity types in the particular conflation of its status as product and service, commodity and experience. The rapid way that motion pictures are consumed and are required to be unique, matched with acute uncertainties about how any single film will perform in the market or be confirmed by audiences, has worked to produce particular conditions for managing risk in the proverbial manufacture of dreams.

Ever since film emerged as a mass entertainment in the first decades of the twentieth century, the motion picture business has sought to control its own industrial vagaries. It has done so through the formation of production and distribution oligopolies but also, at the level of competition between dominating firms, through a range of branding strategies adapted from the advertising industry. These strategies were rationalized when the motion picture industry standardized film as a product in the 1910s and began to concentrate on high-cost feature films that required individual treatment in terms of their advertising. As explained by Robert Cochrane, vice-president of Universal in 1927: 'We cannot standardize our pictures as a soap manufacturer standardizes his soap. They must all be different. So must all our advertisements. We may standardize "brand" advertising, but each film presents a new problem' (cited in Staiger 1990: 6). It was in this context that company names such as Biograph or Pathé, which had initially formed the basis of a movie's brand appeal, were subsumed in the 1910s and 1920s by specific product features such as stars, plots, genres and spectacle. According to Gerben Bakker, the large sums paid by the early Hollywood studios for stars and stories (specifically, adaptations of novels and plays) were part of a process of establishing movies as instant and self-standing brands. He suggests: 'The main value of stars and stories lay not in their ability to predict successes, but in their services as giant "publicity machines" that optimised advertising effectiveness by rapidly amassing high levels of brand awareness' (Bakker 2005: 76). This awareness could extend across products (the image of the star becoming tradeable within and between different films) or could otherwise deepen the life cycle of a single product in the form of licensing agreements and merchandising tie-ins with retail manufacturers and department stores. In each respect, strategies of branding were intrinsic to the development of film as a mass cultural industry between the 1900s and the 1940s, basic to the function of the Hollywood studio system in selling and promoting its wares.

With the breakdown of this system in the immediate postwar period, the function of branding changed. The Paramount decrees of 1948 brought about seismic shifts in the industrial organization of the motion picture business. Divesting studios of their theatre chains, the decrees ushered in a period that, in combination with the rise of television and the boom in postwar leisure consumerism, saw Hollywood struggle with plummeting box office revenues. While this led to new interdependencies between film and television, it also signalled the rise of fewer but more expensive films, inaugurating a blockbuster economy with an inflationary logic that would define Hollywood's output from the mid-1970s. Despite changes in the industrial climate, entertainment branding retained important continuities with the studio system in its focus on stars and stories. The value of 'name' actors and directors and the significance of 'pre-sold properties' still largely determined the branding of individual film events. However, an important underlying difference resides in the crucial shift in power relations that took place in the American film industry between the 1950s and the 1970s. This signalled Hollywood's transition from a studio system where moguls exercised significant control over production rosters and technical and creative talent, to a package-unit system where studios came to finance and distribute film projects put together by agents. As Edward Jay Epstein writes, 'The main task of today's studios is to collect fees for the use of the intellectual properties they control in one form or another and then to allocate those fees among the parties – including themselves – who create, develop and finance the properties' (Epstein 2006: 107). The result has been to redefine the significance of brand names. In the bidding wars and deal-making processes that underwrite the landscape of contemporary film, the brand name of the star, the director, the film property or concept, has become central to competition between rival studios as they seek in their role as distributors and financial 'clearinghouses' to cohere the temporary networks of money, talent and labour that form to make and market a film.[1]

Loosened from the binds of studio contracts, the struggle over brand names has given enormous power to elite stars and directors, who often form their own production companies (such as Mel Gibson's Icon Productions and Steven Spielberg's Amblin Entertainment) to rent out their acting and publicity services. In a series of ways, the rise of agents and the move to a package-unit system has given branding new currency in the way that stars and directors have become their own marketable sub-industries. From Elizabeth Taylor to Arnold Schwarzenegger, stars have increasingly sought to license their image rights and protect their public personas, just as star directors have nurtured their own trademark status.[2] The names of 'Alfred Hitchcock' and 'Steven Spielberg', for instance, have both come to signify brands that have been commercially leveraged within the context of developments within the New Hollywood era. While the cultivation of Hitchcock's creative persona in the 1950s gave rise to the television series (and silhouette title sequence) *Alfred Hitchcock Presents*, orchestrated by the industry power broker Lew Wasserman and produced by a subsidiary of the MCA talent agency, Spielberg parsed his particular brand identity in the early 1990s into the foundation (and fishing cloud logo) of the privately owned studio DreamWorks SKG. From the selling of suspense to the marketing of spectacle, public image has become a vehicle of 'commercial auteurism', to use Timothy Corrigan's term (1998), a form of brand value that has served, not least, to author(ize) texts and ventures beyond the exclusive control of the major studios.

Despite the significance of creative talent to the way that brand names function within the contemporary Hollywood system, my concerns in this chapter are less with stardom and celebrity image than with the development of branding as a *business model* in the age of the vertically integrated entertainment conglomerate. Following on from a wave of mergers in the 1960s between film studios and large manufacturing and service industries, this concentrates on the 1980s and 1990s. This was a period during which key changes in the media environment, including the accelerated conglomeration of the film industry and the emphasis placed on exploiting motion pictures across diversified business structures, helped to reformulate the economic and textual status of film as a commodity. Here, we return to the emblematic (although not strictly conglomerated) case of Disney.[3] Describing Disney's television texts of the 1950s, Christopher Anderson suggests that programmes such as *Disneyland* were 'propelled by a centrifugal force that guided the viewer away from the immediate textual experience toward a more pervasive sense of textuality, one that encouraged the consumption of further Disney texts, further Disney products, further Disney experiences' (Anderson 1994: 155). In seeking to integrate different segments of commercial culture after the war, Disney sought to establish an inhabitable world of corporate-cultural signification that targeted the family audience through a range of mutually interlocking products and services. Such principles of cross-promotion would return with a vengeance at Disney in the 1980s under the helm of Michael Eisner. After a period of corporate stagnation in the 1970s, Eisner helped steer Disney's revival in ways that were both informed by, and informing of, an industrial and regulatory climate defined by mergers and acquisitions, and that would concentrate the possibilities of new ancillary and global markets. It is not my intention to rehearse the details of what is, by now, a well-told story of corporate and technological change, of leveraged corporate deals and the emergence of pivotal technologies such as cable, home video and personal computers (see Prince 2000: 40–141). Instead, I want to draw from it those elements that comprise, and define, the gestalt of 'total entertainment' to which branding has become lynchpin and signature key.

The law of synergy, the language of the franchise: branding comes centre stage

> I'd never heard anyone talk much about 'the brand' before Frank [Wells] and I arrived at Disney. To me, a brand was a marking that you put on horses and cattle. Brand management sounded very austere and serious – something that people did at Procter & Gamble, but perhaps not in a creative business.
>
> Michael Eisner (1998: 234)

In evaluating the significance of his role at Disney, Michael Eisner considers the state of the Disney brand name at the time of his arrival in 1984. Acknowledging the unusual potency of the name 'Disney' to signify and promise a certain kind of experience – what he associates with 'wholesome family fun appropriate for kids of any age, a high level of excellence in its products, and a predictable set of values' – Eisner also writes in his autobiography of a brand that had become 'awkward, old-fashioned, even a bit directionless' (Eisner 1998: 234). It was in this context that Disney's new management team, including Eisner, Frank Wells and Jeffrey Katzenberg, sought to refresh the brand, exploiting the company's valuable assets while extending and diversifying the business. 'Our job wasn't to create something new, but to bring back the magic, to dress Disney up in more stylish clothes and expand its reach, to remind people why they loved the company in the first place' (ibid.: 234). Eisner was not the first to import the concept of brand marketing to the 'creative business' of entertainment. Walt Disney had already made significant headway in the 1950s, the same period that Procter & Gamble had begun to organize its product engineering process according to marketing principles. However, the new team at Disney was instrumental in refining the strategies of cross-fertilization, or synergy, which would be widely emulated as a branding model in the 1980s and 1990s.

According to Michael Wolf, the key to a successful brand is the way that it 'captures the psychological and emotional turf of a particular cultural value' in order that it may be universalized (Wolf 1999: 251). Branding, in this sense, is a question of the degree to which a product or company can naturalize an emotional relation or set of values. In Disney's case, this process has long been organized by the rhetorical 'magic' and 'innocence' attached to values of the family, in particular the white, nuclear, middle-class family. As with all claims to universality, the Disney brand is far from innocent in its articulation of cultural and social relations. For Henry Giroux, Disney values are ideologically invested in a series of ways, such that 'Disney's power and reach into popular culture combine an insouciant playfulness and the fantastic possibility of making childhood dreams come true with strict gender roles, an unexamined nationalism, and a notion of choice that is attached to the proliferation of commodities' (Giroux 1995: 46). While Giroux is rightly aware of the complex, contradictory and potentially subversive way that Disney products may be experienced and consumed by audiences, questions remain about the enchantments of Disney culture and the way that its range of texts and pleasures help serve, and mystify, an aggressive corporate-consumerist agenda. It was the very success of this agenda, however, that drew attention within executive boardrooms and the marketing and entertainment trade press. The company's remarkable turnaround in the 1980s and 1990s – moving from an under-performing studio propped up by theme parks to a global entertainment juggernaut – presented a compelling business model for others, a multitude of companies in the nineties, according to Michael Wolf, 'recognizing the need for an emotional connection' that might underpin their organizational activities. For cultural and consumer businesses alike, Wolf wrote, 'everyone is trying to create a brand. Actually, everyone is trying to be Disney' (Wolf 1999: 224).

What does it mean to be like Disney? For the contemporary motion picture business it has meant pursuing the international family audience. Peter Krämer makes the point that, since the late 1970s, Hollywood has been shaped by the 'return of the family audience' (Krämer 2006). This has been governed by demographic shifts. With the sizeable baby boom generation reaching parenthood in the 1970s, spawning a bulging generation of 'echo boom' children (born between 1977 and 1995), there emerged in America a powerful prospective family market (see Allen 1999). This inclined the major studios towards the 'Disney model', moving away from dependencies on the youth market and 'returning family entertainment to the centre of their transnational multimedia operations' (Krämer 2006: 188). From *Star Wars* to *Shrek*, *Home Alone* to *Harry Potter*, family entertainment has been at the forefront of Hollywood's contemporary industrial strategies and branding efforts. Disney has been attuned, in this regard, to wider transitions in the composition and construction of the domestic and international movie audience. This is especially marked as the film industry has sought formulas that will cross over markets in a territorial as well as a textual sense, building franchises that can span multiple regions, outlets and audience constituencies. It is in the management of this process, however, that Disney has really shaped the mainstays of brand practice in the entertainment industry, bringing together promotional synergy with ruthless assertion of intellectual property rights.

Within Eisner's regime, the role of synergy was formalized in the 1980s, signalled not least by the creation of a vice-presidential position responsible for its implementation. Increasingly, synergy lay at the heart of Disney's identity as a major entertainment and media company. As Janet Wasko explains, Disney's success, which gained purchase in the second half of the 1980s, was linked to a number of calculated strategies. Together with limiting its exposure through cost-cutting measures and the creation of corporate partnerships (such as the ten-year agreement signed in 1996 with McDonald's, the fast food chain paying $100 million for exclusive licensing of all Disney features), Disney increased film production, it successfully revived its animation business, and it moved to exploit a host of ancillary markets. This ranged from the release on home video of classic titles drawn from its animation library, to the creation of branded ventures – including Disney Stores, the Disney Channel, EuroDisney, Disney Theatrical Productions, Disney Cruise Lines, and so forth – that would extend and consolidate the company's stake in leisure attractions, consumer products, television and theatre (Wasko 2003: 28–69). While Disney's creation of Touchstone Pictures in 1984, its purchase of Miramax in 1993 and the pivotal acquisition of ABC/Capital Cities in 1995 (giving the company a major news and entertainment network as well as the premium cable brand ESPN) demonstrate a concomitant desire to broaden the company's range of products and distribution channels, Disney's brand empire was borne of a single name. This would differ from global media companies like Time Warner and the News Corporation that were more decentralized in their organizational structure and in their management of brand assets. As Michael Eisner explained in the company's 1995 annual report:

> We are fundamentally an operating company, operating the Disney brand all over the world, maintaining it, improving it, promoting it and advertising it with taste. Our time must be spent insuring the Brand never slides, that we innovate the Brand, experiment and play with it, but never diminish it.
>
> (Eisner, cited in Collette 1998: 128)

Eisner's assessment is revealing of the degree to which 'the Brand' is conceived of as a 'living entity'. Despite the growing difficulty of Eisner's imperial management style after the death of Frank Wells in 1994 and the poor performance of Disney film and media ventures at the start of the twenty-first century, what Eisner and others called the 'Disney Decade' of the 1990s carried a lesson, demonstrating, quite simply, the necessity to exploit and extend the 'totality' of the brand in cultural space.[4]

Just as significant as the formalization of synergy in this respect was 'the need to pay more attention to protecting the brand … to think more rigorously about what represented an appropriate use of the Disney name and characters, and what seemed excessive or gratuitous' (Eisner 1998: 239). Primacy was given, in other words, to issues of copyright and trademark protection. This has become a defining concern of the Disney Company, enforcing intellectual property rights or lobbying for their extension at every possible turn. This can be understood within a global moment where copyright trade, including the pre-sale of rights to films, images and characters, has become a leading export sector for countries such as the United States. In 2001, revenues generated by the principal copyright industries (film, broadcasting, music recording, computer software, advertising, newspaper and book publishing) contributed $531.1 billion to the US economy, accounting for 5.25 per cent of gross domestic product (Wang 2003: 28). It is in this context that Disney, along with other major entertainment companies and trade organizations such as the MPAA, have sought to shape intellectual property law for its own needs, drawing where required on arguments of American national interest. That Jack Valenti should describe the battle over digital piracy and unauthorized copying in the early 2000s as a 'terrorist war' is indicative in this respect, elevating the moral language of 'robbery' and 'theft' to new heights of industrial-cum-national panic (Streitfeld 2002: 12).

Disney has sought to extend and exploit the judicial enforcement of intellectual property law in two key respects. At one level, it has tried to protect the company's exclusive right to reproduce works for which, in copyright law, Disney is seen as the 'author'. As copyright law protects authored works for a designate period of 75 years – including cartoon characters like Mickey Mouse and feature animation such as *Snow White and the Seven Dwarfs* (1937) – Disney has lobbied to extend legal protections in order to prevent its properties falling into the public domain. This culminated in the Copyright Extension Act of 1998, a Congressional bill that extended copyright protection for an additional twenty years, rescuing Mickey from his original copyright expiration date of 2003. As significant in legal terms, however, is the function of trademark law under which Mickey also falls. This offers protection to rights in the sign (a name or a symbol) as indicating the source of goods for sale. There is no time limitation in this case and, with the judicial extension of state anti-dilution laws in the US (increasing legal protection against the 'dilution' or 'tarnishing' of a trade name), holders of trademarks have been able to prevent 'misappropriation' wherever they seek to find it (Coombe 1998: 67–73). These issues play into wider debates about the affirmation of proprietary rights within (trans)national legal regimes, and the struggles that take place over the use and meaning of commodified texts. In Disney's case, changes in copyright and trademark law since the 1970s have served to ensconce the brand, regulating and repressing threats to its commercial aura in ways that not only suggest a legal system poised to protect prominent corporate symbols, but that support Shujen Wang's claim that 'in the new global informational economy of signs, intellectual property has indeed become the real property' (Wang 2003: 30).

Disney is emblematic of the emergence of branding as an entertainment business model. However, its activities must also be set within wider shifts in the cultural industries during the 1980s and 1990s, deregulation and technological change catalysing what Jennifer Holt calls 'a sweeping realignment of the corporate terrain' (Holt 2001, 2003). This turns centrally on the rise of the entertainment conglomerate, the creation of Time Warner in 1989 becoming its pristine expression. Based on the growing significance of entertainment to Wall Street investors, built on the rollback of anti-trust legislation and designed to exploit the collapsing horizontal and vertical boundaries of the media system, conglomeration has transformed the contemporary entertainment environment. Most significantly, it has seen the rise of a new media oligopoly whereby a small number of global corporations – Viacom, News Corporation, NBC Universal, Time Warner, Sony, Disney, Bertelsmann – manage vast entertainment empires, controlling within the United States alone 96 per cent of film rentals, 98 per cent of advertising revenue on prime-time television, 80 per cent of pay television subscribers and 70 per cent of broadcast television viewing (Epstein 2006: 83).

In popular accounts, such concentration of power is often understood as an expression of competition between moguls (Wolf 1999; Epstein 2006). In this corporate struggle of wills, the attempt by Steve Ross (founding CEO of Time Warner) to exploit the power of vertical integration by owning entertainment content and cable delivery is matched by the desire of Akio Morita (founding CEO of Sony) to connect stakes in hardware and software in selling home entertainment to consumers. Meanwhile, the global ambitions of Rupert Murdoch (founding CEO of News Corporation) to extend his media holdings through international control of news outlets, networks and satellite broadcasting is duplicated in the attempt by Ross and Sumner Redstone (founding CEO of Viacom) to assemble ever-widening global interests in film, radio, television, cable, print journalism, sports teams, theme parks and new media. The corporate realignments of the 1980s and 1990s are of course not reducible to individual personalities. However, the period witnessed the innovation and implementation of particular business strategies that moved, or were steered, in a similar general direction: towards global economies of scale and scope, towards the strategic marriage of content and distribution, towards the importance of the home audience and, as a function of the above, towards the strategic value of film in driving ancillary and cross-promotional opportunities.

The new emphasis on branding emerged as a feature of the changing structures of the entertainment complex; it became a means of tapping into volatile and differentiated global markets while, at the same time, connecting and recycling content across multiple media platforms. With technologies of communication such as cable and home video helping to subdivide media audiences and with entertainment conglomerates focusing both on mass markets and narrow but high-spending niches, the will-to-brand developed in line with the institutionalization of market research. According to Justin Wyatt, one consequence of the first wave of conglomeration in the film industry was the growth of statistical marketing research in the late 1970s. This process, developed as a means of rationalizing corporate decisions about what and for whom movies should be made, helped to reconstruct the movie audience into a series of target markets. In particular, Wyatt concentrates on the example of 'high concept' film (typified by a series of movies made by Paramount in the 1980s such as *Top Gun* (1986)) that were inspired by the aesthetics of music video and were marketed to youth audiences through a range of affiliated media, notably soundtracks (Wyatt 1994). As in the case of high concept, synergy was never the exclusive preserve of Disney. Rather, it developed within a period of corporate restructuring where branding sought to respond flexibly to audience taste and to synchronize a range of products for maximum commercial gain.

Whatever the organizational particularities of a conglomerate in this restructuring process – brand synergy being applied most successfully within Disney's integrated corporate structure – the move towards media consolidation in the 1980s and 1990s had a profound effect on the motion picture business. Indeed, as the film industry was taken up and reconfigured within a burgeoning global entertainment sector, the importance of movie-related brands and licensed merchandise grew exponentially, central to a regime where the creation and control of intellectual property formed, and continues to form, a core strand of corporate profitability. In economic terms, film has become less important as a discrete commodity than as a brand platform that can be transfigured across industries and cultural fields. In the telling words of Aida Hozic, film has become the 'epiphenomenon of its alternative identities: it is not film as the mechanical reproduction of reality that is relevant, but film's permutation into consumer goods, travel options and software programs' (Hozic 2000: 216). This describes the sum and substance of the film franchise. As a term borrowed from consumer and fast food industries, a franchise in this case denotes the partnership between Hollywood, as the owner of a business system offering a branded product or service, and the network of individuals licensed to sell that brand in accordance with the system's regulation of trademarks, logos and intellectual property rights. While the history of the movie franchise can be traced back to the lucrative developments in merchandising associated with *Star Wars* (1977), the increasing need for movies to become a hub of commercial opportunity and brand exchange via product placements, merchandising, licensing, promotional tie-ins and ancillary media moved the logic, as well as the language, of the franchise to the heart of the motion picture business in the 1990s.

It is in relation to the franchise that proclamations about the transformation, even the death, of cinema have been made. Robert Allen, for example, suggests that shifts 'from audience to markets, from film as celluloid experience in a theatre to film combined with so many other manifestations over a longer period of time … not only alters the logics by which films are made and marketed, but also alters what film "is" in an economic sense and, by extension, in both an ontological and epistemological sense as well' (Allen 1999: 119). Coterminous with the decreasing significance of box office revenue to a film's overall profitability, Allen makes the point that film is 'no longer reducible to the experience of actually seeing it'. This speaks of a key alteration within the tradition of cinema and cinematic performance: of the blurring boundaries of commercial and audiovisual culture and of the interpretive status of film as text and event. In this, film is no longer simply a screen experience but something apprehended and understood through a wide environment of cultural encounters, such that the screen experience may not always even be a beginning or end point. If, as some argue, theatrical film is one long marketing device for a range of ancillary products (videos, DVDs, soundtracks), extra-textual experiences (theme park rides, video games) and non-filmic consumables (toys, soft drinks, fast food), then branding has become the lynchpin of a new gestalt of 'total entertainment', central to a consolidated media moment transforming the status of the motion picture as commodity and aesthetic object.

It is the nature of 'total entertainment' that I want especially to explore. My intention, so far, has been to sketch the development of branding as a business model in the entertainment industry since the 1980s. This has been coextensive with changes in the contemporary media environment, brought about by transitions within industrial, technological and legal infrastructures that have both reorganized corporate relationships according to the laws of synergy and centralized control over rights. To understand the significance of brand culture for the emerging global image business, however, it is necessary to account in more detail for the gestalt of 'total entertainment'. This term can be understood in two distinct ways. Firstly, it can be seen as an industrial principle, describing the attempt by global media conglomerates to create an expansive entertainment and communication environment in which they have a disproportionate, near total, stake in terms of ownership and control. Secondly, it can be thought of as a particular form or horizon of cultural and textual practice, growing out of the permeable boundaries and newly 'immersive' modalities of commercial entertainment media. The term that captures best these parallel, although by no means complicit, industrial-aesthetic logics is that of 'convergence'.

While convergence became synonymous with a host of dizzying corporate theories in the late 1990s, a byword for the combining of information and entertainment services on broadband networks, there is something in the term's more general suggestion of connectivity that gets to the economic and epistemic crux of total entertainment. According to Henry Jenkins, understanding the 'cultural logic of media convergence' requires that two seemingly contradictory trends are kept in mind at the same time: the 'alarming concentration of the ownership of mainstream commercial media' that has taken place in recent decades and the capacity of new media technologies and an expanding range of delivery systems to enable 'consumers to archive, annotate, appropriate and recirculate media content in powerful new ways' (Jenkins 2004: 33). Rather than develop monolithic theories of media hegemony or audience sovereignty, Jenkins finds in convergence a process marked by ambivalence; it signals a transitional moment where the proliferation of media channels and the portability of new computer and telecommunications technologies have given power to media giants but have also reshaped relationships between consumers, distributors and producers in unforeseen ways. The impact of digital file sharing on the music industry (and to a lesser extent the film industry) is perhaps the most obvious illustration of these equivocations. If, as Jenkins suggests, convergence represents 'a reconfiguration of media power and a reshaping of media aesthetics and economics', I want to examine how transformations in the media landscape have been felt and addressed by a major studio. My aim is not to dismiss the evident monopolization of media power by the likes of Disney and Time Warner. Rather, I want to acknowledge Michael Wayne's point that 'the simple demonstration of the tendency towards monopoly does not really grasp the processes by which this is achieved or the contradictions and tensions this involves' (Wayne 2003: 83). As a means of focus, I will concentrate on Warner Bros., the key company of Time Warner's 'filmed entertainment' division.

Trajectories of total entertainment

Warner Bros. is now a total entertainment company, made up of movies, television, video, consumer products, stores, international theatres and international theme parks. We've fulfilled our original game plan to build a broad-based entertainment company that doesn't rely on any one business in any given year.

Robert Daly (Time Warner 1997: 19)

Exactly twenty years after Steve Ross turned Warner Communications (WCI) into the prototype for the modern entertainment conglomerate, owning Warner Bros. and a host of cable and media concerns, Ross levered a deal that would transform his company into a global media player. This came as the result of the $14 billion marriage between Time Inc. and WCI in July 1989, the most widely discussed and highly trumpeted media merger to occur in a period where size had become the quintessence of corporate survival. According to company statements, the decision by Time and Warner to unite was born of a mutual need to compete internationally: to participate in the globalization of media industries and to achieve 'a major presence in all of the world's important markets' (Time Warner 1989: 1). With subsequent mergers with Turner Broadcasting Systems in July 1996 and America Online in January 2000, Time Warner sought to assert control of production (content) and outlets (distribution) across a diversified range of entertainment media. With bulging assets in publishing, cable, music, film, television, sports teams, retail outlets, theme parks and new media, Time Warner became the epitome of the vertically and horizontally integrated conglomerate, a formidable, if financially burdened, corporate force committed to the synergies of multimedia investment and to ever-deepening global market expansion.

Warner Bros. became the heart of the conglomerate's 'filmed entertainment' division in this context; it belonged to one of several core units that, after the AOL deal, also included 'networks', 'music', 'publishing', 'cable', and 'America Online'. Rather than inherently collaborative in nature, the major companies that constitute these operational divisions – Warner Bros., New Line, Warner Music, HBO, CNN, AOL, Time Inc., Little Brown, to name the most prominent – have invariably functioned as semi-autonomous fiefdoms. This remains especially true of Warner Bros. Made up of film, television, animation, video, consumer products, international theatre, online and comic sub-divisions, and overseeing Warner Music, Warner Bros. was managed by Robert Daly and Terry Semel until their retirement in 1999. In this year, the combined filmed entertainment division (made up of Warner Bros. and New Line) accounted for 29 per cent of Time Warner's revenue, representing the largest source of revenue for the company as a whole. While this percentage would drop slightly after the AOL merger – contributing $8,759 million to AOL Time Warner's total revenue of $38,234 million in 2001 – filmed entertainment has always weighed substantially on Time Warner's corporate balance sheet (Balnaves *et al.* 2001: 63; Wasko 2003: 62). The pressure to maintain performance levels in this corporate context, however, and to find adaptive strategies for a changing entertainment marketplace, has served to transform the business of film and television in a number of key respects. With the decline in the traditional importance of box office revenue and the rise of the multichannel environment, attempts have been made to find successful business combinations that can maximize performance in and between the fluid markets of the so-called 'post-cinematic' and 'post-network' age.

If synergy has become the watchword of this endeavour, it can be understood not simply as a matter of increasing and exploiting the earning potential of particular intellectual properties, but, more precisely, as a strategy of managing risk. By Robert Daly's account, transforming Warner Bros. into a 'total entertainment company' was an attempt at corporate synergy designed to hedge the liability of market squalls, of not relying 'on any one business in any given year'. This need was particularly acute in the 1990s given the rising costs of movie production and the fact that studio profitability was ever more dependent on ancillary revenues such as licensing, video and DVD. As Richard Maltby suggests of the film business, 'While the media mergers have most commonly been accounted for in terms of the synergies they produce, synergy is actually a rationalization of what is in reality a largely defensive commercial practice aimed at spreading the risks of ultra-high-budget movie production into the lower-cost businesses downstream' (Maltby 2003: 211). This defensive principle underwrites other kinds of synergistic expansion. In television, for example, the creation of broadcast networks such as the WB – launched in January 1995 anticipating the removal of the 'Fin-Syn' rules[5] – helped guarantee an internal window for programmes bought and produced by Warner Bros. As a means of cross-promoting media content on a ready-made network, the WB also helped protect the studio from threats of exclusion by the big network gatekeepers (NBC, CBS, ABC, Fox) able, for the first time, to broadcast their own in-house programming (Collette 1998; Holt 2003).

Describing synergy as a 'defensive practice' is not the same as defending it as a practice. The logic of synergy, like that of convergence, is linked to the concentration of power enabled by a deregulated media system where news and entertainment sources and distribution channels are now owned by a few giant conglomerates. In this context, branding provides a way for corporations to differentiate their content offerings and consolidate footholds in the entertainment marketplace. As Time Warner's 1995 annual report made clear, 'brands build libraries, libraries build networks, networks build distribution, distribution builds brands'. By this logic, branding is a means of acquiring competitive advantage by controlling and extending copyright properties (*The Sopranos*, *Batman*, *Larry King Live*) across an integrated system of production/delivery with a corporate brand value of its own (HBO, Warner Bros., CNN). In the words of chief executive Gerald Levin, Time Warner's 'powerful synthesis of branded content and branded networks – the world's most trusted sources for news and entertainment – ensures that we will continue to lead the competition' (Time Warner 1995: 3). As a corporate strategy, branding attributes value to products and platforms in ways that help aggregate multiple niche audiences and establish a basis for industry expansion.

The example of the WB is suggestive here. Along with the creation of studio stores, theme parks and multiplex venues in the 1990s, all extending 'Warner Bros.' as a brand signifier (discussed in Part III), the WB used the studio's brand name to penetrate the burgeoning multichannel environment. With major cable networks such as NBC and CBS wrestling with dramatic losses in market share during the nineties, and with a host of networks like HBO, ESPN, and MTV creating powerful niche constituencies in their place, television networks developed a range of brand strategies in the resulting competition for audiences (McMurria 2003). From promotional campaigns and network tag lines to channel 'idents' and revamped logos, network branding was fuelled in great measure by what John Caldwell calls 'the growing sense that there was simply not enough of an audience to go around, that is, not enough to share (profitably) with all of the competition'. As he suggests, 'branding was the first of many tactics that exploited the instability of the televisual form in the age of digital' (Caldwell 2004: 57).[6] In this case, the WB used the studio's initials and a dusted-down cartoon character (Michigan J. Frog) to signal its emphasis on family entertainment. According to one marketing executive, the WB was designed to 'complement what Warner Bros. means to the public and what the stores have done for the image of the company' (cited in Flint 1995: 14). In key respects, the WB was an instance of Warner's strategic emulation of the Disney model in the 1990s, pursuing young viewers through teen dramas such as *Dawson's Creek* (1998–2003) and *Buffy the Vampire Slayer* (1997–2001) while targeting children through its 'Kids WB' programming block. It is not my intention to outline the complex history of network broadcasting in the 1990s, or indeed that of the WB before its incorporation into the CW Network in September 2006. What *Variety* described as the 'frenzy of network branding' (Levin 1995) in the multichannel environment does begin to raise questions, however, about the relation of brand practice to transitions in the media environment, specifically the way that entertainment companies like Warner Bros. have sought to expand revenue opportunities through flexible corporate frameworks that concurrently pursue broad national/global markets and specific niche audiences.

If vertical integration is 'simultaneously driven by segmentation and unified vision, broad range and specific demographics' (Holt 2003: 11), the WB is an example of corporate attempts to cross-promote and 'window' products for a narrowcast market. For critics such as Jeffrey Sconce, this has given rise to particular textual strategies. Specifically, he considers how programmes such as *24*, *Star Trek* and *Buffy the Vampire Slayer* have sought to foster 'intensified viewer involvement' as a response to the need to compete more aggressively for audiences. For Sconce, 'US television has devoted increased attention in the past two decades to crafting and maintaining ever more complex narrative universes, a form of "world-building" that has allowed for wholly new modes of narration and that suggests new forms of audience engagement' (Sconce 2004: 95). This speaks of a nascent principle of immersion in cultural production, achieved in television both through cumulative series architecture and the spawning of books, websites, chat rooms and phone messaging. More recently, this principle of immersion has been accelerated by multiplatform media properties like *Big Brother* and WB's *Popstars*, reality formats combining television programming with websites, podcasts, e-mail updates, print publications, even music production and concert venues. For John

Caldwell, these examples represent forms of 'convergence television', typifying the new migratory patterns of industrial texts and the impetus to 'calculate, amass, repackage, and transport the entertainment product across the borders of both new technologies and media forms' (Caldwell 2004: 50, 2006). Of interest here is the precept of textual 'inhabitation' and 'interactivity' that has become linked with the branding of commercial entertainment. While Sconce associates 'world-building' with the pursuit of specialized television audiences, a textual effect born of particular institutional instabilities in the multichannel era, a similar impulse to cultivate total environments (as consuming experiences) governs Hollywood's franchise strategy in relation to the global mass audience.

As a 'defensive practice', franchising can be understood as a response to institutional instabilities within the film business during the 1990s stemming from escalating production costs, declining box office margins and the persistent pressure on studios to fulfil the goals of shareholders. With US theatrical rates-of-return falling from 31 per cent to 23 per cent between 1988 and 1999, and dipping as low as 8 per cent between 1996 and 1998, Hollywood was struck mid-decade by an incipient feeling of crisis (Pokorny 2005; Connor 2000). This was catalysed by anxieties about the requirement of $100 million movies to 'open big' on first weekends. The perception of a movie's 'success' or 'failure' at the US box office could, of course, be deceptive. Decline in the importance of domestic theatrical rentals during the 1990s was matched by the increased significance of international and ancillary revenue. While the domestic box office could still potentially determine a film's earnings in other markets, the importance of global/ancillary revenue meant that even the most spectacular box office disasters could prospectively turn a profit. *Waterworld* (1995) and *Godzilla* (1998) are examples in kind, Tom Shone calling the latter 'the world's first $375 million flop, which is to say, no flop at all' (Shone 2004: 272).[7] In addition to a film's residual earning capacity, major studios took measures in the nineties to distribute the risks associated with high-budget films, limiting their exposure through co-production deals and spreading investment across a portfolio of projects whereby successful films, invariably 'tent-pole' movies, would pay for the losers.

By all accounts, 'risk' is a relative term in the motion picture business. While strategies of diversification have tempered the commercial instabilities of the industry, the fact that a very few successful films make up a studio's earnings – a billion-dollar blockbuster can transform a studio's annual performance single-handedly – has given rise to the feverish preoccupation with 'megabrands'. As Richard Maltby suggests, 'the integrated entertainment marketplace is most receptive to multi-media franchises, and once the majors created a corporate structure designed to maximize the benefits of synergy, they found themselves inevitably obliged to develop products capable of "synergistic brand extension"' (Maltby 2003: 211). As he goes on to suggest, however, franchise movies have their own risks. While the demands of techno-spectacle have continued to spur massive cost inflation, franchise movies may exhaust themselves in the market or simply fail to launch a resonant brand identity that can underwrite a film's calculated commercial afterlife. This creates a precarious situation where, even with the aggressive pre-selling of licensing rights and blanket pre-release publicity, big-budget films can still threaten to incur monumental losses for studios and their partners. These were issues facing Robert Daly and Terry Semel at the end of their tenure at Warner Bros.

For much of the early 1990s, Warner Bros. relied on movies with established stars like Clint Eastwood and on proven formulas such as the *Lethal Weapon* and *Batman* series. It effectively specialized in star-driven, high-budget movies, a strategy that maintained Warner Bros. as one of the top two performing studios for much of the 1980s and early 1990s. The dismal theatrical performance of *The Postman* in 1997, however, combined with stuttering sequels such as *Batman and Robin* (1997) and *Lethal Weapon 4* (1998), precipitated a box office slump that led to a re-evaluation of the studio's roster and marketing approach. One Hollywood exec-utive surmised: 'the most successful films recently have been in the $70m–$100m range, and that is what Warner does. The problem is, it has been putting the wrong kinds of pictures in that budget level' (Hazelton 1998). Finding the right picture became a priority in this context. Striving to invigorate its output of movie block-busters by recruiting talent from the realm of independent cinema – the Wachowski brothers moving from the low-budget *Bound* (1996) to the heights of the *Matrix* trilogy (1999–2003), Christopher Nolan and Bryan Singer translating their 'indie' pedigree to *Batman Begins* (2005) and *Superman Returns* (2006), respec-tively – Warner Bros. also sought to extend more fully the economic-aesthetic logic of the franchise. In short, it sought to invest in films with commercial 'world-build-ing' capacity. While these tendencies were first signalled in *Batman* (1989), which was the studio's inaugural franchise blockbuster directed by Tim Burton, Warner Bros. intensified its concern at the turn of the millennium with serials, spin-offs and genres that were based quite specifically on the filmic realization of a pre-sold, inveterately marketable, narrative universe. This governed the studio's primary investment in animation (*Looney Tunes, Pokémon, Scooby Doo*), fantasy (the *Harry Potter* franchise, *Charlie and the Chocolate Factory*), comic book adaptations (*Batman Begins, Superman Returns*) and science fiction (the *Matrix* trilogy). Seeking films that could be targeted at the global audience and that could mutate into other products, Warner Bros. amplified its stake in movies that could imagine inhabitable worlds (and generate licensable characters) for children, teenagers and adults alike.

The origins of this impulse go back to *Star Wars*, what Scott Bukatman describes as 'less a movie than an extended multimedia universe' (Bukatman 1998: 248). Marking the arrival (or revival) of a cinema defined by spectacular excess and sensory involvement, *Star Wars* is a key instance for Bukatman of the means by which film can expand beyond the screen, 'something to inhabit rather than watch'. If the act of play is central to 'the expansion of cinema into a more environmental and ambient form', the logic of convergence, as witnessed in the television industry, has facilitated patterns of play *across* media, movies giving themselves to expansion not simply through toys and merchandise but through active interrelation with other cultural forms. Concerned with shifting formations of audience pleasure and 'gameplayer agency', P. David Marshall associates this with 'the new intertextual commodity'. Specifically, he outlines a mode of cultural production based on structured forms of interactivity designed to meet, and take advantage of, the permeable boundaries of film, television, publishing, consumer products, websites, video and computer games. Describing the 'intensification and elaboration of the intertextual matrix' that accompanies multimedia events, he writes:

> The culture industries are providing a circumscribed agency for the new audience by providing complex patterns of engagement and exploratory architectures. Wedded to this development of the complex and new inter-textual commodity is the expansion of the pleasure of anticipation through more elaborate strategies of product promotion. Various forms of promotion are aligned with providing background information on cultural forms that are designed to deepen the investment of the audience in the cultural commodity.
>
> (Marshall 2002: 80)

If we accept Marshall's portrait of the entertainment industry as one defined by the attempt to generate depth of engagement with commercial media, presuming as it does a more active spectator who can (and will) follow new forms of transmedia flow (Jenkins 2006), it is perhaps not incidental that one of Hollywood's most self-consciously immersive and 'exploratory' films of the nineties should be called *The Matrix* (1999). Just as television has sought to reinforce viewer commitments through niche strategies of network branding and narrative 'world-building', Hollywood has been quick to establish its own spectacles of total entertainment as a means of deepening the significance of film events for the global mass audience. It is in this respect that we might turn by way of illustration to Warner Bros.' most distinctive franchise project of the 1990s and to a film that in many ways captures the episteme of total entertainment at the turn of the twenty-first century.

Brand regimes: enter *The Matrix*

> We know we've bought something cool. We don't know what it is.
> Warner Bros. executive to the Wachowski brothers
> (*The Matrix* Revisited 2004)

For Warner Bros. production executives such as Lorenzo di Boniventura, *The Matrix* was a speculative investment in bringing something 'innovative' and 'cutting-edge' to the studio. Not insignificantly, it was put into production in 1997, the same year that Warner Bros. experienced a significant slip in its market share. As a cinematic object, *The Matrix* is much discussed, generating a raft of popular and academic literature about the film's relation to computer games and kung-fu choreography, its premillennial sensitivities, as well as the transmedia storytelling represented by the franchise phenomenon as a whole (see Clover 2004; Gillis 2005; Jenkins 2006). While *The Matrix* lends itself to critical readings of various kinds, I am particularly interested in the film's inscribed status as a cinematic brand. Arguing that *The Matrix* is most significantly 'about life as we lived it around 1999', Joshua Clover identifies a contradictory impulse in the film that reflects uncertainties about the power of technology and spectacle within its contemporaneous visual digital moment. He contends that the film is 'a historic advance in digital entertainment that is unpacifiably anxious about the dangers of digitality; it's a critique of spectacles that is itself a spectacle' (Clover 2004: 15). If this suggests a residual ambivalence about the status of big-budget Hollywood movies at the end of the nineties – blockbusters becoming a growing focus of cultural and economic life in their global mobilization of images, goods and hyperrealized fantasies – one might extend Clover's paradox by saying that *The Matrix* is a critique of branding that is itself a pervasive media brand.

In different ways, the spectral, and spectacularly visualized, world of *The Matrix* returns us to the altered logics by which movies are made and marketed, and to the ontological and epistemological definition of what contemporary film 'is' or takes itself to be. There are three ways in which *The Matrix* is an especially suggestive illustration of the brand regimes of total entertainment at the close of the nineties. The first two relate to questions of style and storyworld. Undoubtedly, a key source of brand identification for *The Matrix* was its distinctive visual look. From the spectacle of 'bullet-time' to the sleek costuming that gave sartorial cachet to shades and leather trench coats, the film was influenced by, and influencing of, the surrounding culture of advertising and fashion. Its visual register 'jacked in' to the world of branded lifestyles. While bullet-time techniques (of circling objects and bodies stilled in flight) had been used previously in advertisements for Smirnoff and The Gap, Pamela Church Gibson observes that the simulated reality of the Matrix was 'designed and presented using many of the visual conventions associated with commercials, fashion shoots and even catwalk shows' (Church Gibson 2005: 117). She suggests that the pleasure of costume spectacle in the grid of the Matrix, linked to the display of cars, cellphones and other lifestyle products, indicates the complete immersion of Hollywood in fashion and style, even as the film establishes this world as something to be demystified. Although it is commonplace for Hollywood movies to impress a marketable look through product styling (the raining green code of *The Matrix*) and fashion-inspired images (the battle-ready figures of Neo, Trinity and Morpheus), the identity of the film was based on the extravagance of its 'cool' visual appeal.[8] As Claudia Springer writes, *The Matrix* 'not only looks cool, it is also about the attainment of cool, about the transformation of a geek into an icon of incomparable cool' (Springer 2005: 89). The film becomes a performance of style in this respect; the fashioning of identity is played out in a gleaming and spectacular world which the film critiques but emphatically plays within.

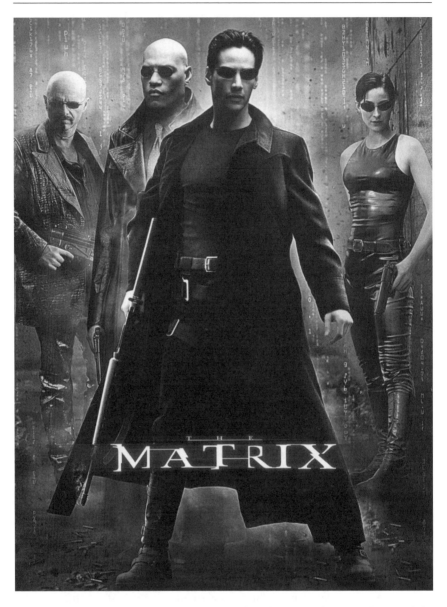

Figure 2.1 Media 'cool' and *The Matrix* brand (1999). Courtesy of Warner Bros. and the Ronald Grant Archive.

At one level, *The Matrix* ministers to the politics of style, taste and youth subculture in its calculated cool factor; it solicits cult fascination amongst its digitally savvy, brand-literate target audience. The film invokes a host of philosophical allusions, however, in ways that also seek to extend the popularity of *The Matrix* beyond a core young male audience. The official website 'whatisthematrix. warnerbros.com' featured lengthy discussion about the film's representation of the world, servicing a highbrow fan constituency enthralled to its metaphysical overtures and express postmodernism. That *The Matrix* should reference Jean Baudrillard through a momentary glimpse of his classic work *Simulacra and Simulation* (1983) is unsurprising given the tendency of the film (and series) to wear philosophy on its sleeve. It also marks the ambiguity of the film's relation to brand signification, however. While visually steeped in codes of advertising and fashion, the film constructs a mythos based on struggles fought within and against the phantasmagoria of signs. In his gloomy predictions about the 'death of the real', Baudrillard reserves special antipathy for branding. He suggests 'the lexicon of brands ... is doubtless the most impoverished of languages: full of signification and empty of meaning. It is a language of signals. And "loyalty" to a brand name is nothing more than the conditioned reflex of a controlled affect' (Baudrillard 1988: 17). *The Matrix* gives allegorical freight to this vision of control. Literalizing a world experienced entirely through code, it offers up the nightmare that Naomi Klein finds in nineties-style branding, a situation where marketing mavens take the cultural and social experiences associated with products 'out of the representational realm and make them a lived reality' (Klein 2000: 29). Envisioning the triumph of the (commodity) sign, the world of the Matrix can be seen as the ultimate brandscape, the struggle of Thomas Anderson/Neo representing the interminable struggle against a world of (capitalist) simulation.

And yet, here the paradox of *The Matrix* becomes fully evident. While both the style and storyworld of the film, at some level, mediate contemporary brand culture, it becomes itself a branded cinematic object par excellence. As Jonathan Romney observes of the franchise: 'The most glaring paradox of the *Matrix* project, of course, is that while it proposes a fictional programme for liberating ourselves from a dominating system – implicitly global capitalism and the entertainment complex – there isn't a single commercially available piece of the puzzle that doesn't somewhere bear the inscription "© Warner Bros"' (Romney 2003: 27). This describes the aggressive proliferation of the *Matrix* name in the marketplace, the success of the first film (grossing $450 million) creating the impetus for two high-budget sequels and a number of textual permutations. The latter would include a heavily marketed series of anime stories relating to the world of the *Matrix* called *The Animatrix* (2003), a comic series, a computer game titled *Enter the Matrix* (2003), the multiplayer game *The Matrix On-Line* (2004) and a host of licensed products. Together, these would generate complex narrative interplays, *Matrix*-based stories developed in and across a network of texts. Creating a world in which contexts, characters, events and back-stories are realized through 'multiple degrees of iteration across all the different media, crossing boundaries of both media and versions of stories' (Wood 2005: 15), the *Matrix* franchise was distinctive in the way it encouraged audiences to participate actively in a transmedia environment.[9] This can be seen as an expression of aggressive franchise commodification by Warner Bros., but also something more. The visual and narrative 'architecture' of the

Matrix series was informed by a concept of immersion responsive to shifts in the media landscape. Specifically, it expressed a particular re-thinking of content brought about by the convergence of media ownership and technology at the end of the 1990s. This figured centrally around the capacity of digital binary code to unify media commodities of all types (Murray 2005). With digital technology reducing the costs of creating, storing and transferring content from one format to another, the *Matrix* franchise was emblematic of the increasingly liquid nature of media content and the attempt by Hollywood to harness and protect its stake as an anchor, or entry-point, to branded media experience.

Describing the mutability of *The Matrix*, Patricia Mellencamp suggests that the film 'represents a confluence, a grid, of aesthetic and structural forms – theater, film, graphic arts (particularly comic book drawing and stories), television, and centrally, I think, computer games' (Mellencamp 2001: 84). In key respects, *The Matrix* was a reaction to the multi-billion dollar games industry that challenged Hollywood's economic dominance at the end of the 1990s.[10] It is perhaps no surprise given the phenomenal success of games such as *Tomb Raider* (1996), and other titles made for the burgeoning console and computer market, that *The Matrix* should invoke their interactive style. Often replicating the *mise en scène* and point-of-view of digital games, notably in fight sequences and the use of bullet-time, the *Matrix* films establish a graphic architecture with deliberate affinities with the immersive feel and playable aesthetic of contemporary video games. The concept of entering a (virtual) world would translate neatly to the *Matrix* games. However, the principle of textual exploration was not restrained to the activity of gamers and committed fans. It was also figured in the market *The Matrix* helped create, that of DVD.

Joining in partnership with the Japanese electronics giant Toshiba in 1992, Time Warner had a key stake in the development of DVD as a replacement for video. Introduced in 1997, the Digital Video Disc penetrated the market faster than any previous entertainment technology, its self-denoting 'versatility' and promise of superior digital quality positioning itself to become 'an intimate and indispensable part of a high-tech universe of home and personal technologies' (Klinger 2006a: 364). According to Barbara Klinger, the ascendance of DVD, made all the more swift by the economic incentives of cheap manufacturing costs, cost-effectiveness in renting/retailing and the falling price of DVD players, helped redefine 'how movies are offered to and experienced by home viewers'. While Klinger is ultimately concerned with the dynamics of household film consumption, she outlines features of a 'DVD film culture' that has implications for the production and marketing of film itself. The ability of viewers to watch scenes repeatedly through precision time-shifting, for example, has arguably reinforced the importance of generic spectacle (fight scenes, car chases) as well as the minutiae of *mise en scène* (background detail, body display), both increasingly subject to the powers of digital replay and freeze-frame. In a different vein, movies are now routinely accompanied by the production of special editions and 'behind-the-scenes' extras, what Klinger examines as the presentation of 'insider' knowledge about film technique, meaning and industrial process. The spectacular effects, narrative intricacies, and production history of *The Matrix* gave themselves to home viewing's new invitation to explore, becoming the first runaway DVD hit, selling 1.3 million copies in its first week of release. Joshua Clover writes of the film:

> Successful in the theatre, it was a watershed in the home, essentially inventing a market. This sort of superpresence is far from being solely an economic fact. It chimes rather harmoniously with the script's conception of immanent image projection: like the Matrix, *The Matrix* is the movie that's everywhere, and was designed to be so.
>
> (Clover 2004: 49)

The DVD release of *The Matrix* helped cement the film's status as a phenomenon.[11] It was also indicative of attempts by Warner Bros. to establish the principle of total entertainment for different kinds of viewer, creating 'a unified, expansive sphere that immerses the home viewer, the filmgoer and the gamer equally' (ibid.: 55). Through films, games, DVD and other media – each offering exploratory pathways into the layered totality of a brand/world – the *Matrix* franchise was a calculated attempt by Warner Bros. to establish an 'emphatic sense of presence' in the global media market. This derived from strategies such as the back-to-back global release of the second and third parts of the series (the studio designating 2003 'The Year of the Matrix'), but it also stemmed from the manner in which 'presence' became a question of audience encounter: creating a new depth of engagement through the kinetic visual spectacle of the films themselves, through the navigation of DVD chapters, scenes and bonus material, through storyline iteration across a range of discrete and interplaying texts, through the interactivity of *Matrix* gaming and online fan-writing sites, or through multiple combinations therein.

Distinctive in its experimental transmedia structure, *The Matrix* is suggestive of the way that the 'mass audience no longer refers to one simultaneous experience so much as a shared, asynchronous cultural milieu' (Curtin 1996: 197). In effect, the franchise became a global media event that sought to organize and exploit different points, or vertices, of audience involvement. Simone Murray relates this content strategy to a new enthusiasm amongst global media corporations for 'streaming' branded products. She writes:

> At the core of the contemporary phenomenon of media branding lies the abstraction of content from the constraints of any specific analogue media format. Content has come to be conceptualized in a disembodied, almost Platonic, form: any media brand which successfully gains consumer loyalty can be translated across formats to create a raft of interrelated products, which then work in aggregate to drive further consumer awareness of the media brand. Given the dominance of film divisions within global media conglomerates, the content package driving this process is frequently a feature film. Yet a

key aspect of content's new streamability is its unpredictable, multi-directional impulse.

(Murray 2005: 417)

The unpredictability of 'content streaming' gets to the root of the tensions and ambivalences of media convergence, especially as it bears on the contemporary movie business. While the Hollywood blockbuster may well drive synergistic operations within global media companies, questions remain for studio executives about the place and profitability of film as a self-standing industry: how to manage the rising costs of movies as they seek to compete as must-see 'events', how to respond to changing viewing habits as industrial-textual hierarchies (between film, television, video games, new media) continue to blur, how to manage and control the way that content is anticipated, discussed and downloaded by audiences. The *Matrix* trilogy is in many ways symptomatic of the attempt by Warner Bros. to position itself within a broadening, and ever more complex, entertainment environment. A studio franchise carefully attuned to its own brand status, *The Matrix* is a corporate property revealing the anxieties, as well as the ambitions, of Hollywood in continuing to remodel the motion picture as a multipurpose object.

In this conjuncture lies the status of film itself. That the Warner Bros. logo should be cast in phosphorous green in the title sequence of *The Matrix* is not a frivolity. As the next chapter will show, it speaks to the way that film has sought to announce itself in a changing media world. Despite pronouncements about the end of cinema, by which is often meant the end of a particular type of film (celluloid in matter, narrative in style) seen and experienced in a movie theatre, Robert Allen makes the point that 'movies continue to want to claim the ground of authenticity, as the originating site of experience' to which other texts and licensed products relate (Allen 1999: 120). Despite the way that high-budget films are now leveraged across multiple media platforms and transfigured into a host of non-filmic commodities, movies still seek, in Allen's words, 'to retain their power to enchant'. With box office performance determining the success of a movie's earning capacity in other markets, the event-based promotion of film, and filmgoing, remains critical to the activity of global media corporations. The gestalt of 'total entertainment' has not, in this sense, altered the function of contemporary Hollywood studios in selling the commodity 'film' and the service 'cinema'. Rather, its significance lies in the way that film and cinema have increasingly come to be understood as something environmental, a spectacular experience to enter and inhabit. The manner in which this has been constituted as a specific *brand* experience is the subject of the rest of this book.

Part II

Brand logos

Chapter 3

Studio logos and the aesthetics of memory and hype

In August 1993, the *New Yorker* expressed concern that the torch-bearing figure in the monumental trademark of Columbia Pictures had lost weight, transformed from a marble statue to a lifelike figure with a passing resemblance to Hillary Clinton. Purchased by Sony in 1989, Columbia moved to update its logo, refiguring the studio's identity for what corporate executives labelled a 'new phase in its history' (Barry 1993: 25). This was not the first such modification. While the US flag had been removed from the logo in 1941, replaced with plain drapery, the 'Lady' was removed altogether in 1975, giving way to an abstract logo that set the image of torchlight against a black crescent design. Signalling Columbia's diversification into the key markets of film, video and television, the abstract logo symbolized the company's desire to 'light up all corners of the entertainment world' ('The Lady may be gone' 1975). In significant ways, the 1993 redesign was part of a widespread tendency among studios to refashion corporate identity in times of change. However, it happened in a period in which branding had become an especially powerful imperative for both new and established media companies, serviced by a growing number of brand consultants, logo specialists and graphic design boutiques.

In the 'transaction-rich nexus of markets' (Lash and Urry 1994: 111–44) that surrounds and supports media industries, brand consultants flourished in the 1990s, responding to changing orthodoxies and technologies of promotional imaging. Within broadcast industries in particular, branding practices based on the development of specific kinds of programming content were matched with a proliferation of network slogans, screen logos ('bugs') and channel identifiers ('idents'). Graphically innovative brand campaigns became a routine feature of a network landscape defined by the pressures and economics of channel differentiation.[1] Meanwhile, the early 1990s saw a flurry of modifications to studio logos in response to broad changes in corporate management and the launch of specific entertainment divisions. From refinements to Columbia's torch-bearing Lady to the appearance of Bugs Bunny and lion cubs on the family entertainment banners of Warner Bros. (in 1993) and MGM (in 1994) respectively, logos became indicative symbols of global media restructuring in a period that the executive vice-president of Columbia, Sid Ganis, described as 'about richness, depth, and, yes, the grandeur of Hollywood, but also about emotion and communication' ('What's In a Logo?' 1993). Logos were vital in the perceived need to update corporate identity for prospective entertainment futures. In visual terms, this involved the use and incorporation of digital effects, rendering logos in creatively engineered and increasingly panoramic forms. High-tech resuscitations were able to hold in balance the glories of Hollywood's past with the promise of something adaptive and new. While studio logos function in a different way to the brand idents of network television – figured as discrete corporate signatures within a film's tailored publicity rather than as a means of cohering specific kinds of programming content – Hollywood trademarks have nevertheless been influenced by the dynamic modes of logo projection that have arisen in what Michael Curtin calls the 'neo-network era' (Curtin 1996).

This term is used by Curtin to describe a new volatility in contemporary culture industries, encompassing film as well as television. It approximates the reorganiza-tion of the US culture industries around neo-Fordist models of flexible accumula-tion, describing an industrial configuration where production, marketing and distribution systems have become increasingly diverse and decentred. Foretelling the difficulty facing large corporations in controlling the distribution of cultural forms, Curtin suggests that, just as IBM lost its dominant organizational position in the computer industry, Hollywood studios and network broadcasters face a similar risk. He writes: 'we may be witnessing a shift away from an emphasis on hardware and limited channels of distribution towards software and flexible corporate frameworks. Rather than a centralized network structure anchored by New York finance, Hollywood studios, and state-regulated technology, the neo-network era features elaborate circuits of cultural production and reception' (ibid.: 190). In a period characterized by industrial transition – when a mass audience can no longer be dependably constructed, systems of copyright governance have been chal-lenged by the emergence of digital piracy, and electronic technologies are threat-ening to eclipse the basis of long-held network and studio empires – entertainment companies have sought to project their logos as a means of confirming specific kinds of industrial authority and viewing pleasure.

For Hollywood studios this endeavour has involved the dissemination of tradi-tional brand signatures (or variations thereof) throughout the multiple consumer and exhibition windows of the global entertainment sector, carrying trademark labels across video, consumer products, animation, television, family entertain-ment and theatrical divisions. It has also shaped the logo aesthetics of motion picture features. Indeed, studio logos were given crisp visual makeovers in the 1990s and were often customized for specific blockbuster events.[2] While, as mentioned in the last chapter, the Warner Bros. shield transformed into a fore-boding green circuit board in *The Matrix* (1999), in *Harry Potter and the Philosopher's Stone* (2001) owls and bats flew from its corners. Meanwhile, the world logo of Universal became both the diluvian setting of *Waterworld* (1995) and the desert sun in *The Mummy* (1999). Consistent with its overt theatricality, *Moulin Rouge* (2001) even staged a musical prelude to the cinematic unveiling of the Twentieth Century

Fox searchlights. Studio logos have come to play a more pronounced role in the formal, stylistic and thematic unfolding of Hollywood trailers and credit sequences, inviting questions not only about the nature of corporate branding in post-classical Hollywood, but also about how logos act upon, and can give meaning to, a film.

With the growing complexity of production and distribution deals, and the tendency of the majors to spread risk through agreements with other companies, credit sequences can find themselves prefaced with a volley of corporate logos. Those of the studio majors may appear for a number of reasons: if the movie was financed and developed exclusively for a studio, if it was created for a production company based at the studio, or if the studio functioned as the distributor. David Cook notes that during the 1970s, when studios reconfigured their power base in distribution, the majors would brand independent productions as their own, 'bolstering their image as purveyors of feature films to the nation' (Cook 2000: 21). This trend has continued on an international scale, adding to the general complexity of who makes, owns and profits from what. Logo sequences can include a range of narrativized brand signatures, including those of distributors and production outfits, as well as technical trademarks such as THX and Dolby (examined in the next chapter). In a period in which entertainment companies compete for, and seek to extend, presence in the global media market, and in which audiovisual libraries have become an important source of brand value in their capacity to be figured as equity, corporate logos have acquired a dynamic function in the cultural economy of filmed entertainment.

It is the projection of entertainment logos that I want to explore in Part II of *Brand Hollywood*. Before analysing the franchise properties that occupy much of the discussion about motion picture branding, I feel it is instructive to consider the on-screen thresholds that routinely commence, and thereby pattern and set expectations about, the experience of film. At one level, the 'performance' of entertainment logos relates the practice of branding discussed in Part I to what Vivien Sobchack calls 'our sensual experience of the cinema'. By inviting audiences to encounter or inhabit the world of the trademark, corporate logos have become increasingly tactile, appealing from the outset of film experience to 'the way we are in some carnal modality able to touch and be touched by the substance and texture of images' (Sobchack 2004: 65). Sobchack is ultimately concerned with the capacity of film, including promotional trailers, 'to physically arouse us to meaning' (see Sobchack 2005). While sharing certain of her interests, it is not my intention to address logos in ways that make claims about cinema's phenomenological characteristics, or that otherwise measure the effects of branding upon audiences.[3] Instead, I consider how the *poetics of branding* within institutional signatures, specifically the process of 'bringing to life' corporate logos, relates to particular negotiations of studio identity and trademark power.

Henry Jenkins suggests that 'since the breakdown of the studio system, Hollywood has entered into a period of prolonged and consistent formal experimentation and institutional flux with a media-savvy audience demanding consistent aesthetic novelty and difference' (Jenkins 1995: 114). Studio logos reveal a telling history in this context. Evoking the legacy of the studio system while announcing the novelty of contemporary film events, studio logos are bound in a representational economy of memory and hype. This chapter will examine these dynamics by drawing upon the logo history of Warner Bros. and Paramount. Seeking to develop an expansive purview of corporate branding associated with motion picture features, I will consider expressions of studio branding and logo design in key moments of the post-classical period. As a symbolic inscription of media memory and industrial advertisement, studio logos provide an acute means of analysing the expressive history of entertainment branding in the era of package-unit production; they offer a specific entry point into what Thomas Elsaesser has described as the 'micro-links and macro-level synergies that hold today's media culture together' (Elsaesser 2002: 13).

On the history of studio logos

In her discussion of the history and theory of film advertising, Janet Staiger suggests that Hollywood's promotional activities must be analyzed in terms of the normative procedures that have been established in specific periods of time. While Hollywood has frequently imitated the strategies of modern advertising practice, she suggests that the film industry has also had to adjust and innovate marketing methods for its own needs and problems. Staiger writes that from the period of early cinema 'it was not at all apparent that what the industry had to sell was a product. Rather it was the *experience* of an entire show that had to be sold: a show that eventually would feature one special film that would run for only a certain period of time and be replaced by a similar – but different – movie' (Staiger 1990: 3). In the first decade of the twentieth century, the motion picture industry advertised and distributed its product by way of the company brand. With films conceived as a relatively standardized commodity (offered on one-reel films), the brand name of the production company – Biograph, Vitagraph, Lubin, Pathé – took precedence. With the rise of the star system, however, a shift occurred in the public mind from brands to stars (Bowser 1994: 103–19). By 1913, changes in the industry system – including the development of the feature film, the emergence of fan magazines and other formal means of achieving close identification with actors – set in place a transition that reduced production companies, and later studios, to the background of promotional activity.

This did not lessen the need to invest in corporate trademarks. Indeed, they became an integral part of the studio system in demarcating particular kinds of 'house style' in the context of greater uniformity within Hollywood's industrial practices. Based on the organization of stars and genres, and what became an aggregate pattern of movie output based on the tastes and dispositions of key producers, logos became the manifestation of a studio's 'corporate personality'. Thomas Schatz relates this to the series of institutional forces – including production operations, management structures, talent pools, narrative traditions and marketing strategies – that comprised the output and identity of the integrated majors from the 1920s (Schatz 1998). Logos became a signature of product differentiation within a still fairly stable system of marketing and sales. While the Warner Bros. shield became associated with films of a certain narrative and technical economy, expressed in the studio's hard-bitten and stark foundation genre of the gangster film, the MGM lion primed the high-gloss and glamour of the studio's numerous prestige spectacles. This puts the case simply, of course, for brand association was figured around a constellation of product cycles and the inveterate pursuit of novelty and innovation on the part of the majors. Nevertheless, logos were associated with a particular repertoire of expectations, mapped according to the competitive dynamics and house styles of the classical studio system.

Studio logos from the classical era have proven to be resilient. Despite complex transformations in ownership and the emergence of conglomerate business structures, Warner Bros., MGM, Columbia, Paramount, Twentieth Century Fox and Disney remain potent corporate trademarks. In comparing the logo histories of these corporate brands, patterns emerge that connect specific changes in the use and design of studio logos to particular forms of institutional and industrial transition. This can be illustrated by the major logo designs of Warner Bros. between 1923 and 2003.[4] In formal terms, the Warner Bros. shield has undergone a series of refinements that can be used to establish the changing shape of cultural/corporate signatures.

The first logo to appear (1923–9) saw a narrow shield on a black background, a picture of the Warner Bros. studio in the top part of the shield and the bottom part containing the elongated lettering 'WB' (figure 3.1). With the move towards national advertising campaigns in the 1920s, and with developments in the use of trailers (Warner Bros. opening its own in-house trailer operation in 1928), company logos were part of the standardization of advertising practice that occurred as studios grew in size and began to accentuate their identity as vertically integrated majors. If Warner Bros. framed its studio facility within a fraternal coat of arms, the Paramount peak (allegedly based on Wadsworth Hodkinson's personal memory of a mountain in Ogden, Utah) was crowned with a halo of stars after Alfred Zukor criticized the new distribution company as sounding 'like a brand of cheese or woollen mittens' (cited in Dick 2001: 9). Although characterized by factory-like organization and the use of mass-production methods, the nascent film industry used images of historical and cultural grandeur to establish and legitimize its particularity as a manufacturer of entertainment products.

In the second design (1929–36), 'Warner Bros Pictures, Inc.' appears above a small shield containing the stylized 'WB' lettering. Gone is the picture of the early studio at Sunset and Bronson. New to this design, however, is a waving flag and the promotional lettering of 'the Vitaphone Corp', the company established between Warner and Western Electric to develop the pioneering sound technology that would truly consolidate the position of Warner Bros. in the emerging studio system. Reflecting Hollywood's co-ordinated investment in technological innovation as a means of creating (and pronouncing) competitive advantage, the new

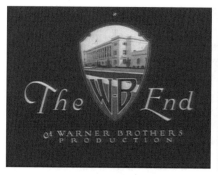

Figure 3.1 Warner Bros. logo, 1923.
Courtesy of Warner Bros.

Figure 3.2 Warner Bros. logo, 1967.
Courtesy of Warner Bros.

Figure 3.3 Warner Bros. logo, 1972.
Courtesy of Warner Bros.

Figure 3.4 Warner Bros. logo, 1999.
Courtesy of Warner Bros.

studio logo was used at the beginning of studio pictures and (with an additional ring of concentric circles) feature animation. According to David Bordwell, the advent of sound cinema canonized the narrativization of the credit sequence, encouraging a higher degree of graphic and aural play in the initiation of film narrative (Bordwell *et al.* 1985: 25–9). While studio logos still had a limited narrative function at this point, they were becoming resonant indicators of particular kinds of production value.

The third and fourth logos, introduced between 1936 and 1948, see a now familiar design whereby an enlarged Warner Bros. shield is superimposed over an image of clouds, with 'Warner Bros Pictures, Inc.' appearing over the shield or as a line across the shield. This is the first logo to use zooming, the shield design moving up to the screen. Developments in the use of colour film stock saw this version of the logo appear in sepia, accompanied musically either by the beginning of the movie's theme, or the sound of a majestic horn. This style was effectively 'cleaned' between 1949 and 1967, comprising a fifth logo design where the border, banner and text of the shield widen and appear in gold, set against a blue cloud background. This represents the formalized logo of the late studio era, more precise in terms of visual definition but unmistakably developed from the early brand design. This also became the base for a number of variations that marked the Warner Bros. television signature in the 1950s and 1960s. Becoming one of the predominant suppliers of network television programming in the late 1950s, Warner Bros. developed logos that would distinguish the studio's theatrical feature films from its television products. Television serials often superimposed the Warner Bros. logo onto scenic action, while animated cartoons saw characters such as Bugs Bunny and Road Runner lean against the famous shield, a design that would be replicated in the 1990s. With the demand for television programming increasing the book value of the majors' film libraries to two and three times the value of its stock, studios became ripe for corporate takeover; the shift to television production in Hollywood signalled a growing trend toward the integration of media industries. Often discussed as representing a key transition from Old to New Hollywood, this ushered in a period of change in the form and currency of studio logos (Anderson 1994).

Between 1967 and 1972, the Warner Bros. logo saw three variations of a design that reflected transitions in ownership and the formation of Warner Bros.-Seven Arts in 1967 and Warner Communications Inc. in 1972. While two of these designs retained the original Warner Bros. shield (changing the background palette to solid blue and cutting the shield with the words, 'A Kinney Company'), a more radical design was signalled by the brief introduction of a new logo that saw the Warner Bros.-Seven Arts shield combine a squat W with an arching 7 (figure 3.2). While this ligature was justified by the designers, Scope advertising, as having a 'daring simplicity' symbolic of the 'clear thinking men who are the company's leaders', for others it diminished an essential part of cinema experience, namely the 'excitement and anticipation of trademarks appearing on screen' (Pratley 1968). For Gerald Pratley, writing in *Variety* in 1968, the new symbol was a pitiless result of the merger between Hollywood studios and industries with no connection to motion pictures, a symbol that appeared to be a 'cross-bred animal that turned out a freak – a mutation looking back at what's left of its former self with shocked surprise' (ibid.). The design, colour and graphic lettering of corporate logos have long been used to index the brand identity of new corporations and product lines, establishing associations or effects that are linked to particular discursive registers and specific ideas of taste. In the 1970s, media logos took on a stylized and contemporary edge, moving away from pictorial logos – which had come to represent the heavy weight of profitability crisis in the case of the major studios – towards abstract graphics and block colour that were cast by studios as 'more attractive, tasteful and progressive'.[5]

The tendency towards abstract design was typified between 1972 and 1984 by the ninth major version of the Warner Bros. logo. Heralding the creation of Warner Communications Inc, a red abstract W was introduced, consisting of two slanted elongated circles and a shorter elongated circle, zooming in towards the middle of the screen (figure 3.3). Not only did this logo challenge the traditional Warner Bros. shield, it transformed Warner's brand colour from blue and gold to a combination of red and black. This must be set against the backdrop of the movie industry's deep slough in the late 1960s and the need to revitalize performance. According to Connie Bruck, when Kinney acquired Warner in 1969, Steve Ross 'considered the Warner Bros. movie production company the weak sister in the deal', announcing a write-down of $59 million on the asset value of all movies, including those in process and just released (Bruck 1994: 64). Having lost its sheen as a moneymaking studio, and with the onset of the brave new world of entertainment conglomeration, Warner's logo was revamped to express a regime change in the style and purpose of media operations. From Warner's new system of autonomous divisions (with film overseen by Ted Ashley) to its ranging stake in developments such as cable and video, the 1970s saw the emergence of film as one of many possible profit centres, and no longer the gravitational focus of corporate/brand identity.

The restabilization of Hollywood as an industry within this structure led to the return of the classic Warner Bros. shield, indicative of film's centrality to the synergistic aspirations of increasingly streamlined entertainment conglomerates in the 1980s and 1990s. The tenth logo design, between 1984 and 1998, returned to the golden Warner Bros. shield, set over the blue background of clouds. A succession of corporate names have appeared under the shield: 'A Warner Communications Company' (1984–90), 'A Time Warner Company' (1990–2), 'A Time Warner Entertainment Company' (1992–2001, figure 3.4), and 'An AOL Time Warner Company' (2001–3). In most cases, the logo is silent or combined with the beginning of a movie's theme but, since 1998, a computer-generated logo marking the 75th anniversary of Warner Bros. has used a sepia impression of the Burbank studio, shimmering towards the screen in the rotating form of the company's traditional shield. Exploiting new techniques of computer generated imagery and digital sound, this design is indicative of the move towards three-dimensional logos, characterized by swooping aerial panoramas and clean orchestral fanfares. Many of the major studios have developed anniversary trailers of a similar kind, heightening audiovisual impact while capitalizing on the growing and strategic investment in brand nostalgia. When Paramount introduced its 90th anniversary logo in 2002, using the famous peak, Jonathan Dolgen, chairman of Viacom, remarked: 'We wanted to maintain the integrity and historical value of our original logo while incorporating design elements commemorating our 90th anniversary' (cited in Dunkley 2002). Integrity and historical value are keywords here, central to the brand capital of studios whose contemporary franchise potential and extensive film libraries have become highly prized by conglomerates for their strategic function as multimedia content providers.

My intention in tracing this logo history has been purposely broad, and I have sought to draw out general patterns of change that can be applied more widely to other Hollywood studios. Across the majors, there are marked similarities in the evolutionary stages of logo branding. This includes the successive development of classical design (experimenting with variations of image, colour, sound and perspective), the introduction of logos that differentiate theatrical from television product, the move from pictorial to abstract symbols in the early periods of media conglomeration and the contemporary renaissance of classical design, enhanced by digital technologies.

It would be wrong to present the history of studio logos as necessarily sequential. Different logos may circulate in the same historical instance according to particular corporate or creative imperatives. Since 1995, Warner's abstract logo from the 1970s has been used as the logo of WarnerVision International, one of the company's television distribution arms. Conversely, modern logos can be used to sell and package old or 'classic' products. If a renewed interest in the cinematic past has become one of the by-products of the new relationship being forged in the age of video, cable and DVD between institutions, texts and viewers, logos both construct and complicate ideas of Hollywood history. While using the original MGM logo in the DVD release of *North by Northwest* (1959), the film was packaged in 2001 with the contemporary logo of Warner Bros. (the MGM back catalogue being owned by Turner Entertainment, a subsidiary of Time Warner). By replacing or refreshing old studio signatures, media corporations have been able to claim proprietary rights over Hollywood's past, a form of brand annexation tied to the appropriation and circulation of competing logos. This must be seen in the context of developing transmission technologies and exhibition windows that have given film an extended product life cycle, and for which copyright ownership has become essential in spinning out corporate profits at as many levels as possible.

If studio logos are an integral part of the history of film advertising and marketing practice, one might ask in what particular ways their function and development can be understood as especially, or in any way, post-classical. Within Hollywood historiography, accounts of continuity and change have focused on varying periods and industrial/aesthetic pressures in demarcating the constituent territories of Old (classical) and New (post-classical) Hollywood (see Maltby 1998; Krämer 1998b). Murray Smith suggests that tracing smaller-scale shifts and changes is perhaps a more productive analytic mode than postulating some epochal break between classicism and a putative post-classicism (Smith 1998). If studio logos indicate one such shift, they began to function differently with the increasing move towards package-unit production and event-based filmmaking. This, of course, reflects the history of the blockbuster, conventionally traced to the 1950s, accelerating in the 1970s, and dominating industrial practice from the 1980s. It is in this period that logos become more dynamic, both in the way they index corporate dissemination and change, and in the way they are 'brought to life' in relation to film texts themselves. At each level, studio brands are taken up within affective media economies based around the memory of Hollywood's past and the promise of contemporary spectacle.

Aida Hozic suggests that the 'intense and continuous battle over brand names between Hollywood's producers and merchants' is a key to understanding the disparate threads of Hollywood's economic development since the 1960s (Hozic

2000: 206). While this is linked to industrial struggles over stars and products, it also grounds the discourse of branding that would envelop Hollywood studios in their transformation into what Hozic calls the 'franchiselike media organizations' of the contemporary period. In essence, the major studios sought to foster and exploit their brand capital in a number of ways as they were refigured within global entertainment companies. This would include the development of theme parks, studio stores and network broadcasting platforms as environments for the selling of brand-based properties. However, it has also seen the dynamic projection of logo signatures onto film products as companies have sought both to leverage the profit potential of the movie past and to assert market control in the present.

The revival of the cinematic past is linked in no small part to the branding imperatives figured around what Jan-Christopher Horak calls the 'Hollywood history business' (Horak 2002). This describes the investment in film history as a viable commodity that can be marketed on television and other electronic media. In brand terms, this bears heavily upon the equity vested in film libraries. When Ted Turner bought MGM/UA in 1986 for a staggering one billion dollars, anxious to secure the prized film catalogue for use on his cable networks, it was clear that studio brands carried enormous financial rewards. If brand equity describes the calculated price difference that a brand adds to a company over and above its material assets and total annual sales, the equity of a major Hollywood studio is closely tied to the value of its library. In 1996, this had become worth fifteen to twenty times the value placed on them in 1980, Wall Street weighing libraries heavily in valuing stock and banks ready to accept them as collateral. For movie studios, brand identity generally develops through composite and layered meanings built through specified relationships with their productions. For the majors, this includes the history of these relationships across time. In economic terms, classic studio brands (whether owned or licensed) have become a core asset within the entertainment economy, something to manage and maintain, protect and project.

If the management of entertainment libraries (and their associated logos) is one dimension of the incentive to protect the cultural and financial standing of contemporary media companies, the graphic projection (or bringing to life) of studio logos has become a concurrent brand strategy, linked to the negotiation of presence and identity in a diversified entertainment economy. Jerome Christensen examines this in allegorical terms, reading *Batman* (1989) as an inscription of the larger corporate tensions produced in the historic merger between Time and Warner in 1989. He writes:

> If Vicki Vale is explicitly linked with Time, the character of disguised hero Bruce Wayne/Batman strongly suggests an impersonation of Warner. Batman is primarily associated with the privatised technological space of the batcave, set up as a television control booth. His eventual triumph over the forces of evil involves the installation in the heart of Gotham of a projection system that evokes the apparatus used by a motion picture studio during the

production of premieres. Climactically, the image of the projected batsign visibly rhymes with the enskyed Warner Bros. trademark that opens the film.

(Christensen 2003: 599)

Batman is an exemplar of the branded entertainment property, literally projecting a brand signature into manifold ancillary markets. However, the film also projects Warner Bros. as a *corporate* brand. While Christensen reads this as an allegory of the calculated desire by Steve Ross 'to save Time in a world supervised by a Warner superhero', the incorporation of studio logos can be analysed more specifically as part of the aesthetic tendencies of 'industrial advertisement' that Michael Allen associates with Hollywood's ongoing desire to promote itself through the form of the blockbuster (Allen 2003a). In being increasingly tailored to the aesthetic propensities of specific blockbusters – *Batman*'s gothic WB shield differing from the binary code shield used for *The Matrix* – studio logos participate in what Allen calls the film industry's dual attempt to '(re)confirm the unique range of pleasures it can offer its audience, and [to signal] its continued survival in an increasingly threatening media landscape' (ibid.: 113). The transfiguration of studio logos into the atmosphere (and even the diegesis) of Hollywood film is something that I want to explore in the next section, turning to the question of how logos act upon the films they frame.

Moving the mountain

While fleeting, studio logos provide a link between, what Thomas Elsaesser calls, the macro and micro levels of film's particular bringing together of capital and desire. If the macro level describes the film industry's place within forms of modern capitalist business practice, the micro level describes particularized forms of pleasure that invite 'a kind of repetition compulsion that ties the cinema experience to recollection and expectation' (Elsaesser 2002: 16). Elsaesser's suggestive if generalized point is that blockbusters can mobilize certain internal connections based around time: a folding movement that draws upon history, childhood and the memory of watching film. In providing the most obvious signature of Hollywood's corporate form and invested pleasure principle, one might argue that studio logos function at the very intersection of recollection and expectation, or what might be called the blockbuster's aggregation of memory and hype.

Hollywood has long used the aesthetics of logo design for expressive cinematic ends.[6] However, the graphic projection of studio logos really emerged when the studio system began to disintegrate and the notion of film style shifted from a studio-based to an individual context. With the majors steadily refiguring their power base in distribution, logos took on a different register, no longer tied to production in any necessary fashion. While Paramount produced ten of the twenty-two films it released in 1973, it produced only five of twenty in 1975. This would become a dominant pattern across the majors, linked to investment strategies attuned to the enormous profit potential of the blockbuster. Richard Maltby writes that 'by the mid-1970s the post-Paramount attitude of regarding each production as a one-off event had reached a point where none of the majors any longer possessed a recognizable identity in either its personnel or its product' (Maltby 1998: 31). In other words, studios were no longer associated with even the vestiges of a distinctive house style. And yet, the 'one-off event' gave rise to specific and playful instances of studio signification, symptomatic of the desire to accentuate their place in a changing media landscape. In a period where the majors were increasingly absorbed within integrated media structures, and where 'corporate personality' was becoming more opaque, studio logos took on a more significant role in the coding of the 'presentational prowess' that Steve Neale associates with the visual and aural dimensions of (selling) film spectacle (Neale 2003).

Two films map this neatly and introduce the projection of the Paramount peak to this chapter's study of logo aesthetics. Both *The Ten Commandments* (1956) and *Raiders of the Lost Ark* (1981) use Paramount's logo in ways that situate the studio in the discursive and textual *habitus* of each film. While *The Ten Commandments* was symbolic of Paramount's reliance on blockbuster strategies during the 1950s, overseen by Barney Balaban and George Weltner, *Raiders of the Lost Ark* was released in a different industrial and aesthetic moment, as part of the rejuvenation of Paramount's fortunes within the new conglomerate structure of Gulf & Western, steered by the management of Barry Diller and Michael Eisner. While Paramount Pictures may have been 'engulfed' by corporate Hollywood, to use Bernard F. Dick's term (2001), studios nevertheless sought to project their identity as a means of consolidating their position within competitive industrial hierarchies.

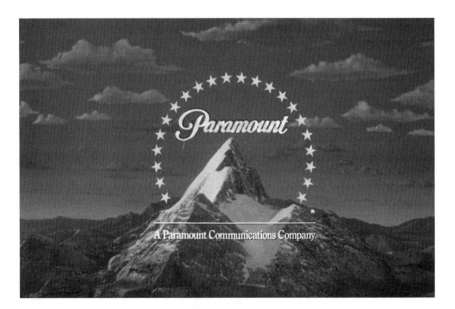

Figure 3.5 The topography of a logo: the habitat of Paramount's mountain. Courtesy of Paramount Pictures and the Ronald Grant Archive.

The Ten Commandments begins with a frame of the widescreen Paramount logo, introduced in 1954 to accentuate the technological grandeur of VistaVision and its objective of 'filling the screen'. Instead of the mountain peak, the logo creates a more expansive perspective, heightening the sky and widening the mountain base to reveal a mist-covered forest. In the case of *The Ten Commandments*, the logo is further customized in colour and design. Instead of the usual cloud-strewn blue sky surrounding the peak, the mountain is set against a red sky. While the peak reflects the light of snow, the logo is filled with deep shades of red throughout. On closer inspection, the peak is not that of Paramount but of Mount Sinai itself. While the Paramount logo has seen variations in the size and shape of the mountain, in *The Ten Commandments* it becomes figured as God's veritable 'high place, his temple'. As the frame develops, accompanied by the film's orchestral score, the still picture of the red mountain is ringed by Paramount stars. Finally, the words 'A Cecil B. DeMille Production' appear at the bottom of the screen before the logo fades to black and the title of the film appears on the cover of a red Bible.

What interests me here is the way that Paramount becomes part of the film's symbolic tableau. Michael Allen suggests that the technical systems which have frequently been allied to spectacular blockbusters (whether sound, colour, widescreen or digital effects technologies) have been used to make apparent 'the true hierarchy of the industry. Who are the companies who can afford to showcase them in big-budget movies? Who cannot?' (Allen 2003a: 103). Separating major and minor studios, and distinguishing film from the competition of television, Paramount sought to bolster its increasingly vulnerable position in the 1950s with a technically well-endowed blockbuster. If VistaVision 'brought a new look to motion pictures, a permanent new look', *The Ten Commandments* enabled the studio to project its own corporate prowess within the presentational and thematic unfolding of a biblical epic that placed a mountain at its dramatic core. Exiled from Egypt, and gazing upon Mount Sinai with his future wife Sephora, Moses asks if God lives on the mountain. Sephora replies: 'I do know that the mountain rumbles when God is there, and the earth trembles, and the cloud is red with fire'. In a film concerned with the spectacle of seeing (widescreen/God), the sublime gaze rests upon a mountain peak as the source of wondrous happenings. The conflation of Paramount and Sinai in the film's logo makes apparent, and individuates, the corporate force behind epic cultural spectacle.

The Paramount logo has offered itself up for various kinds of symbolic adoption. As an indicative 'nostalgia film' of the early 1970s, *Chinatown* (1974) used the logo in historically refractive terms, opening with the Paramount logo of the 1940s (featuring the mountain peak) and closing with the abstract blue logo of the 1970s (comprising a ring of stars and the word Paramount, *sans* peak). This helped code *Chinatown*'s complex temporal identity, refashioning Hollywood's tradition of noir through a lens of stylistic pastiche (what Roman Polanski would describe as 'a film about the thirties seen through the camera eyes of the seventies' (cited in Cook 2000: 189)). In significant ways, *Chinatown* drew on a signifying blend of memory and hype, using logos to index the atmospheric mood of the classical studio era while locating in time its own lavish production values. It is within the modern blockbuster economy, however, that studio logos have been more assiduously 'brought to life' in ways that engage both the chords of studio memory and the extant delivery of movie spectacle.

The contemporary impulse to project logo identity has emerged alongside graphic and representational shifts within movie form in general. However, it must also be seen as a function of the competitive dynamics of the entertainment market. In an industrial context governed by the commercial logic of the pre-sold property, studios have sought to formularize, but at the same time differentiate, a limited range of big budget movie events. Branding is a key tool in this context. While seeking to rationalize and control its product lines, branding enables Hollywood to create a feeling of novelty and difference amongst its product offerings. This can readily inflect the projection of studios themselves, anxious to assert their identity and output by trying to imbricate themselves in the blockbuster's nexus of capital investment and consumer desire.

Both *Raiders of the Lost Ark* and *Star Trek: Insurrection* (1998) provide examples of contemporary logo projection. In *Raiders*, the Paramount peak bleeds into the actual diegesis of the film. Beginning with the standard Paramount logo, the image slowly fades into the opening sequence, replaced with a literal mountain scene replicating the pictorial logo. Over the mountain, the titles appear, beginning with 'Paramount Pictures Presents'. The back of a silhouetted figure, wearing a hat, then strides in front of the camera, partially obscuring the mountain. The next title reads 'A Lucasfilm Ltd Production'. Walking towards the mountain, and revealing a bullwhip at his side, a third title reads 'A Steven Spielberg film'. The silhouetted figure then stops and looks at the mountain, hands on hips. 'Raiders of the Lost Ark' appears on screen before the camera dips and moves upwards, passing the mountain out of shot.

The title sequence is direct and playful in situating Paramount within the diegesis; the mountain becomes a reference point for character action and is central to the *mise en scène* where Lucas and Spielberg (literally) write themselves on the back of a mysterious hero. If *Raiders of the Lost Ark* is structured according to the serial format of the B-movie adventure story, the Paramount peak is promotionally dialogic. Based around the pursuit of tablets spectacularly formed in *The Ten Commandments* thirty years before, the opening sequence nods to Paramount's studio history while at the same establishing the ground for both the generic rekindling of the action cliffhanger and the formidable prospect of a high-budget movie by Lucas *and* Spielberg. As an autobiographical aside, Spielberg 'thought it would be fun to start with the Paramount mountain', not least because his first production company was called Playmount Productions, 'Spielberg' translating as 'Playmount' in German.[7] This form of corporate self-projection would later be echoed by Mel Gibson in *Braveheart* (1995), a film that J.D Connor reads, in part, as an allegory of Gibson (and his company Icon Productions) moving allegiance from Warner Bros. to Paramount. If in *Braveheart* 'Warners faced what amounted to its own Scottish rebellion' (Connor 2000: 54), it is telling that the film opens with a sweeping panorama of a recognizable mountain, the topography of Paramount's logo adjusting effortlessly from jungle subtropics to sparse Celtic borderlands.

Paramount's symbolic projection in the opening sequence of *Raiders* is more than a clever narrative gimmick. As with Gibson's claim of independence in the mid-1990s, Spielberg and Lucas had reason to foreground Paramount. Essentially, it was the sole studio willing to meet a bullish contractual offer where their joint services could be secured in exchange for complete financing ($20 million), director and producer fees ($1.5 and $4 million, respectively), the waiving of all overheads, distribution fees and ownership rights, and with percentage profits weighted in favour of Lucas (50 per cent once rentals had reached $50 million) and Spielberg (10 per cent once rentals had reached $40 million) (Dick 2001: 186–7). While tendered to all studios, only Michael Eisner at Paramount took the deal seriously, part of a strategic move towards high concept filmmaking that Justin Wyatt suggests defined the 'personality' of Paramount in the 1980s in terms of visual style, genre and marketing approaches (Wyatt 1994: 104–8). Major independents such as Miramax and New Line, and studios ranging from Pixar to Ghibli in Japan, all rely on a notional brand style in their demarcation of identity. The majors have the industrial muscle to be more varied in their project investments, but this does not preclude the accretion of brand style in specific moments, and around particular film cycles. At the time, *Raiders of the Lost Ark* was Paramount's most profitable film ($363 million in rentals) and was emblematic of the studio's focal interest in developing individual entertainment brands. The projection of the Paramount logo was linked to the fusion of stylized and saturated genre narratives that Wyatt sees as the principle method used by Paramount to differentiate its product in the 1980s.

The *Star Trek* franchise grew out of this history, developing as a result of Paramount's decision to cross-fertilize with other corporate divisions in a model of prospective synergy. By 2002, the nine *Star Trek* films released since 1979 had collectively made $1.2 billion, with merchandise sales exceeding $4 billion (Cloud 2002). Much could be written of *Star Trek*'s brand status, but my interest is in the specific projection of the Paramount logo in the trailer sequence of the 1998 release, *Star Trek: Insurrection*. While standard corporate logos had, until this point, framed the *Star Trek* franchise, *Insurrection* witnessed the digital integration of the Paramount peak into the narrative milieu of the film. Specifically, the trailer sequence begins with a scenic view of the valley that surrounds the Paramount peak, gradually fading into a live action habitat that we learn to be the valley utopia of Baku. As the stars ('Paramount') and brand lettering ('A Viacom Company') disappear, the base of the mountain and surrounding forest come into view as the camera perspective withdraws across a digitally rendered valley. An eagle is heard but not seen as the camera moves behind and down a valley slope, obscuring the mountain and, slowly, its peak. When the mountain can no longer be seen, the shot seamlessly fades into a valley habitat that becomes the backdrop for narrative action, members of the Starship Enterprise fighting battles on snow-capped mountains, and villagers fleeing hillside slopes.

This example of logo projection is emblematic of the dynamic and digital character of studio branding within trailers and credit sequences of the 1990s and 2000s. Developments in computer generated technology have provided greater potential for the movement, zooming and narrative integration of logos. As a result, the creative embellishment or 'defacement' of corporate logos has become a discernible trend within modern movie trailers.[8] Outlining modes of 'audience address' in classical and contemporary trailers, Lisa Kernan identifies two different and historically traceable types: a 'vaudeville mode' which announces something for everyone and a 'circus mode' that more directly encourages audience participation, symbolized in the injunction to 'see/hear/feel' (Kernan 2004: 17–24). If, as she suggests, the 'circus mode' is seen repeatedly in contemporary trailers for blockbusters and event films, the heightened performance, or bringing to life, of studio logos has become part of the promotional motif 'which lures audiences to see the film by inviting them inside the screen as if they are stepping into a sideshow tent, to participate in the film's discourse in some way' (ibid.: 22). More generally, and not uncritically, Kernan suggests that contemporary trailers 'frequently utilize the convention of promoting the film's narrative world, assuming audiences' desire to experience the unfolding of the contemporary event film more as surrounding environment than as a causal chain of activity' (ibid.: 215).

Whether or not we accept Kernan's misgivings about the extended (commercial) environment of contemporary Hollywood – what she equates negatively with 'the promotional discourse of the high-concept era' (ibid.: 204) – the customizing of studio logos in trailers and credit sequences has become an identifiable feature of the modern blockbuster economy. In an immediate sense, the pliability of corporate logos can be linked to greater levels of manipulation brought about by digital graphics and non-linear editing systems, technologies with significant bearing on the current and future development of cinematic form. However, the impetus to transfigure studio logos also relates to the new liquidity of film content in the era of 'total entertainment', a period in which media brands have been increasingly designed, and digitized, so as to flow across windows, products, signs, screens and computer interfaces. Prominent in the promotional address of franchise blockbusters (e.g. *Star Trek*, *Spiderman*, *Harry Potter*, *The Matrix*), contemporary logo projection is a symptom of the general impulse to 'sign' media products with enhanced, engineered and essentially playful signatures. By the logic of the 'new intertextual commodity', discussed in chapter two, logo projection has developed, and can be understood, as a means of conferring status on the blockbuster as brand. While studio logos may be a stamp of corporate authorship, their projection is also revealing, I would say, of the 'historically determined industry imaginary' (Lury 2004: 35) shaping Hollywood's assumptions about the desires, and intermedia dispositions, of the contemporary movie audience.

Through various forms of logo projection in the three films briefly described, audiences are taken inside a habitat imagined to surround the Paramount peak. The corporate mountain is situated in and between the imperatives of industrial advertisement and each film's particular narrative imagination. This gives expression to what Thomas Elsaesser calls 'situation synergy', a term for the different levels of corporate/cultural referentiality that connect film as production and cinema as experience (Elsaesser 2002: 20). Tapping the linked awareness that filmgoers invariably develop of companies, films and the memory of going to the movies, studio logos inscribe a dual sense of recollection and expectation that can provide them with their own form of enchantment. Despite their inherent evanescence, logo signatures are part of the affective history of film as screen entertainment, providing a way for established studios to lever the felt durability of their corporate/cultural legitimacy.

Throughout its history, Paramount has sought to exploit its trademark advantage as a major film distributor, using its logo to authenticate and differentiate its film product. While film distribution is highly concentrated, it is also distinguished by uncertainty,[9] intensified by the growth of rival entertainment media and the development of electronic technologies that raise questions about the function of Hollywood in a world of prospective media convergence. It is in this context that the majors have sought to exploit what Richard Maxwell terms the 'accumulation over time of consumer preference', accentuating the memory of studio logos as a mark of quality and trust (see Miller *et al.* 2001: 146–70). However, logos have also come to function in a more adaptive fashion, helping to accentuate the event status of Hollywood film against the many possible alternatives for consumer spending within a diversified entertainment field. It is the aesthetic/affective combination of studio memory and blockbuster hype that can be applied more widely to the symbolic economy of post-classical logos. By tailoring the form and appearance of logos for specific presentational ends, and by occasionally insinuating themselves into a film's (promotional) diegesis, logos have helped code the event status of the modern blockbuster while visibly asserting the industrial history and position of their corporate progenitors.

The culture of contemporary logos

As this book explains, branding has become an instrumental part of Hollywood's production and dissemination of filmed entertainment, central to a blockbuster economy reliant upon revenues drawn from merchandising, franchising and product placement. From James Bond to *Jurassic Park*, the branded media property is both an advertising space for the placement of consumer logos, and a synergy-driven logo in and of itself. Although film logos have been commonly analysed as a function of product differentiation – examined from perspectives that explore the 'high concept', 'dispersible' or 'post-Fordist' nature of particular marketing strategies – much less has been made of the cultural significance of studio logos within this brand economy. While publicity executives such as Warner Bros.' Barbara Brogliatti insist that entertainment companies 'concentrate on promoting our content and not ourselves' (Brogliatti 2003), studio logos have nevertheless developed a profligate life in the entangled networks of licensing, financing and distribution.

This has been particularly marked with the emergence of flexible conglomerate structures. Michael Curtin suggests that in a period in which production operations are no longer centralized with a placed and permanent labour force, in which new modes of electronic communication are making channels of distribution more fluid and in which the focus on a national mass audience is cross-cut by the pursuit of distinctive audience subsets, industrial infrastructures are marked by a tension between global consolidation on the one hand (based around Fordist strategies of mass production, marketing and consumption) and cultural fragmentation on the other (based around neo-Fordist strategies of flexible production, dispersed marketing and niche consumption) (Curtin 1996: 190). Studio logos function variously in this context. Just as they suggest a certain moviemaking 'home' within a globalized production system,[10] they can also be deployed according to flexible marketing requirements. I have been concerned with the *projection* of studio logos, but this should not downplay their potential for effacement. Thomas Austin notes that Warner Bros. consciously removed its logo in the British marketing of *Natural Born Killers* (1994) to reinforce the film's 'unofficial, "underground" and subculturally hip image' (Austin 2002: 159). As this example suggests, logos are subject to the needs and dictates of flexible corporate frameworks that connect mass market operations to niche and localized initiatives. It remains the case, however, that logos have been brought to life more often than they have been hidden, erased, or momentarily put to rest.

Since the vertical reintegration of the film industry in the 1980s and 1990s, the projection of studio logos has functioned in the context of collapsing boundaries between film/television/cable/Internet and between production, distribution and exhibition outlets. Entertainment companies like Warner Bros. and Paramount have sought to channel and disseminate their corporate logos across the media terrain. Clearly, the multiple exhibition windows of the entertainment industry give studio logos a cultural, creative and copyright resonance beyond that of theatrical film alone. However, the modified logos of motion picture features have become a recurrent example of, and key site for, the reconstitution of cinema's affective address. In the case of filmed entertainment – and especially the logos tailored for the 'launch pad' of theatrical release – this address is distinguished by a brand economy of memory and hype. Studio logos are part of the creative and industrial armoury of the majors, used in the competitive struggle to associate themselves with cinema's past and experiential pleasures in the present.

While characteristic of the majors, this brand economy has also been seized on and developed by contemporary film studios seeking to challenge the oligopoly of the leading distributors. This was especially notable in the case of DreamWorks SKG before it was sold to Viacom (owners of Paramount) in 2006. Established in 1994 around the troika of Steven Spielberg, Jeffrey Katzenberg and David Geffen, DreamWorks was the first movie studio to be set up in more than seventy years. As such, it devised a logo that proffered instant memory value. Using the fantasy image of a boy fishing on the crescent of a moon, the logo tracks up, and then across, to reveal the name of DreamWorks in a pillow of clouds. Reminiscent of the archetypal figure of Elliot flying against the moon in *E.T.* (used in the logo of Spielberg's production company Amblin Entertainment), Warren Buckland suggests that the logo provides an 'overarching, visionary image', constructing an emotional experience of childhood innocence (Buckland 2003: 94). As a pure content company with no significant library, DreamWorks sought to invent its own tradition through the extension of Spielberg's brand status as New Hollywood's auteur storyteller. Meanwhile, the logo's highly narrativized digital sequence gave the studio a simultaneous association with technological and presentational edge.[11] While the film majors have sought to invest in their brand status, patterning the memory of their past and the promise of contemporary spectacle, the same combination of memory and hype has informed the promotional strategies of even the most recent studio ventures.

My intention here has not been to provide a comprehensive history or reading of studio logos across time or to exaggerate moments of logo projection. Instances of heightened brand performance exist alongside standard (and more static) forms of logo signature. However, in drawing out patterns of change, I would argue that logos have become more pliable as studios have become more uncertain about their status in a consolidated media market that supports, yet threatens, their power. Associated with the move from the mass production system of classical Hollywood to the package unit system of event-based filmmaking and high-budget blockbusters, studio logos have been 'brought to life' in accordance with specific industrial, aesthetic and technological pressures on film's particular equivocation of profitability and pleasure. As a means of demarcating corporate/presentational prowess, studio logos can be read as an index of film's status within the changing dynamics of the entertainment economy and as a significant dimension of Hollywood's enduring, if not interminable, brand history. If, as John Frow suggests, 'signature and brand name are shifters, markers of the edge between the aesthetic space of an image or text and the institutional space of a regime of value which frames and organizes aesthetic space' (Frow 2002: 71), I have outlined some of the ways in which studio logos mark the 'edge' of film as it has been historically sold as commodity and experience. In the next chapter, I want to expand my consideration of this brand threshold, examining the logo history of a trademark that has uniquely shaped the 'excitement and anticipation' associated with the selling of modern cinematic entertainment – the name and signature of Dolby.

Chapter 4

Dolby and the unheard history of technical trademarks

In 1982, Dolby Laboratories produced a sound technology demonstration for public exhibition. Eight-minutes long, and given the promissory title '*listen* …', the film was intended for screening as a short prior to theatrical features. Incorporating live action and animated sequences, the film was designed to accentuate the presentational possibilities of stereo technology; it interwove a number of scenes that could exemplify the range and heterogeneity of multichannel sound. Cast by Dolby as a 'sight and sound journey', the demonstration included scenes of a trickling brook, a cannon salute, a string quartet, a church organ, the sounds of children at play and the thundering lift-off of an Apollo rocket. Together with a Jiffy Test film, made available to theatre owners and projectionists to evaluate the performance of theatrical sound in particular venues, these promotional initiatives responded to ongoing industrial concerns about the quality of film exhibition in the 1980s. With the emergence of rival technologies of home video, and a sense among exhibitors and distributors that theatrical venues in the United States were inadequate to the needs of the market, companies like Dolby were instrumental in promoting the discourse of 'quality presentation' that would transform the history of the multiplex in the 1980s and 1990s and, with it, the status of cinema as event.

'*listen* …' was produced with two promotional functions in mind. Primarily, it was designed to embed and naturalize expectations around sound quality. Rather than deliver an explicit sales message for Dolby (although Dolby was virtually synonymous with sound technology at this point), the demonstration film sought to attune audiences to the intense sensory experiences that new sound technologies could deliver.[1] At the same time, it enabled theatre owners to market potential investments in exhibition technology. While Dolby had been striving to shape industrial stakes in the presentation of film since the late 1970s, exhibitors were initially cautious about the investment risks of sound conversion, Dolby Stereo requiring new theatrical equipment and installation expertise. In 1978, 700 theatres were equipped for Dolby Stereo and 25 films had been released in this format, most notably *Star Wars* (1977) and *Close Encounters of the Third Kind* (1977). By the mid-1980s, Dolby had over 6,000 installations worldwide and over 1,000 films had been released in Dolby Stereo. This represented a move towards the standardization of Dolby technology within industrial practice, bringing with it new imperatives for marketing and promotion, both for Dolby as a licensed trademark and for distributors and exhibitors seeking to retool the place of cinema in relation to alternative media forms.

The expansion of home video created a particular impetus to reconstruct the spaces and spectatorial conditions of the motion picture theatre. '*listen* ...' was in many ways a forerunner of the promotional place that sound technology would develop in the 'permanent marketing campaign' for cinema undertaken by the film industry during the 1980s and 1990s (Acland 2003). This was linked to broad industrial reconfigurations extending the principle of 'total entertainment' across cultural and consumer markets. In terms of public film exhibition, sound was linked to the multiplex boom and the ensuing development of the megaplex, new theatre design in the 1990s installing screens and sound systems that could heighten immersion in the spectacle offered by Hollywood blockbusters. With global revenues linked to a film's profitable media afterlife, however, the home would also become a pivotal exhibition environment, increasingly defined by the promise of audiovisual quality. As Barbara Klinger has shown, the importance of domestic film consumption became especially linked in the nineties to 'the successful positioning of home theatre as the apotheosis of digital entertainment technologies' (Klinger 2006b: 22). As a 'self-proclaimed "total" entertainment system', home theatre offered technological excellence within domestic surroundings. One consequence of these developments, as Klinger duly notes, was to amplify the blockbuster's cultural presence in private as well as public media space, confirming its status as a 'central principle of contemporary viewing'.

Dolby Laboratories has played an integral part in the substrata of marketing strategies that promote, and set expectations of, Hollywood film in this context. Specifically, sound has become a mark of the 'sensory surge' (Chion 1994) associated with technological developments deployed and construed in the formulation of contemporary cinematic experience. This has been especially apparent with the emergence of digital audio technologies that have placed (surround) sound at the centre of theatrical claims of 'big screen' experience while, at the same time, increasing the centrality of television for film viewing as linked to the phenomenon of home cinema. As Gianluca Sergi notes, 'sound has never been such an important marketing force as it is today' (Sergi 1998: 163). Not only has sound become central to the visceral aesthetic of the contemporary blockbuster, it has become a key factor in the reconstruction of public and private exhibition space. In significant ways, the acoustic architecture of the cinema complex, as well as the living space of the home, has been increasingly redesigned to maximize the 'lure of sound'. In the post-Dolby era, this represents for Sergi 'an evident shift in the weight given to the figure of the spectator as listener' (Sergi 2001: 124), the expectations and enticements of sound technology becoming a certifiable mark (literally in the case of theatres carrying the THX logo) of quality presentation.

This chapter examines the place of Dolby's multichannel sound technology in what Rick Altman calls cinema's 'event-oriented aesthetic' (Altman 1992: 15). Rather than explore specific instances of sound technology in filmic examples, I concentrate on the means by which Dolby has become an instructive logo for the film industry and its audiences. This builds on my analysis of studio logos in chapter 3, providing a different vantage point from which to consider the brand invitations of cinematic entertainment, and the aesthetic and institutional histories revealed in the performance of corporate trade names. While film branding is most often associated with Hollywood majors, it is important not to ignore the function of the technical brands (and supporting trademarks) that shape, influence and cue the encounter with film. Just as consumer branding cannot be reasonably contained by the catch-all examples of Nike or McDonald's, entertainment branding should not be reduced to Disney, Time Warner or other global media corporations if one is to understand the complexity of our current promotional culture, and the wide range of companies, institutions and bodies driven by the will-to-brand. My approach to Dolby, in this respect, is to consider the company's marketing history, rather than to present an outline of its technological achievements. Firstly, this chapter considers the capacity of sound technology to create 'added value' in the synchronism between sound and image, situating the brand capital of Dolby Laboratories through early industrial and promotional initiatives. Secondly, it explores the function and presence of Dolby as a licensed trademark, including its value as an intermedia sign. These provide a basis for examining, finally, the brand battles fought over digital sound in the 1990s. Analysing a number of Dolby trailers that update the sensory principle of '*listen* …', I consider the way that Dolby Digital has sought to enliven its market presence in a competitive audio field. Critically, this chapter considers different stages in the trademark life of a key sound technology, concentrating on the way that Dolby formats have been naturalized, standardized and commercially imagined. In so doing, the chapter asks questions about how the sensory affect of sound has been made visible in brand terms.

'Making films sound better' – the added value of sound

In theorizing dimensions of sound analysis, Michael Chion adopts a term beloved by account planners and brand managers, that of 'added value'. In the mercurial world of corporate branding, this describes 'assembling together and maintaining a mix of values, both tangible and intangible, which are relevant to consumers and which meaningfully and appropriately distinguish one supplier's brand from that of another' (Murphy 1998: 2). For Chion, it means something more specific, based on the formal history and reciprocal development of sound/image synchronism. Put simply, it describes the 'expressive and informative value with which a sound enriches a given image', a principle based on the impression of 'an immediate and necessary relationship between something one sees and something one hears' (Chion 1994: 5). In each case, qualities of affect are set forth, measured in relation to the experiential value of particular products/services/technologies. In the history of contemporary film, Dolby sound technology has an especially

significant place at the intersection of these commercial and technological definitions of 'added value'; the tangible and intangible value of Dolby as a technology
and corporate name has become central to the patterning of cinematic expectation and pleasure.

Before considering the circulation and refinement of Dolby as a technical brand,
it is helpful to locate the 'added value' of stereophonic sound in ways that draw
attention to the seeding of 'Dolby' as a recognized trademark. The foundational
impact of Dolby on the development of multichannel sound has, of course, been
far-reaching, giving rise to an experience of film sound that is more prominent and
layered in the complexities of sound track and in the very hierarchies (industrial
and aesthetic) governing relations *between* sound and image (Sergi 2004). Replacing
magnetic-strip with stereo optical print formats in the 1970s, Dolby noise reduction and recording techniques dramatically increased the possibility to extend and
layer the sound environment of theatrical film. In aesthetic terms, the capacity to
employ different tracks in the recording and orchestration of cinematic sound
meant that films (and filmmakers) could experiment with the three-dimensional
qualities of sound, essentially moving beyond the edges and boundaries of the
visual frame. This was a process that could achieve loudness but also subtlety in
layering and directionality. Michael Cimino measured the significance of optical
stereo in the following terms: 'What Dolby does is give you the ability to create a
density of detail of sound – a richness so you can demolish the wall separating the
viewer from the film. You can come close to demolishing the screen' (cited in
Schreger 1985: 351).

The idea of 'demolishing' or 'breaking through' the screen was, and remains, an
important metaphor in the aesthetic and marketing potential of post-classical
sound. However, in seeking to shape industrial wisdom about audio technology in
the late 1970s, Dolby Laboratories took initial steps to assuage misconceptions that
'Dolby' had a characteristic sound of its own, often conceived as a particular brand
of loudness. Rather, information campaigns cast Dolby Stereo as a *process* rather
than a specific effect, playing down the impression that multichannel sound was
principally a means 'of making the moviegoer think he has a typhoon between his
ears' (Schreger 1985: 351). Emphasizing the creative and commercial implications
of heightened 'sound realism', attempts were made to draw out the *use value* of
stereophonic technology for directors, sound mixers, projectionists and other relevant personnel. Indicative here is an advertorial 'Progress Report' written by
Dolby Laboratories and published in *Variety* in August 1978.[2] In being associated
primarily with the recording business, the Dolby name and logo was at the time
largely associated with stereo components and as a built-in extra for home cassette
recordings. The report in *Variety* put forward a series of facts, assurances, guarantees and promises, organized around a vision of Dolby Stereo as a threshold technology for the motion picture industry.

The rhetorical moves of this advertorial report are suggestive of the formation of
Dolby's early technological and trademark status. Guarding against the perception
that Dolby Stereo is 'some "magic box" which turns a mediocre soundtrack into a

wonderful one', the report defines the technology as a 'new artistic tool' ripe for creative and commercial exploitation. In this, it constructs a set of appeals based on artistic control, technical efficiency and attractiveness to Hollywood's core youth audience. By creating value in 'the life-like reproduction of sound' (Dolby 1978), Dolby Laboratories sought to move beyond the science fiction and rock music genres to which its sound technology had become coupled in the late 1970s, instead investing audio quality with envisioned meanings of cinematic possibility and prestige. (Terrence Malick's *Days of Heaven* (1978) was one of the first major 'quiet' films to see the value of Dolby Stereo.) As a privately owned company located in San Francisco rather than Los Angeles, Dolby Laboratories nurtured an ethic of independent consultancy, projecting its singular commitment to sound technology in meeting a range of industrial needs. Within the Progress Report, Dolby establishes both an informative portrait of multichannel sound technology – what it can do, who it can benefit, how much it costs – and of Dolby's status as a technical laboratory unaffiliated with any major studio. The brand appeal of Dolby Stereo only really emerges, however, when the 'added value' of sound is mapped onto the expectations and economics of the contemporary movie audience. It is perhaps unsurprising that the Progress Report ends on this point:

> [Dolby] is becoming so widely accepted primarily because good sound is good business – and Dolby Stereo makes good sound possible in a technologically and economically practical format. Today's relatively young and affluent moviegoers have grown up with high-fidelity stereo sound as part of their lives. They appreciate it when the sound in a movie theatre matches the picture. According to a recent article in *Daily Variety*, 'Of those responding to a random telephone survey last July in cities where *Star Wars* played in Dolby Stereo, 90% said it added depth to the picture … [and it] was rated equally as important as the visuals.
>
> (Dolby 1978)

Star Wars is generally credited with initiating a large-scale conversion to four-channel Dolby Stereo. However, this did not happen as a matter of course; Dolby continued to invoke wider transitions in audio sensibility to construct an industrial argument for stereo sound as the untold future of film. Far from an established or inevitable force within industrial lore in 1978, the Progress Report indicates the cultivation of common sense regarding the function and capacity of multichannel sound for producers, distributors and exhibitors. Signed with the symmetrical double-D logo (representing the perfect symmetry of the encode-decode noise reduction process), the report casts Dolby Stereo as a tool that 'will take a while for everyone to use to its most exciting advantage' but that has the capacity to realize itself as an industry standard.

Information campaigns of this sort were designed to shape prevailing wisdom about trade practice. They set the ground for marketing strategies, however, addressed more specifically to the cinematic spectator. If, as Gianluca Sergi suggests, 'the combination of heightened expectations and increased aural sophistication has produced a highly demanding, active and discerning listener of Hollywood films' (Sergi 2001: 126), Dolby has shaped these expectations in quite deliberate ways. As the company's first theatrical trailer, '*listen …*' was a strategic means of investing multichannel sound with *sign value*, a marketing initiative responsive to the particular means by which multichannel sound was being developed in relation to the visual field, and in relation to new ideas about the active listener. This brings into focus the reciprocal relationship between (cinematic) sound and (screen) image at the level of promotion.

Optical stereo technology was a pivotal development for Hollywood cinema in the 1970s and 1980s, but this does not mean to say that choices were not made about its particular form and development. Michael Chion contends that Dolby favoured the development of 'passive offscreen sound'. This describes the balance and activations of sound on the spectator in an environment where sound is enabled to come from points other than from the screen. Linked to speakers offscreen and to one side, audiovisual space in the post-Dolby era has been given greater fluidity and breadth. Chion suggests that Dolby accentuates the potential for offscreen sound but in ways that 'provide the ear a stable place'. In other words, the spectator may be subject to a greater sensory feel for sound but will not be disorientated by aberrant sounds that exist disconcertingly 'in-the-wings' (Chion 1994: 84). This effect is not, in fact, inherent within Dolby Stereo but describes the relational compact between sound and image as it has been drawn and codified within particular styles of editing, scene construction and sound design. Essentially, sound in contemporary Hollywood has been given far greater density and precision but has been anchored to screen image in providing the 'gathering place and magnet for auditory impressions' (Chion 1994: 143).

It is for this reason that Dolby has employed cinematic trailers such as '*listen …*' to announce the launch or refinement of particular audio formats. If, as Chion puts it, the 'sound-camel continues to pass through the eye of the visual needle', Dolby

Figure 4.1 Trailer still from '*listen …* ' (1982). Courtesy of Dolby Laboratories, Inc.

has used screen visuality to magnify the splendour of the company's audio achievements, nurturing expectations of sound quality among audiences as a means of
standardizing its use and appeal for exhibitors. While relatively inexpensive to
install by industrial standards (costing approximately $5,000 in the late 1970s),
exhibitors were reluctant to commit themselves to multichannel sound conversion.[3] Robert Altman was quick to note the paucity of investment in reproduction
technology in the late 1970s, commenting: 'most of the problems with sound in
film today are in the reproduction. Sound in theatres – the overwhelming majority
of them – is just terrible' (cited in Schreger 1985: 354). In this respect, however
good a recording might be, sound reproduction would often be compromised
without requisite equipment and forethought to acoustic design.

Initiatives such as '*listen* ...' catered to the specific needs of theatre owners in
encouraging full multichannel sound conversion. Specifically, it enabled theatre
owners to *market* sound as a form of experience and pleasure, providing a basis for
audience choice about the location of film consumption. Dolby vice-president,
Ioan Allen, wrote in 1983: 'maintaining and promoting the very high quality
attainable in theatres right now, with today's practical soundtrack and formats and
playback equipment, can contribute significantly to the growth and stability of our
industry' (Allen 1983: 19). This was part of a larger argument – current within
industrial talk of crisis and reconfiguration – based on the core premise that 'to
remain competitive, the moviegoing experience must be unique'. According to
Charles Acland, attempts to stabilize cinemagoing in the 1980s gave rise to a
specific understanding of theatrical exhibition; it led to a particular organization of
audience space where 'upscaling, comfort, courteousness, cleanliness, total entertainment, and prestige emerged as qualities to be offered through the services
provided and through the design of auditoriums' (Acland 2003: 106). Synonymous
with prestige sound, Dolby Stereo took on a significant trademark life in this
context. As sound technology was taken up in the reformation of the reproductive
environment, the Dolby name became a means through which exhibitors could
help audiences meaningfully differentiate one theatre from another and appropriately distinguish the immersive potential of cinematic sound from the flatter audio
effects of domestic television.

'*listen* ...' helped figure sound quality as something that could be openly advertised and exploited. It set the precedent for a number of subsequent trailers and
theatrical marketing initiatives by Dolby Laboratories and the likes of THX that
established the cinema complex as a space for new kinds of sensory experience.
This has been captured in specific logos that pointedly address the active listener,
from the 'deep note' crescendo of THX with its tag line 'the audience is listening',
to the various trailers by Dolby gathered under the rubric 'we've got the whole
world listening'.[4] Before analysing these in relation to digital sound, it is necessary
to widen the discussion of Dolby as a licensed trademark. At one level, the dissemination of the Dolby name across the terrain of entertainment media and electronic
consumer goods demonstrates the interconnections of hardware and software
industries, and the means by which different industries have drawn upon Dolby

(and its logos) to sell products through a notion of audio quality. At a more immediate level, however, the case of Dolby invites questions about the circulation and
regulation of technological trademarks, especially as it relates to the accretion of
brand value across cultural and consumer markets.

'Breaking sound barriers' – the circulation of technological trademarks

In discussing the effect of modern cultural technologies on modes of replication,
Celia Lury suggests that trademark has replaced copyright as the preferred legal
framework of the cultural industries in protecting the inherent mobility of its
images, characters, names and logos. If, as she suggests, the 'culture industry is
increasingly organised in terms of a regime of rights characterised by branding',
this has developed in accordance with a specific understanding of intellectual
property, constituted in relation to audience practices. She writes: 'the commercial exploitation of new technologies of replication has required a new emphasis
on the processes of reception rather than the authorial moment as the basis of
defining the terms of intellectual property' (Lury 1993: 56). By accounting for the
increasing significance of 'exhibition value', trademark law effectively supports
the exploitation of an image, character or logo across a multiplicity of reproductive forms, establishing the legal basis for licensing. While critical work has
focused on specific entertainment properties in this context, much less has been
made of the way that technologies themselves can circulate as a form of licensed
trademark.

With the widespread adoption of multichannel sound technology by audiovisual
industries in the 1980s, Dolby Stereo began to proliferate as a licensed technology,
traversing industrial borders as a marketing device for the added value of high-
fidelity sound. In many ways, Dolby has come to function as an intermedia sign,
appearing in and between different sectors of the entertainment industry. From
music and gaming to film and television, Dolby is a ubiquitous name attached to
various forms of entertainment software and hardware. If Dolby is unusually
present as a logo in the cultural terrain, it is the result of systemized licensing agreements that include specific guidelines about when and how the Dolby name can
and should be used.[5] These agreements serve a mutually beneficial promotional
function for licensor and licensee: they allow Dolby Laboratories to extend itself as
a recognized trademark, naturalizing its position in the field of audio technology,
while enabling electronics and consumer industries to exploit Dolby's accumulated
brand renown.

It is through the process of trademark standardization that Dolby has worked to
assert and regulate its brand authority. Indeed, the protection and monitoring of
corporate trademarks is linked inextricably to the maintenance of brand value. If
trademarks serve to indicate consistency in the qualities or associations attached to
goods and services, trademark standardization is a process of building and
protecting the cultural and capital value attached to corporate signs. Significantly,

the control of trademark identity prevents goods and services from becoming generic names and therefore vulnerable to cancellation as intellectual property on these grounds. Dolby has been careful to protect itself from generic drift by maintaining its status as a brand sign, establishing a number of provisions within licensing agreements that protect the value-added status of its name, logos, slogans and soundmarks. These include rules about the use of 'Dolby' as a word, about the size and placement of logos when used to sell encoded material (DVD discs) and consumer products (DVD players), and about the correct use of specific logo variations.[6] Together, these help foreground Dolby as a brand name related to specific technological innovations ('Stereo', 'Surround', 'Digital') and prevent it from being used as a *generic* term for enhanced sound quality, or confused as a manufactured consumer product in its own right.

If the history of Dolby can be read through its use and introduction of trademarked technologies, these have been organized around promotional initiatives that link Dolby to new sensory and affective possibilities for experiential listening. Dolby Laboratories has fashioned itself as an instantly recognizable brand name that makes 'cutting-edge, in-demand audio technologies and renowned trademarks available to all sections of the electronics industry' (Dolby 2003a). Whenever Dolby has introduced a new technological innovation, the basic 'double-D' trademark has been refined, announcing developments at the 'cutting-edge' with new visual and audio signatures. This has been particularly marked with the development of digital and surround technologies, the proliferation of logos (Dolby Digital, Dolby Digital EX, Dolby Surround Pro Logic, Virtual Dolby Surround) serving to create an array of distinctions in the type and degree of sound experience available in theatrical and non-theatrical venues. While setting expectations of sound quality in movie auditoria, these logos have also become significant in the particularized economies of taste associated with developments such as home cinema.

In particular, Dolby Surround (the consumer designation for the home theatre version of Dolby Stereo) has become central to the sensory reinvention of domestic space. According to Barbara Klinger, this is co-joined to a discourse of elite television viewing. Klinger suggests that, in attempting to transform domestic space into that of a movie auditorium, home theatre technology 'depends on the aestheticization of digital technologies for domestic use, a development which parallels the contemporary rebirth of the motion picture theatre through the promotion of digital advances in visual and audio representation and consequent upgrading of theatre facilities' (Klinger 1998: 16). As a key digital trademark, Dolby has become a hallmark of viewing distinction in the domestic fusion of sound and image, instrumental to what Klinger calls a 'semiotics of class superiority, refinement and good taste', or what she otherwise labels home theatre's 'aristocratic techno-aesthetic'. Using Dolby Pro Logic or Dolby Digital AC-3 processors to separate the audio signal into five channels, passed through five speakers, the 'Dolby Surround' trademark offers up a promise of active spectatorship for particular social groups. Technological capacity, in this sense, is inextricably linked to the cultural capital associated with bringing cinematic audio technologies into the home.

Much could be written of home theatre's recreation of big screen sound. In discussing the brand value of Dolby, home theatre demonstrates that trademark status is never 'standardized' in discursive terms, but is given meaning through socially determined frameworks of consumption and spectatorship. Moreover, home theatre provides a potent example of the increasingly blurred boundaries between forms of audiovisual culture, and the contributory role that sound plays in the 'total entertainment environments' created by and for particular kinds of audience. In a period in which hardware and software industries have moved closer together, and in which cultural industries have based operations on the expansion of media platforms and exhibition windows, Dolby resonates in the relations *between* film, television, music, video, gaming, and electronic media, drawing upon the sensory promise of sound for broad audiences and specialized taste segments.

As a licensed technology associated with processes of recording (software) and reproduction (hardware), Dolby has acquired brand capital across a spectrum of entertainment machines and media. While often parsed as a 'third party trademark' – occupying a residual position in logo terms 'to ensure that consumers do not mistake another company's advertised product or service as one provided by Dolby Laboratories' (Dolby 2003b) – sound has come to prominence in the delineation and marketing of audiovisual 'experience'. This has encouraged proactive strategies by Dolby to calibrate and brand this experience, becoming especially significant in the 1990s with the competitive developments of digital sound. Sound has not only become more visible in discursive terms, it has also been visualized quite literally by Dolby Laboratories in brand initiatives designed to accentuate the industrial and affective significance of its technologies. I want now to analyse this in the form of the cinematic audio trailer. While Dolby is an intermedia trademark, cinema has become the privileged form through which new audio technologies are showcased, reconstituting the active listener – or at least the expectations of cutting-edge sound – in ways that reverberate through the wider channels of moving-image culture. Specifically, I will consider a number of digital trailers that were produced by Dolby Laboratories in the 1990s for use in movie theatres, but which also 'played' on applications such as DVD, broadcast television and videogames. Announcing the audio effects of spectacular sound – with titles such as Train, Aurora, City, Canyon, Egypt, Temple and Rain – these convey a particular scenic inhabiting of the Dolby universe.

'We've got the whole world listening'™ – advertising the sound event

In June 1992, Dolby launched a striking trailer for its new Dolby Digital format. Entitled 'Train', the trailer was designed and mixed by Randy Thom and Skywalker Sound, the visuals undertaken by an independent digital workshop called Xaos. Thirty-two seconds in length, the trailer focused audiovisual effects through the scene of a sepia steam-train, its wheels slowly emerging and then gathering momentum through billowing clouds of grey smoke. The choice of a train was not incidental. In practical terms, it offered up a range of illustrative audio effects. Beginning with a hollow clanking (set to a blank screen), the heavy movement of carriages (grey smoke) gives way to the compressed movement of steam and metal (train wheels), the billowing smoke (pistons) matching the rhythmic acceleration of a heavy locomotive across a track (train moving into the near distance). Fading to black, the scene is followed by a silver Dolby Digital logo, turning gradually to gold.

In discussing the heterogeneity of sound, Rick Altman invokes the railroad to explain how molecular sound is essentially a vibration carried by a transmitting medium (e.g. air, water, rail) in the form of changes of pressure (Altman 1992: 17). 'Train' was designed to amplify this heterogeneous quality through the power of digital and surround technology. For all its promise of the digital audio future, however, the trailer went backwards in time in a representational sense. In significant ways, the monochromatic 'Train' invoked the legacy of Lumière and the first public actualité presentation around which legends of audience wonder have grown. While the famous *Arrivée d'un Train en Gare le Ciotat* (1895) created sensory thrall, and with it the apprehension that a locomotive would break through the screen, so 'Train' rehearsed this moment in sonic terms, producing dense layers of sound effect and pressure in ways that gave the audiovisual scene a sublime physical presence. According to Vivien Sobchack, drawing upon the phenomenological work of Gaston Bachelard, the Dolby trailers (and especially 'Train') were 'purposefully oneiric – "dream devices" that constitute both an intimate and immense poetic space in which one can wonder at, as Bachelard puts it, "hearing oneself seeing … hear[ing] ourselves listen"' (Sobchack 2005: 3).[7]

Unlike '*listen …*' which in 1982 sought to normalize expectations around sound quality, 'Train' was a more determined brand initiative for audiences accustomed to high definition sound and what Michael Chion calls 'a more lively, spasmodic, rapid, alert mode of listening' (Chion 1994: 99). 'Train' was, in short, a more determined advertisement for Dolby multichannel technology, set squarely in the 'sound war' being waged in the move from analogue to digital. Indeed, digital sound systems developed by DTS (in which Universal swiftly bought a share after the technology was fully developed) and Sony (SDDS) quickly rivalled the Dolby Stereo Digital System, introduced with *Batman Returns* (1992) and promptly rolled out in prestige theatres. These systems were not interchangeable. While each system could perfectly reproduce the range and variety of sound captured by sophisticated multitrack film recording, the digital formats produced by Dolby and Sony were on-film systems, encoded on the movie soundtrack itself, compared with DTS that synchronized a movie's visual track with sound from a CD-ROM. While DTS could be offered to theatres at a much lower price, Dolby's six-track system offered name recognition and reliability, compared with SDDS which offered an improved eight-track system but that required extra speakers. As a result, fierce corporate battles emerged to control the industrial and technological promise of digital sound, creating new competition for what the *Los Angeles Times* called 'the hearts and ears of US moviegoers' (Natale 1995: D1).

These struggles were propagandist in nature, incorporating information campaigns and marketing initiatives designed to persuade exhibitors to convert to their own system. In doing so, the motion picture theatre became an enlivened space for the constitution of the sound event. Marketing the technical apparatus of sound played an especially significant part in defining what cinema, and cinemagoing, might represent in experiential terms during the 1990s.[8] In its pitch to exhibitors, Dolby Laboratories described how digital sound would give theatres a 'competitive edge' in 'keeping "going out to the movies" a unique entertainment experience' (Jasper 1998). Reformulating claims made for multichannel sound in the 1970s, Dolby argued that audience expectations were being shaped by familiarity with improved sound quality (notably through use of CD players) and by the desire for a heightened sense of 'show business' relegated by domestic video. 'When it comes to film sound', the company proclaimed in a promotional leaflet in 1992, 'no name is more familiar to audiences than "Dolby". When it comes to the latest technology, nothing means more to audiences than "digital". Put them together – in your theatre, on your marquee, in your ads – and you have a winning combination'. In the industrial endeavour to formulate expectations of cinemagoing pleasure, Dolby Laboratories has continued to sell the lure of sound both to producers and exhibitors. As the above statement suggests, this is linked to marketing initiatives designed to accentuate the value of (Dolby) sound as a renewable form of consumer enticement. It is for this reason that Dolby Laboratories, in its own words, supplies exhibitors 'with a *choice* of exciting digital trailers that audiences regularly applaud, and issues new ones on a regular basis'.

Dolby Laboratories does not oblige filmmakers or exhibitors to use its tailored brand materials. Marquee signs, lobby posters and trailers are made freely available to cinemas that have installed Dolby equipment. The promotion of sound in theatrical space must be understood within contexts of industrial competition and alliance, including the inscribed rivalries and collaborative relations of extant technologies. While rivalry can be witnessed in the struggle between Dolby and DTS for dominance in the market for worldwide theatre installations, collaboration can be seen between Dolby Laboratories and Lucasfilm THX in the development of Dolby Digital Surround EX.[9] If this represents a tension between studio-sponsored initiatives in sound development and those developed by specialist audio and effects-based companies, leverage has been sought through sound-reliant event movies. While Universal's *Jurassic Park* (1993) launched DTS and obliged theatres to upgrade to the studio's own sound system, Dolby Digital Surround EX premiered with *Star Wars: Episode 1: The Phantom Menace* (1999), along with strong recommendations from George Lucas about the necessary sound technology required by theatres to exhibit the film. Trailers, such as those made available by Dolby, are a means of asserting market presence and of distinguishing one name in sound technology from another. In the process, however, the affectivity of sound has become manifest within certain kinds of brand aesthetic, significant in demonstrating both the contours of sound marketing in the 1990s and the patterning of audio experience.

According to Michael Chion, contemporary sound quality is based on the 'realization of the modern ideal of a great "dry" strength' (Chion 1994: 100). This is organized less around fidelity than on the 'technical capacity to isolate and purify the sound ingredients' with very little reverberation. This is captured for Chion in the short THX sound trailer that he summarily describes as: 'a bunch of glissandi falling towards the low bass register, spiralling spatially around the room from speaker to speaker, ending triumphantly on an enormous chord. And it's all at an overwhelming volume that leads the audience to instinctively react by applauding in a sort of physical release' (Chion 1994: 100). The soundmark of THX is made up of a 'deep note' crescendo that highlights the capacity of THX to reproduce sound with the quality and power intended at the point of production. This is matched, in aesthetic terms, by the solid physical presence of the THX initials that encapsulate a visual feeling of clarity and bulk.[10] For Ann Brighouse, director of marketing at THX: 'THX cinema trailers have become tremendously popular among moviegoers. Audiences anxiously await our signature Deep Note crescendo; it creates a sense of anticipation and eagerness for the feature presentation' (THX 2003). In a familiar gesture, partic-ular claims are made here about the significance of trailers in shaping the active (and applauding) listener; trailers are seen to act physically upon the audience in establishing the sound event. Vivien Sobchack develops the point, suggesting that 'the trailers are exciting to watch and often applauded by audiences less for their computer-generated bravura than for their primary function of visibly articulating sound – and, more importantly, of visibly imagining and articulating sound *as such*' (Sobchack 2005: 8).

While THX has come to rely in its trailers on the dynamic strength of theatrical sound, Dolby has used a number of atmospheric scenes to project particular audi-tory impressions. These can be seen in defined stages during the 1990s that corre-spond with the launch of Dolby Digital (1992) and Dolby Digital Surround EX (1999). In considering how the affectivity of sound has been made visible in brand terms, it is worth considering the supportive visual elements that have been given to the sound mix in Dolby trailers. Broadly speaking, Dolby trailers have come to present sound either in terms of natural elements (light/water/fire) or through forms of embodied space (canyons, temples, cities). In each case, digital sound is figured as a world to be explored. While the industrial argument for digital sound invoked a host of familiar themes from the 1970s about quality presentation, the forms of brand marketing that accompanied this were more attuned to a sound-sensitive audience.[11] Gianluca Sergi suggests that the technologically advanced space of the film theatre has become 'a sonic playground in which the spectator actively participates, making sense of what is around him or her, and discovering new pleasures' (Sergi 2001: 121). While the idea of sound as discovery is nothing new in promotional or discursive terms, it was parsed in striking audiovisual forms as Dolby sought to assert its claim on the digital market.

'Train' was in many ways anomalous in this respect. Having established the significance of Dolby Digital in terms that echoed the very birth of cinema, subsequent trailers played with themes of exploration, enabling audiences to behold Dolby through the exotic vistas of 'Canyon', Egypt' and 'Temple', all made in 1996. In each case, the audience moves through monumental space; the trailers present ancient structures that, filled with contrasts of sunlight and shade, reveal the Dolby Digital logo as an imposing tablet or hieroglyph. Created by the same company (Digital Artworks), these provide a supporting visual environment for a sound mix designed 'to demonstrate that Dolby Digital does not make only loud sounds more impressive, but also makes subtle, quieter sounds crisper and cleaner' (Dolby 2000). This must be set in the context of complaints (by exhibitors) about the loudness of theatrical trailers. Precipitating the formation of the Trailer Audio Standards Agreements (TASA) in 1997, forged between sound engineers, exhibitors and major studios, Dolby Laboratories created scenic trailers as a direct response to industrial concerns about the imposing physicality of sound. Where 'Train' relied on bold contrasts in the level and directionality of sound, linked to the movement in narrative space of a heavy mobile object, Dolby's scenic trailers spatialized sound around rhythmic and kinetic sensations. The use of syncopated drums, cymbals, bells and other percussive instruments – all marked as exotically non-Western – add to the discrete sound design in this respect, reinforcing the impression of Dolby as a world to inhabit rather than a simple technology to employ.

'Canyon', 'Egypt' and 'Temple' rely on the figurative representation of lost worlds, invoking ancient myths and anthropological fascinations to make sound itself an object of discovery. If the moniker 'explore our world' has become a banner for Dolby Laboratories, this has become further manifest in trailers that

Figure 4.2 Trailer still from *Canyon* (1996). Courtesy of Dolby Laboratories, Inc.

Figure 4.3 Trailer still from *Egypt* (1996). Courtesy of Dolby Laboratories, Inc.

deepen Dolby's status as a brand. As previously mentioned, new sound technologies are commonly unveiled through, and in relation to, their associational development with particular films. While Dolby Digital was launched with *Batman Returns* and DTS with *Jurassic Park*, SDDS premiered with *The Last Action Hero* (1993). In 1998, Dolby launched a trailer called 'Rain' with *Star Trek: Insurrection.* This saw colliding water droplets passing through a strobe light. Designed to illustrate how 'clear', 'pure' and 'quiet' a movie trailer could be, it also introduced a symphonic soundmark that identified Dolby Digital with an auditory signature. Unlike the deep note crescendo of THX, this was made up of a delicate five-note theme, a continuation of Dolby's primary association with sound definition rather than dry strength.

The introduction of the soundmark was conceived in a moment where Dolby Digital was beginning to attain screen dominance over DTS. Indeed, 1998 was the first year since the release of DTS that Dolby surpassed its rival in terms of worldwide theatrical installations. While Dolby had a total of 13,073 auditoriums, DTS had 12,800, leaving SDDS with a mere 5,201. With the release of Dolby Digital Surround EX, Dolby would increase this to 20,000 installations in 1999, compared with 15, 881 for DTS (largely based on the launch of its DTS-ES upgrade) and 6,675 for SDDS (Hindes 1998a, 1998b).[12] The adoption of a soundmark was significant in pressing home Dolby's growing advantage over DTS in a period where the majority of major film studios (including Universal from 1998) were distributing films in all three formats. According to *Variety*, this left 'exhibitors able to make their equipment purchasing decisions based on a system's price and performance, rather than on distributors' corporate allegiances' (Hindes 1998c). Cost and functionality became a more determined basis for theatrical adoption. In selling sound investment to audiences, however, use value was rarely divorced from a technology's sign value, and the means by which installation could be advertised by theatres as a recognized signal of commitment to high-quality presentation.

Accordingly, the soundmark would accompany the Dolby Digital logo in all future trailers and on other Dolby applications. This included 'Aurora', designed specifically for the launch of Dolby Digital Surround EX and the much-hyped release of *The Phantom Menace*. Swiftly adopted in the scramble to secure bookings for the most eagerly anticipated film of the decade, Dolby Digital Surround EX represented a new surround system employing a 6.1 format using an additional rear centre channel. For Gary Rydstrom, who spearheaded the initiative, the aim was 'to open up new possibilities and place sound exactly where you would hear them in the real world' (cited in Olsen 1998). Consequently, 'Aurora' was developed (by a digital workshop called yU + Co) to emphasize the rear channel effect, taking the viewer through the development of an aurora borealis in space. In this, sound came from behind the camera, sweeping down and around the audience so that, beginning in the rear channel, it filled out from back to front. Rather than the 'organic' sound of water droplets, the trailer was distinguished by a choral rendition of Dolby's soundmark, audiences encircled by the celestial fanfare of a trademark that first came to prominence with *Star Wars* in 1977 and that marked its association with the franchise twenty years later as a stellar brand of its own.

Figure 4.4 Trailer still from *Aurora* (1999). Courtesy of Dolby Laboratories, Inc.

Dolby has continued to refine and reinvent the visual tropes of materialized sound. In 2003, it launched 'Perspectives', a live-action trailer made in collaboration with theatrical percussion group Stomp. This was based on a vibrant rhythmic demonstration of its Dolby Digital Surround EX format. Through different forms of audiovisual trailer, digital sound has been framed as a ranging and exploratory dimension of the cinemagoing experience. Trailers draw attention to the sound event, enabling, in the words of Michael Chion, 'sensations to be perceived for themselves, not merely as coded elements in a language, a discourse, a narration' (Chion 1994: 152). For Chion, this can be seen as a defining aspect of sensory cinema. He continues: 'Cinema is not solely a show of sounds and images; it also generates rhythmic, dynamic, temporal, tactile, and kinetic sensations that make use of both the auditory and visual channels. And as each technical revolution brings a sensory surge to cinema it revitalizes the sensations of matter, speed, movement, and space'. Capitalizing on the possibilities of digital technology, Dolby Laboratories has been quick to brand the affective potential of the contemporary sound event. In the effort to maintain Dolby at the forefront of cinematic audio technology, brand strategies have moved toward a more concerted vision of Dolby as a source of experiential wonder. If branding is based on emotive, rather than informational, appeals in the commercial patterning of value, Dolby has sought to distinguish itself not only through demonstrations of the depth and directionality of digital sound, but through a concept of the audiovisual sublime, inscribed variously in cinematic ('Train'), monumental ('Canyon', 'Temple', 'Egypt'), and even cosmic ('Aurora') terms.

Selling spectacular sound

To speak of cinema as an 'experience' or 'event' brings with it a number of questions about the very space of cinema as a site of social interaction and cultural practice. James Hay suggests that film is 'practiced among different social sites, always in relation to other sites, and engaged by social subjects who move among sites …' (Hay 1997: 212). Sound is constituted in and between these sites. It has been used to sell the 'unique' experience of the motion picture theatre, just as it has been figured as the ultimate commodity of home cinema. These two sites are linked by an industrial concept of 'total entertainment', specifically the creation of environments that, according to Barbara Klinger, situate cinema within 'diverse technological and aesthetic economies that create a kind of *Gesamtkunstwerk* of the possibilities of fusing sound and image … with the utmost veracity and impact' (Klinger 2006b: 23). Within this framework, sound has become something to brand, a form of 'added value' that has developed new (or renewed) significance in the constitution of film's 'event-oriented aesthetic'.

By concentrating on the sign value of Dolby technology, one can situate the developing place of film sound within the industrial and affective economies of contemporary cinema. Critically, this chapter expands the horizon of entertainment branding to include the technologies that lie at the core of contemporary audiovisual spectacle, instilling specific kinds of sensory promise. If the challenge of sound criticism has been to wrest the analysis of film from its dependence on visual and text-based analysis, I have sought to investigate the way that sound technology has a promotional and discursive history, anchored to conceptions of the active listener. While Dolby is an intermedia sign, having been forged through a range of hardware and software licensing deals, its status as a brand has been especially refined in the battleground of digital sound. Having naturalized multichannel sound for the film industry and its audiences, Dolby Laboratories had to imagine its relation to sound in more determined ways in the 1990s as a means of asserting itself against its rivals. This meant developing new digital systems but also a provision for selling (and standardizing) its trademark technologies within new theatrical and consumer markets. With the widespread adoption of digital sound technology across film and electronics industries, Dolby has remained a pivotal trademark but one that has also tried to stabilize its hold in the audio market through promotional initiatives that territorialize the affectivity of sound.

Selling sound is nothing new; it can be seen as part of the film industry's enduring use of technology to heighten sellable notions of 'realism' and 'spectacle' (Allen 1998). And yet, the significance of sound has been increasingly realized through a regime of branding where audiences are solicited not simply through a company's name recognition, but through an invitation to inhabit and figuratively enter the very world of the trademark. This goes to the heart of contemporary brand practice, what Elizabeth Moor characterizes as a set of strategies designed to expand the potential spaces of marketing and where 'consumer experience itself is increasingly both the object and subject of brand activity' (Moor 2003: 42). Rather than function as a sign of quality, branding relies on linking products, services, and technologies to 'sensual and memorable' experiences. This provides the principle means of engaging with consumers, forging durable affective connections in the interplay between branded objects and consumer bodies, or what might equally be seen as the relationship between sounds and spectators. If 'total entertainment' describes a mode of experiencing a 'world of new images, sounds, and specially fabricated sites', Dolby has sought to visualize itself *as a world* for audiences that have come to recognize sound quality as a component of choice in their encounter with film and its ancillary entertainments. If, indeed, Dolby has got the 'whole world listening', this has been achieved in no small part through strategic efforts to maximize and enliven Dolby's brand identity as a way of maintaining industrial and audience appeal.

In examining different kinds of logo history in Part II, I have sought to examine the poetics of branding in the fleeting but distinctly familiar life of entertainment trade names. Revealed within these histories are particular forms of industrial positioning, film studios and technology companies seeking to project status within the entertainment marketplace, as well as naturalize their relation to it. In one sense, logos can expose the strategies through which established industry trademarks have sought to manage and maintain their hegemony. At the same time, the study of logo aesthetics – in particular the projection or 'bringing to life' of logos that prefigure the modern Hollywood blockbuster – reveal the modalities of sensory involvement that define the commodity of film in the era of total entertainment. As tactile and somatic entry points, logos and trailers enable us to trace formal changes within promotional texts, but also 'to discern who the film industry *thinks* it is addressing' in specific periods of time (Kernan 2004: 3). Through acts and representations of (immersive) seeing and hearing, the logos of the post-classical period address a hypothetical spectator who has become notionally more active in the capacity to inhabit the movie/event. This understanding of the audience is consonant with shifts in the synergistic structure of media industries and the development of new audiovisual (in particular, digital) technologies that have served to rationalize and accelerate the reproduction of cinematic culture as a world, environment or lifestyle to encounter. Having analysed what might be seen as the promotional 'ephemera' of studio logos and audio trailers – linked as they are to historically determined brand strategies and conceptions of film experience – I want to concentrate in the final part of this book on the function of branding within the core operations of the contemporary motion picture business. Examining situated instances of entertainment branding, set in relation to the production, distribution and exhibition of film, I turn by way of focus to the studio that provides a key and deliberate thread in *Brand Hollywood*, that of Warner Bros.

Part III

Brand spectacle

Chapter 5

Licensing the library
Of archives and animation

Describing the realization by the film industry in the late 1980s of 'how enormous merchandising could be driven by toy manufacturers', one-time Warner Bros. executive Peter Guber explained: 'It had been tested with *Star Wars* and several other films but it wasn't yet the concept of the franchise picture: the idea that you could build a series of pictures out of it' (cited in Shone 2004: 186). Substantiating the franchise concept was a film that Guber first brought to Warner Bros. in 1982 – *Batman*. Released in 1989 after a seven-year hiatus, and giving rise to a formidable array of merchandised images and licensed products, *Batman* became a totem for the emerging pattern of corporate synergy governing high-budget studio movies in the 1990s. Coinciding with the $14 billion marriage of Time Inc. and Warner Communications Inc. (WCI), there was something consonant in the film's timing, arriving on the very threshold of the largest media merger in corporate history.

Eileen Meehan suggests that *Batman* can be understood in terms of the external business pressures and profit requirements of WCI in the late 1980s; the film was a calculated in-house blockbuster designed to maximize the company's developing integration of entertainment and media concerns (Meehan 1992). As in other business sectors of the American economy, WCI had begun to shed unrelated market segments in the mid-eighties, divesting peripheral non-media interests in cosmetics, restaurants and sports teams to concentrate on its key operations in filmed entertainment, cable and broadcasting, recorded music, and publishing. This process of reorganization helped facilitate the company's merger with Time, a marriage designed to combine media interests so as to gain maximum competitive advantage within global markets. Hollywood business practice was influenced in light of such corporate manoeuvres. Jon Lewis suggests that, since the early 1980s, 'increasing deregulation and a dramatic reinterpretation of anti-trust guidelines, the introduction of junk-bond financing and its use in leveraged mergers and acquisitions, and the growing consolidation of assets and power by large corporations within the deeply incestuous and collusive industry subculture have dramatically altered the way that business is conducted in Hollywood' (Lewis 1998: 87). In a period where decisions about viable studio projects are now routinely based on a movie's ability to exploit different media outlets, *Batman* became an archetype of industrial thinking about how films should earn their investment. Much like

Meehan, Lewis regards *Batman* as the logical consequence of the growing integration of the entertainment business during the 1980s. As 'the quintessential product' of 'this newest of new Hollywoods' (ibid.: 104), the market and merchandising success of *Batman* established benchmarks for the way that mass media properties could be simultaneously organized as 'text and commodity, intertext and product line' (Meehan 1992: 62). Not without significance, the film established a platform for a rich vein of comic book and character revivals that would continue throughout the next decade.

Given the scale of *Batman*'s commercial exploitation – grossing over $250 million at the domestic box office and channelled across a host of ancillary markets by the film, television, publishing and licensing divisions of Warner Bros., making a total in excess of $1 billion – it is not unreasonable to establish a symbolic equivalence between the cultural hype surrounding *Batman* and the corporate hype enveloping the Time Warner merger. As media 'events', they both marked a watershed of sorts, if not the general tendency towards media consolidation and franchising, then at least the realization of their long simmering commercial ambitions. While Meehan finds in *Batman* a pristine example of the growing interpenetration of media industries and the desire to find profitable and cost-effective ways to manufacture culture, Jerome Christensen suggests allegorical associations between the film and the Time Warner deal itself (Christensen 2003). In a series of ways, *Batman* has been figured as an indicative 'corporate expression', the product of a global entertainment complex seeking to establish renewable identifications with bedazzling and culturally dispersible logos, trademarks, slogans and brands.

The idea that *Batman* and the Time Warner merger have equivalence in their integration of merchandising and media entertainment provides a starting point for Part III of *Brand Hollywood*. Having examined the practice and poetics of branding in the contemporary motion picture business, I want finally to examine how the will-to-brand has influenced the activities of a major studio in its approach to the production, distribution and exhibition of film. Warner Bros. is a suggestive case, not simply because it is a major distributor commanding a significant share of the contemporary film market but also because its parent company, Time Warner, is particularly revealing of both the dominance and dysfunctions of global media power. Time Warner is a colossus of media concentration. At the same time, it has been weighed down by enormous debt and fractious managerial infighting. As corporate structure has an impact on cultural production, I am interested in moments of equivalence in and between the turbulent corporate history of Time Warner and the conglomerate's filmed entertainment division, focusing principally on Warner Bros. but also that of New Line.

My intention is not to outline a strict business history of Time Warner since the pivotal merger in 1989. The turns of this corporate saga have been taken up elsewhere (see Bruck 1994; Lewis 1998; Klein 2003). Instead, I want to consider how, in a period defined by the vertical and horizontal integration of media industries, the concept of 'total entertainment' has been expressed, or rather strategically mediated, by a major film studio. The idea of total entertainment is understood here both as a form of cultural/textual practice and as a principle of corporate ownership. Methodologically, the remaining chapters focus on key vehicles and indices of brand spectacle: animation, fantasy and themed space. These are used to pose questions about Hollywood's promotional culture of production. Specifically, to what end are certain films produced and figured textually within a brand-based economy? How are modern (franchise) movies marketed? Where are Hollywood films exhibited and how does this relate to the practices, and public spaces, of contemporary cinemagoing? To be clear, I am not suggesting an essential relation between, say, animation and the question of production, or fantasy and the question of marketing. Rather, I have chosen to emphasize different parts of the industrial process through different, but indicative, brand examples. Within this analysis, I seek to draw out the *politics of branding* within contemporary cinematic culture, in particular the ideological stakes of Hollywood's tendency towards (what I will define as) commercial obviousness, corporate obfuscation, and purported cultural homogenization. By examining case studies in the recent history of Warner Bros., I want to provide a portrait of branding across the traditional divisions of the film industry apparatus (production, distribution, exhibition), relating my analysis to wider debates about global consumer culture. In each chapter, my examples relate to decisive moments of corporate expansionism in the entertainment industry during the 1990s and 2000s. While this chapter considers the production of Looney Tunes feature animation against the background of the merger between Time Warner and Turner Broadcasting in 1996, the next chapter explores the marketing of *Lord of the Rings* and *Harry Potter* in the context of the tumultuous marriage between Time Warner and America Online in 2000–3. Finally, the last chapter examines the Warner Village multiplex chain in terms of the globalizing premise upon which the Time Warner merger first took place, one that proclaimed, by design and for the future, 'the world is our audience'. Together, Part III considers specific entertainment texts, properties and spaces as they reveal dynamics of brand meaning and power.

I am especially concerned in this chapter with the production of branded family entertainment. Here, we return momentarily to *Batman*. As an instance in the political economy of culture, *Batman* transfigured the memory of a comic superhero into a complex brand commodity. While not the first time that old comic book characters had been revived by Hollywood – Warner Bros. turned *Superman* (1978–83) into an early vehicle of synergy – *Batman* intensified the commercial possibilities of the process, appealing to various demographic markets in its advertising and licensing approach. In a series of ways, *Batman* showed how a popular icon might offer itself up in the service of corporate branding requirements. Re-energizing old products for new markets, *Batman* was suggestive of a livening corporate impulse to examine the inventory of vaults, to focus the profit potential on characters rather than actors and to accelerate the flow of branded media content across delivery channels for strategically differentiated mass market appeal.

This chapter picks up critical concerns that emerge with *Batman* but that mature as an industrial strategy in the 1990s. According to the president of Warner Bros.

Consumer Products, Don Romanelli, the biggest lesson learnt from *Batman* 'is that movie marketing and merchandising can exist hand in hand. Before, this was not the case' (cited in Sandler 1998: 12). Inspiring the urtext of nineties brand merchandising, *Space Jam* (1996), the movement from comic books to cartoons is my focus as I turn from the revival of bats to the unburrowing of rabbits. Kevin Sandler suggests Warner Bros. characters such as Bugs Bunny and Daffy Duck 'are now at the forefront of its marketing and corporate identity' (Sandler 1998: 8). In this context, I consider how the animated history of Looney Tunes has been used to mediate the commodity logic of total entertainment. Critically, this chapter takes up the suggestion by Constance Balides that, to understand the imbrications of economy and culture in the contemporary moment, it is necessary to ask 'how economic and textual systems of meaning are "productive" in relation to one another' (Balides 2000: 141). For my purpose, this means getting to the bottom of the unapologetic, indeed quite self-satisfied, comment by Time Warner CEO Gerald Levin that '*Space Jam* isn't a movie. It's a marketing event' (cited in Handy 1996: 78). First establishing the significance of the archival/animated past within corporate power plays of the 1990s, I move on to consider the aesthetics of synergy in *Space Jam* and *Looney Tunes: Back in Action* (2003), two arch studio films that, in concert with other 'family adventure' movies of the period, make their brand economics abundantly clear.

Raiding the archive

In 1956, Jack Warner made a costly mistake. Without anticipating the value that a major studio's film library might one day hold, he sold Warner Bros.' entire pre-1948 film collection to a television syndication company (Associated Artists Productions) for the sum of $21 million. The library included work by stars such as Bette Davis, James Cagney and Humphrey Bogart, together with a full roster of Warner Bros. cartoons by Tex Avery and Bob Clampett. So began a forty-year odyssey of external ownership, the library subsequently acquired by United Artists Corporation in 1958, MGM in 1981, and Turner Broadcasting Systems (TBS) in 1986, before returning to Warner Bros.' control in 1996, a result of the corporate merger between Time Warner and Turner (Murphy 1995; Mallory 1996). While the value of film libraries had become painfully evident to Jack Warner fairly soon after his impromptu garage sale – designed at the time to inject cash into Warner Bros. Pictures – by the early 1990s libraries had become a major site of acquisitive interest. Ever since Ted Turner purchased the MGM/UA back catalogue in 1986 to service a roster of new cable stations, including Turner Classic Movies and the Cartoon Network, the proliferation of media channels and digital technology platforms had transformed libraries into highly strategic assets. In a media climate with a voracious hunger for programming content, entertainment companies sought in the nineties to consolidate library catalogues and buy up smaller collections with the intention of licensing rights to channel operators or becoming 'packagers' in their own right, establishing studio-branded cable and satellite channels (Klady 1996).

It was in response to the proliferation of television outlets, and to the cost-effective trend for restoring and re-releasing old films, that studios began founding their own archives. With libraries becoming an evident source of profit potential, studios transformed their once neglectful relationship with the collective movie past and began to protect their historical assets. While Disney had always been careful to preserve its prints and collections, Warner Bros. established the first fully-fledged studio archive in 1994 (Horak 2001). This would include a museum on the studio's lot in Burbank, which was designed to exhibit memorabilia, correspondence and shooting scripts from the studio's past along with props and costumes from 'classic' movies and those in release. While the declared mission of the museum was to 'share memorable pieces of the studio's past with friends of the industry, film historians and the public' (Warner Bros. 1996), the desire to safeguard the past and make history visible was fed by a powerful commercial impulse. Although questions of film preservation had come to the fore in a series of debates about film heritage, notably expressed in the conflict over film colourization in the late 1980s (Grainge 1999, 2002), the fact that studios were willing to spend considerable sums on the restoration of film prints, and in gathering the miscellanea of studio history, was linked in no small part to the realization, in the words of preservationist Robert Rosen, that 'their holdings are not dead storage but capital assets' (cited in Slide 1992: 151). That Ted Turner could restore *Gone With the Wind* (1939) for $350,000 and net $7 million in profit from its reissue on film and videotape was merely a precursor to the boon that DVD would provide in the late 1990s. Here, the 'hardware aesthetic' of home entertainment would be matched by the transformation of film into collectible artefact, old movies reissued with the 'added value' of lost footage, censored sequences, original trailers, film historical shorts and other archival extras (Klinger 2006b).

Jan-Christopher Horak suggests that 'at all the studios, the desire to collect film history was motivated and driven by marketing and branding considerations, rather than any altruistic urge to preserve history' (Horak 2001: 34). This was aptly demonstrated by the Looney Tunes display that occupied the second floor of the Warner Bros. Museum when it first opened in 1996, celebrating, in its own words, '65 years of Warner Bros.' outrageous, sophisticated and timeless animation, both classic and contemporary' (Warner Bros. 1996). This was not the first time that Bugs Bunny had been canonized within exhibition space; artwork from Warner Bros. cartoons appeared in the Museum of Modern Art (MoMA) in 1985 as part of the studio's golden jubilee celebration (Mikulak 1996). While governed less by the need to legitimate art for elite aesthetic appreciation, the Warner Bros. Museum would include framed artwork from the animation process, similar to that of MoMA. Reflecting the place of the museum as a new stop-off on the studio tour, however, the Warner Bros. Museum went a step further; it also sought to 'experientialize' the relation of display, providing 'guests a chance to incorporate themselves into an original piece of animation art'. This interactive element underlined a presentation of animation style and history that served the branding requirements of Warner Bros. in the mid-1990s; it established the cartoon world as a mode of encounter, typical of a wider studio strategy remodelling the animation front as a locus of corporate identification and revenue potential.

In business terms, the revitalization of Looney Tunes in the nineties was a result of the new commercial drive towards character merchandising. This was tied to the development of the Warner Bros. Studio Stores that first opened in 1991, the same year Warner Bros. launched its inaugural Movie World theme park on Australia's Gold Coast. These ventures sought to emulate Disney's success in theme park and retail development – Disney opening its first studio store in 1987. Reaching a global total of 728 outlets by 1999, Disney Stores were designed as brand environments, a dazzling array of merchandise offset by video wall displays, trailers and animation. Warner Bros. swiftly mirrored the success of the Disney Store chain with its stores creating an equivalent feeling of brand inhabitation. The design firm responsible for Warner's flagship store in Times Square described the interior as a 'brand-supportive space that makes customers feel like they're in a cartoon' (Nisch 2002). Accordingly, bright neon signs and saturated colour helped integrate giant sculptures of Bugs Bunny, with multimedia plasma screens continuously looping Warner Bros. cartoons, film trailers and classic movie clips. Unlike the child-centred emporia of the Disney Stores, the Warner outlets were designed more as high-tech adult gift stores. Both were intended as sites for consumer amusement – what corporate publicity described in each case as 'a unique setting in which to present a complete shopping and entertainment experience' (cited in Simensky 1998: 178).

Historically, licensing initiatives based around Warner Bros. animation can be traced back to the character merchandising of Porky Pig in the 1930s and the wide range of toys, ceramics, watches, dolls and colouring books featuring Bugs Bunny that appeared in the forties and fifties. As Linda Simensky suggests, however, character merchandising had become sparse by the 1980s. Only with the creation of a new animation division in 1988, designed to produce daily and weekly television series, did the commercial status of Warner Bros. animation show signs of revival. This was further encouraged by the success of Disney's *Who Framed Roger Rabbit?* (1988), an animation/live action hybrid that marked the turnaround of Disney's corporate fortunes and that featured iconographic Looney Tunes characters. Coinciding with the expansion of Warner Bros.' consumer products division after the Time Warner deal, and the particular triumph in licensing that came with *Batman*, the Looney Tunes were ripe for a new and unprecedented wave of commercial exploitation.

At the level of market competition, this must be seen as a response to the incredible success of Disney in the 1980s and 1990s; the company re-energized its animation library in producing new animated 'classics' such as *The Little Mermaid* (1989), *Beauty and the Beast* (1991) and *The Lion King* (1994) in ways that helped transform Disney into an entertainment powerhouse. Under the managerial supervision of Jeffrey Katzenberg animated characters were taken up as brand equity. This was unsurprising given the practical and legal scope for cartoons to transfer their images into toy likenesses and merchandise. As Jane Gaines and Celia Lury have shown, modern trademark law allows for the protection of a fictional character independently of the original or notionally 'authored' work of which it is a part. This creates a legal shield that 'makes it possible for the original proprietor to transfer the sign to second and third parties for a limited period of time in exchange for royalties' (Lury 1993: 85; Gaines 1991). While this can generate conflict when characters are played by actors (who maintain their own image and performance rights), trademark protections are more fully secured, and often aggressively pursued, when it comes to the circulation and public use of cartoon characters. It is in this context that animation has become a key form of image property, its inherent reproducibility lending itself in equal measure to commercial proliferation and cultural policing.

The dual impetus to proliferate and police animation under the protective authority of trademark law is all the more significant when cartoon images also function as corporate metonyms. While Disney has long sought to equate Mickey Mouse with its corporate brand identity, the Looney Tunes characters have had by comparison a more fluid history, their brand status in relation to Warner Bros. only beginning to coagulate in the nineties. Speaking in 1996, Warner Bros. co-chairman Robert Daly explained that, 'Bugs Bunny to us is like Mickey Mouse is to Disney' (cited in Grove 1996). One might argue that this became more determinately so after *Batman* and the Time Warner merger. Responding to corporate-commercial aspirations, Looney Tunes characters were suddenly licensed across the burgeoning network of studio stores and amusement parks (Warner Bros. opened additional Movie World theme parks in Germany in 1996 and Spain in 2002), they appeared in adverts for brands like Nike and Pepsi, starred in a roster of new animated shorts such as *Chariots of Fur* (1994) and *Carrotblanca* (1995), and became generally synonymous with the banner of family entertainment.[1] As Daly explained, 'animation is a very important part of our strategy because not only are they very profitable on their own and obviously the videos are very profitable, but it will also help our consumer products business and our store business' (ibid.).

It was in this context that *Space Jam* emerged as the culmination of attempts to compete with Disney in the feature animation and merchandising business. Combining the enormous sales potential of Michael Jordan and Bugs Bunny, *Space Jam* was developed to launch the movie career of a basketball icon and to consolidate the $3 billion yearly revenue that Warner Bros. received from Looney Tunes products, merchandise and promotional tie-ins (Lukk 1997: 257). Introducing new animated characters such as Lola Bunny, and establishing a platform for feature animation at Warner Bros., the film would generate $1.2 billion in merchandise sales, far exceeding the film's $125 million production and marketing costs. Growing out of two Nike television commercials made in 1991, 'Hare Jordan' and 'Hare-O-Space Jordan', the film itself was a form of brand hyperbole, celebrating the very principle of synergy. This was reproduced in textual strategies that I will shortly examine. To fully appreciate the film's discursive significance, however, it is necessary to situate *Space Jam* within a particular moment of corporate exculpation, specifically that of Gerald Levin who between 1995 and 1996 – the same period that *Space Jam* went into production and was suddenly rushed to release – undertook negotiations that would culminate in the merger between Time Warner and Turner Broadcasting Systems in July 1996.

This deal brought home with force the gamble that Levin was prepared to make, against shareholder pressure, to expand the depth and scale of the company's entertainment holdings. Despite the crippling debt that had ailed the conglomerate since 1989, Levin sought to enlarge the company and its debt further still. Accordingly, he acquired Turner Broadcasting for its prized cable networks (CNN, TCM, TNT, TBS, Cartoon Network) and substantial film and television library, but also for business holdings in areas such as film distribution (New Line, Castle Rock) and sports teams (Atlanta Braves). Like Disney's $19 billion acquisition of ABC/Capital Cities in 1995, these deals created a hiatus not simply for anti-trust lobbies but also for the conglomerates involved, unleashing a new round of anxiety, friction and bloodletting within operational structures and management hierarchies. While the Disney acquisition would destabilize Michael Eisner's reign (Stewart 2005), it was not clear at the time what effect the Turner deal might have for Time Warner and Gerald Levin. Jon Lewis suggests that 'the entertainment industry will be controlled by two or three conglomerates; in the fall of 1996 it was uncertain whether or not Time Warner would be one of them' (Lewis 1998: 114). With many of its divisions underperforming, a $17 billion debt load constraining the exploitation of assets and a falling company stock price, Levin, in particular, was anxious to draw from the deal indicators of hope and percipience.

Looney Tunes became a pregnant symbol in this context, linked as it was to the sudden massive expansion of Time Warner's film and television library. On 26 September 1996, it was announced that Warner Bros. would take responsibility for the Turner Broadcasting film and television library. This was made up of 3,522 film titles from the MGM, RKO Pictures and pre-1948 Warner Bros. archives, the largest film library in the world.[2] The integration with Warner Bros. created a combined feature film library of 6,000 movies and 28,500 television titles, offering enormous programming and licensing potential. Marketing possibilities were especially notable in the case of animation. Not only did the merger make whole the Warner Bros. Looney Tunes library, Turner also owned the world's largest cartoon library, comprising 8,500 titles from the catalogues of Hanna-Barbera and MGM. Together with the prodigal return of Porky Pig, Time Warner now owned Scooby Doo, the Flintstones, the Jetsons, Yogi Bear and Tom and Jerry, amongst others. While the immediate beneficiary of this consolidation was the Cartoon Network, the Warner Bros. Studio Stores quickly began to stock Hanna-Barbera character merchandise (Mallory 1996). In the honeymoon of asset combination, it was not insignificant that Fred Flintstone and Bugs Bunny appeared on the cover of Time Warner's annual report in 1996. Under the corporate slogan, 'Even Better Together', Levin begged for shareholder patience, he promised better cost-management, but he also confidently announced that Time Warner was now 'strategically complete', a move towards the overall objective of building the 'finest array of creative and journalistic franchises in combination with unmatched global distribution networks' (Time Warner 1996: 4). In a restatement of its corporate philosophy – 'create content, build libraries, grow networks, expand distribution' – Time Warner's prospective future was cast in relation to four totemic brands: Batman, Sports Illustrated, CNN and Looney Tunes.

The fact that Bugs Bunny could appear on the front of a corporate report is in many ways emblematic of what Kevin Sandler suggests to be a full-scale appropriation by Time Warner of the Looney Tunes legacy. This connects questions of corporate expedience in the 1990s to particular effects in the field of representation. If characters such as Bugs Bunny and Daffy Duck had, until this point, maintained a powerful strain of irreverence in their popular iconography, Sandler suggests there was a dissipation or draining of their traditional leaning towards conflict-driven, adult-skewed humour. He argues that Warner Bros. characters were taken up within a new discursive formation, often sweetened or finessed in being 'reconfigured into unproblematic corporate commodities' (Sandler 1998: 9). While the according risks were not lost on Warner Bros., concerned that *Space Jam* may hurt rather than enhance the brand image of Bugs Bunny, the commercial rewards of the family entertainment market, exploited with devastating effect by Disney, were such that the history of the Looney Tunes was swiftly remodelled, shorn, according to Sandler, of 'unprofitable and potentially damaging idiosyncrasies, flaws, or representations' (ibid.). There is more than a hint of fan guardianship in Sandler's account, condemning Disney for corporate blandness while celebrating the complex and once renegade nature of Warner Bros. animation. However, the idea that the Looney Tunes have been taken up within a corporate 'discursive formation' is suggestive. Not least, it establishes a platform for examining the complexities of this formation as it has come to signify in particular kinds of text around different configurations of 'total entertainment'.

Undoubtedly, *Space Jam* was a key expression of the new status given to the Looney Tunes, Bugs Bunny starring in what the *Wall Street Journal* would call 'the ultimate commercial movie' (Lippman 1996). While the film's status as a merchandising vehicle brought about a certain withering of the anarchic brashness that traditionally distinguished Warner Bros. animation, it would be a mistake to write off *Space Jam* on these terms. For Constance Balides, it is the very deliberateness of such texts to make visible their commercial status that give them rich contemporary significance. She contends that instances of commercial spectacle in family-centred movies – her chosen example is *Jurassic Park* (1993) but we might also include the likes of *Home Alone 2* (1992), *Hercules* (1997) and *Monsters Inc.* (2001) – are symptomatic of a moment where high-budget blockbusters are produced quite deliberately as economic objects. This is linked to the global dispersal of their merchandise and to public fascination with their box office success, but also to the way that economics are displayed on the surface of the text. For Balides, it is not enough to decry the impact of commerce on film as though it is possible to meaningfully withdraw from commercialized culture, or disentangle its values from the realm of elite or popular art. Instead, she suggests a form of criticism that investigates how films/spectators are deliberately construed/addressed in economic terms, how in different historical junctures particular meanings, and positions of identification, come to resonate in and between 'the (not necessarily conclusive) economic determinations that form the productive field of a text and the (not simply autonomous) character of a text as a signifying system' (Balides 2000: 141). If, as she argues, the contemporary period is based on 'the imbrication of cultural and economic realms and by pervasive identification with economic rationales', it becomes significant to ask what it means for a movie like *Space Jam* to be cast *so obviously* as a marketing event.

At one level, presenting *Space Jam* as an economic phenomenon offered Gerald Levin a sop to disgruntled shareholders, eager for signs of profit revival after the Turner deal. This can be set within a particular industrial context where the revival of character merchandising became a means of competing with Disney in the lucrative family market, expanding ancillary profits by mining the brand capital of Warner Bros.' film and television library. However, the significance of *Space Jam* does not stop there. As with *Jurassic Park*, the film also clearly mediates the issue of branding within its textual strategies, inviting audiences into an amusement park world aware of its status as such. This differs from *Looney Tunes: Back in Action*, a sequel that is equally concerned with branding but that is focused more on navigations that take place within the film industry and the media archive. In the next section, I examine the degree to which the two Looney Tunes movies released in 1996 and 2003 literally 'speak' the economics of branding. While both films make an obvious point of their corporate-commercial status, they do so on different terms and in ways that highlight the changing industrial conditions governing the aesthetics of synergy at the turn of the so-called 'mi-looney-um' (Grove 2003). Critically, I would suggest that the Looney Tunes movies enable us to examine the specific frameworks of consumption that developed around film between the mid-1990s and early 2000s, the screen career of Bugs *et al.* inextricably tied with two significant developments: the rise and fall of studio stores and the domestication of digital technologies, in particular that of DVD.

Looney Tunes and the aesthetics of synergy

For all the importance of 'synergy' to contemporary media industries, synergistic relationships do not spring ready-made from lists of business holdings. They do not occur by rote but have to be actively implemented and reproduced; synergy relies for success upon a variety of internal and market factors, from the co-operation of divisional units to the performance of the content, or brand, tying those divisions together. While the principle of synergy is central to understanding the way that media companies orchestrate and reinforce the commercial potential of their extensive business empires, it is at the same time necessary to consider how this synergism operates within particular contexts and periods. The treatment of the Looney Tunes within contemporary feature animation is suggestive in this

respect; it provides a means of analysing how the production of 'family entertainment' has responded to transitions in the relationship between industries,
markets, technologies and audiences.

According to Peter Krämer, the most significant production trend in American
cinema since the late 1970s has been the move towards the 'family adventure'
movie. Counting the likes of *Star Wars*, *Jurassic Park* and *The Lion King* amongst his
examples, Krämer argues that such films share certain basic characteristics.
Specifically, 'they are intended, and manage, to appeal to all age groups, especially
children and their parents, by combining spectacular, often fantastic or magical
action with a highly emotional concern with familial relationships, and also by
offering two distinct points of entry into the cinematic experiences they provide
(childish delight and absorption on the one hand, adult self-awareness and
nostalgia on the other)' (Krämer 1998a: 305). If family adventure movies have
become central 'to the economics of the American film industry and to the
moviegoing experiences of the American public', this has been powerfully reinforced by the revival of animation. Typified by a raft of blockbusters from Pixar
(*Toy Story*, 1995, *A Bug's Life*, 1998, *Monsters Inc*, 2001, *Finding Nemo*, 2003) and
DreamWorks (*Antz*, 1998, *Shrek* 2001, *Shark Tale*, 2004, *Madagascar*, 2005), the
development of Looney Tunes feature animation was part of a growing industrial
and creative trend in the 1990s. The lure of the family market, combined with the
new aesthetic possibilities of computer generated graphics, transformed the business of animation in ways that would even threaten the hegemony of Disney.[3]

In market terms, *Space Jam* was a live action hybrid poised to activate the dual
points of entry described by Krämer. At one level, the film casts itself within the
multiple fan catchments of basketball, not simply a defining American sport but a
key source of style and attitude for companies such as Nike who worked hard in the
1990s to authenticate its brand by incarnating its image in African-American
sports stars like 'Air' Jordan (Klein 2000: 57–74).[4] At the same time, the film uses
the Looney Tunes characters in ways that seek to appeal to children and parents
through forms of techno-display that create different possibilities for audience
'absorption' and 'self-awareness'. If absorption is linked to the fantastical possibility of animated characters appearing in the real world, self-awareness is based
on a reflexive comic strain in Warner Bros. animation, not for the first time aimed
at its own corporate authorship. As Janet Maslin commented in the *New York Times*,
'*Space Jam* is as much a tribute to the [Looney Tunes] past as it is a product-plug-
ging, high-tech, hip-hopping thing of the future' (Maslin 1996). According to
studio publicity, the film was 'a calculated throwback to the character's youth,
mixed with the familiarity of years spent before an audience' (Carney and
Misiroglu 1996: 22). *Space Jam*'s admixture of commercial spectacle and cartoon
nostalgia was central to the film's overall market strategy, the Looney Tunes (like
that of Michael Jordan) brought back from retirement – 'rested, recharged and
ready for the future' – as a means of appealing to youth and family audiences.

Fundamentally, *Space Jam* was an exercise of brand consolidation for all parties
concerned. For Jordan and his agent, David Falk, who was instrumental in

developing the project, it was an opportunity to launch the basketball star as a free-standing brand. Not content with endorsing Nike, McDonald's, Oakley, Gatorade, Wheaties and numerous other companies, Jordan used *Space Jam* to establish greater independence over the control of his brand name. For Warner Bros., it offered the chance to revitalize the Looney Tunes characters in order to create synergistic merchandising opportunities in and between the company's film and consumer products divisions. These imperatives structure the film in a number of ways, the intergalactic struggle over the cultural iconicity of 'his Airness and his Hareness' central to the film's basis of humour. On these terms, *Space Jam* is unusually transparent in its linkage of cultural and economic themes, the threatened bondage of Jordan and Bugs (enslaved in an off-world theme park) not without its ironies considering the publicity that multinationals like Nike and Hasbro would later receive about their involvement in exploitative sweatshop labour in distant global territories.

In brand terms, *Space Jam* helped finesse Jordan's iconic status, long defined by a mix of sporting enthralment and product endorsement.[5] The film had a more transformative, and for some egregious, effect on the Looney Tunes characters, however. Rather than a 'tribute' or 'throwback' to the Looney Tunes past, a number of fans, critics and animation veterans worried that *Space Jam* developed an understanding of character that renounced the past for new commercial futures, 'liquidating those memories of theatrical and television cartoon images of the past that challenge present discursive formations' (Sandler 1998: 12). While characters such as Bugs Bunny and Road Runner rarely intermingled in traditional Warner Bros. animation, inhabiting separate cartoon worlds, *Space Jam* brought them together in ways that not only made subtle changes to character design but that also, more significantly, transformed the Looney Tunes into a corporate-commercial family.[6] In separate occasions throughout *Space Jam*, characters pass into a subterranean wonderland, a two-dimensional core beneath the earth's surface whose entrance is marked by the logo of Warner Bros. While passing through the logo helps demarcate movements in and between animated and live action sequences, it also refracts the Looney Tunes through a corporate prism. Sandler notes that while Yosemite Sam and Elmer Fudd may once have been the sworn enemy of Bugs Bunny and Daffy Duck, in *Space Jam* they all exist as 'affectionate residents of "Looney Tunes Land"' (ibid.: 14). The idea that Bugs and his 'Tune pals' exist beneath a golf hole in Los Angeles provides *Space Jam* with a core commercial fantasy – the vision that cartoon worlds are inhabitable and populated by a family of characters who exist to be discovered in order to be consumed.

Presenting the spectacle of brand encounter was of course the modus operandi of *Space Jam* as a 'marketing event'. With more than 200 US and international partners selling *Space Jam* products, the film made no attempt to disguise its commercial ambitions but sought instead to parody and perform its status as a merchandising vehicle. It is here that *Space Jam* offered up 'childish delight' and 'adult self-awareness' as points of entry, helping to make visible the film's relation to a product line ranging from collectible $40 cookie jars to a wide range of toys, action figures,

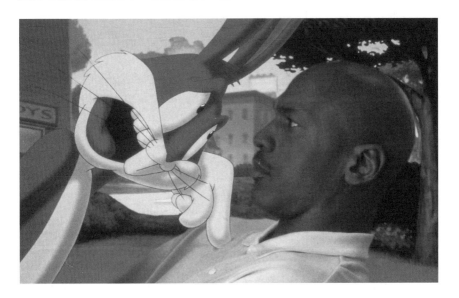

Figure 5.1 Entering the land of the Looney Tunes, *Space Jam* (1996). Courtesy of Warner Bros. and the Ronald Grant Archive.

games, apparel and souvenirs. This is brought out in a key scene that is especially revealing of what Josh Stenger, using the work of Mary Ann Doane, calls a 'cinematic spectatorial mode … fully adequate to a consumer society' (Stenger 1997: 48). Searching for Jordan's sneakers in his suburban family house, Bugs Bunny and Daffy Duck stumble across his daughter's toy-filled bedroom, precipitating an exchange between the two characters about whether or not they have ever 'seen any money' from 'all those mugs, T-shirts and lunch boxes with our pictures on them'. 'Not a cent,' laments Daffy, adding in mock woe, 'it's a crying shame. We've gotta get new agents. We're getting screwed'. Just as interesting as this scene's gonzo referencing of product licensing is the simultaneous playing out of childhood fantasy, specifically the dream possibility that imaginary characters may suddenly come to life. *Space Jam*'s wink to the contemporary exploitation of image rights segues into a scene of childish wonder and wish-fulfilment, Jordan's children helping Bugs and Daffy to escape the clamouring jaws of the family pet. In narrative terms, the Looney Tunes become readable as merchandise *and* mercurial friends, central to the brand relationship that *Space Jam* works hard to achieve on behalf of its merchandising partners and, in particular, the Warner Bros. Studio Stores.

In market terms, *Space Jam*'s project in the mid-1990s was to signify, contextualize and aestheticize consumption practices growing out of the industrial and fan intersections of sports and entertainment. For both Jordan and Warner Bros., the 'retail concept shop' was part of the wider branding impulse. While Jordan opened showcase stores in New York and Chicago for an eponymous line of lifestyle wear (mirrored by the growth of branded ESPN stores), Warner Bros. broadened the base of its retail business to include over 200 studio stores in countries as diverse as Germany, Guam, Singapore, Saudi Arabia, the United Kingdom and the United Arab Emirates. With the ability of cartoons to translate from one country to another, and with the penetration of animation channels such as the Cartoon Network into European, Asian and Latin markets during the 1990s, the extension of retail possibilities for character-based consumption became a branding priority for both Disney and Warner Bros. In serving to 'speak' the economics of branding and synergy, *Space Jam* sought to animate the film's merchandising possibilities in ways that led to the studio store.

Here, it is worth situating the studio store in relation to its parent form – the modern theme park. According to Charles Acland, theming is an organizing principle for the wide range of cross-promotional activities that shape the environment, architecture and forms of sociability inherent within contemporary consumerism. While Disney pioneered the concept of the theme park in the 1950s, it became central to the operation of nearly all the major studios in the 1990s, linking film interests to the development of rides and to associated business concerns in real estate, restaurants and hotel chain ownership. For the 'big five' owners of Disney, Anheuser-Busch, Time Warner, Viacom (Paramount) and NBC Universal, theme parks have become a primal scene of brand synergy (Allen 2003b). However, they are also a particular kind of leisure phenomenon, based around the development of million-dollar attractions, substantial in physical scale and admission price, and generally designed as major tourist destinations. Theme parks are removed, in other words, from everyday consumption practices. It is in this context that Acland suggests a 'miniaturization' of their core principles, witnessed in the 1990s by the proliferation of consumption environments figured around the 'ongoing naturalization of reigning discourses of family, entertainment and public space' (Acland 2003: 203).

Studio stores and ventures such as Planet Hollywood (also first opening in 1991) were indicative of this tendency. Asserting their identity in relation to the shopping mall and the multiplex, they offered customers the accessibility of a synergistic 'experience' organized around the global commodity of Hollywood film. Josh Stenger suggests that the appeal of Planet Hollywood in the 1990s was based on exploding 'the two-dimensional reality of cinema by deploying all the signifiers of Hollywood into a three-dimensional, inhabitable space, a hands-on experience that is at once available at the movies and yet wholly dependent on its unavailability' (Stenger 1997: 48). Buoyed by the glamour of celebrity shareholders including Arnold Schwarzenegger, Sylvester Stallone and Bruce Willis, these signifiers focused on 'the pyrotechnics and special effects of the 1980s blockbuster'. While the studio stores were less muscular and more familial in their projection of Hollywood ideology, each relied as a form of brand space on a principle of interaction with movies. It is perhaps no surprise, in this respect, that dimensionality becomes a spatial theme in *Space Jam* (the capacity to move between worlds) as much as it is a platform for the latest in cartoon compositing (the capacity to integrate live action and 2D animation). The spectacular interplay of flat cartoons and real-life characters presupposes a relationship to brand personalities materialized in the world of the studio store, a consumer space that, to extrapolate from Stenger, obfuscates the process of commercial exchange by transforming the act of visiting into a participatory, quasi-cinematic, brand event.

Studio stores and global franchises like Planet Hollywood became, in many ways, the epitome of Hollywood's self-commodification in the 1990s. And yet, they were far from unencumbered. While Planet Hollywood had become a $2.5 billion restaurant empire by 1997, its success began to wane by the end of the nineties. Suffering from over-extension in domestic and international markets its value dropped by 90 per cent in 1999, forcing the company to file for bankruptcy. Similar kinds of fiscal pressure, born of the capital-intensive nature of retail development and the dangers of brand saturation, also hit Disney and Warner Bros. In each case, studio stores experienced a dip in the late 1990s, losing ground to mass merchandisers such as Wal-Mart in selling DVDs and licensed products.[7] While Disney made plans to refresh the allure of its studio stores, Warner Bros. closed theirs altogether in 2001, moving to an online shopping service (WBShop.com) that enabled AOL Time Warner to shed 3,800 jobs in easing its post-merger debt load.[8]

By the year 2000, studio stores had become less attractive to Warner Bros. as a basis of synergy. While this hardly tempered the licensing and merchandising activities of the Warner Bros. Consumer Products division, it did refocus attention on ancillary revenue streams such as television syndication, movie sell-through and web synergies, enlivened by the growing multichannel environment (incorporating studio networks such as the WB) and by the domestication of new DVD and Internet technologies. This concurrence developed after *Space Jam* and before *Back in Action*, posing questions about their respective forms of cultural-commercial address. I would suggest that bringing the two films into comparison provides an indication of shifts in the branding of animation at Warner Bros. This does not imply any lessening of the commercial significance of toys and tie-ins. The development by Warner Bros. of films based on television cartoons running on its WB network, such as *Pokémon* (1999) and *Scooby Doo* (2002), was defined by the dispersal of merchandised commodities targeted specifically at children. Similarly, Bugs Bunny's licensed image appeared on anything from apparel to postage stamps to NASCAR promotion at the end of the nineties. However, the two Looney Tunes features are suggestive of the way that entertainment companies have also sought to respond to new commercial and viewing habits. If *Space Jam* focused on the dynamics of brand encounter, imagining Warner Bros. as a netherworld to inhabit, literalized in the studio store, *Back in Action* played upon Hollywood studio culture and the navigation of movie and cartoon history. This is especially consonant, I would argue, with the culture and surge in consumer spending associated with DVD in the early 2000s, home video transactions, of which DVD made up 72 per cent, totalling $16.3 billion in 2003 (Kendrick 2005). This compared with an estimated $2.6 billion earned in movie licensing royalties the year before (Wasko

2003). Indeed, while licensing provides a key stream of ancillary revenue for Holly-wood, the phenomenal growth of DVD in the early 2000s threw into sharp relief the economic primacy of worldwide video (and DVD) sales, the film industry's single most important source of income since the late eighties.

As with video, the DVD market forced Hollywood to re-evaluate its archival assets, content-rich companies like Warner Bros. especially anxious to capitalize on the invigorated profit potential of the sell-through market for recently released films and repackaged 'classics' drawn from studio libraries. Indeed, since the introduction of DVD, Time Warner's library had appreciated by $7 billion by 2004 (Epstein 2006: 218). It is perhaps no surprise in this context that *Back in Action* witnessed a calculated re-appraisal of the classic status of Looney Tunes animation. Synchro-nous with the creation of an in-house unit at Warner Bros. dedicated to Looney Tunes productions (the first of its kind since 1961), *Back in Action* announced the studio's figurative return to 'time-honoured tradition' (Littleton and Kit 2002). Mobilizing the Looney Tunes franchise for a second commercial outing, the film sought, in the words of screenwriter Larry Doyle, to emulate 'the irreverence, the biting humor, the nuances in the characters' personalities and the specific styles of animation developed by the legends of the classic Looney Tunes era' (cited in 'Looney 101' 2003). Barely disguising its desire to move away from the 'rested and recharged' characters featured in *Space Jam*, the film's production notes spoke of re-inscribing 'the Looney Tunes' trademark acerbic wit' as a means of redressing 'the period of time where that [wit] got diluted a bit' (ibid.). To this end, *Back in Action* not only revived the long-standing rivalry between Bugs and Daffy – figuring them as Warner Bros. contract players battling for star status within and beyond the studio lot – it gave up the idea of 'Looney Tunes Land' altogether, situating the entire film in a live action world populated by icy entertainment executives, corporate megalo-maniacs and the profit-seeking demands of the 'brothers Warner'.

Like *Space Jam*, *Back in Action* played on two levels, appealing to childish delight through cartoon mayhem while entertaining adults via film parodies and refer-ences to Hollywood's industrial practices. Based around set pieces in Los Angeles, Las Vegas, Paris, Africa and outer space, the film is structured as a series of generic or character 'bursts', demonstrating particular technological proficiencies in the process of live action animation. While 'Las Vegas' provides a showcase for gun-toting slapstick within Yosemite Sam's Wooden Nickel Casino, 'Paris' includes the romantic overtures of Pepé le Pew and a scene in the Louvre where Bugs and Daffy jump inside paintings by George Seurat, Salvador Dali and C. M. Coolidge. Where *Space Jam* turned the Looney Tunes into a familial unit, *Back in Action* relinquished the cosiness that had drawn comparisons with Disney in favour of heightened exposition of cartoon madcap. Like the James Bond franchise the film openly quotes (the central story turns on a mission to recover a powerful diamond and features Timothy Dalton as actor-spy Damian Drake, pitting his wits against an evil corporate nemesis played by Steve Martin), the film is distilled into a number of scenes and gestures that service the brand memory of classic Looney Tunes relationships. This is not to suggest that *Back in*

Figure 5.2 Addressing the 'brothers Warner', *Looney Tunes: Back in Action* (2003). Courtesy of Warner Bros. and the Ronald Grant Archive.

Action was made for adult animation fans. It opened in cinemas in November 2003 as one of a number of pre-holiday releases aimed at the family market. Despite its poor box office performance, grossing a paltry $21 million, the film was designed like *Space Jam* to create new market opportunities for the Looney Tunes franchise, reaching a new generation of children. Unlike *Space Jam*, however, the film's textual strategies were attuned to a corporate moment prioritizing screen rather than store-based synergism, cable networks (such as KidsWB), new media initiatives (LooneyTunes.com launched in 2001) and the wider sell-through possibilities of DVD insinuating themselves more forcibly within Hollywood's ancillary imagination.

This is seen especially in the film's treatment of the entertainment environment, based less on the world of the amusement park than on a cultural landscape defined by the history of Hollywood's past. In the course of the film, textual invocations range from Warner Bros. serials such as *Lethal Weapon* and *Batman*, to other paradigmatic franchises of the New Hollywood era including James Bond, *Indiana Jones* and *Star Wars*. This accompanies more deliberate forms of cinematic parody, from Bugs Bunny's scene-by-scene re-enactment of the shower scene from *Psycho* (1960) to the spoofing of low-budget science fiction films and horror icons from the 1950s and early 1960s. In addition, Looney Tunes characters mix with a host of 'stars' from Warner Bros. film and television shows, Bugs taking an executive lunch among diners including Porky Pig, Speedy Gonzalez, Wile E. Coyote, Michigan J. Frog, Scooby Doo and live cast members from popular studio shows. The extended opening sequence is emblematic of the film's desire to replicate traditions associated with classic Warner Bros. animation, notably the impulse to caricature executives and parody movies from the live film industry (Crafton 1998). Running amok within the boardrooms and sound stages of the Warner Bros. studio, Daffy is chased off the lot in pandemonium that includes his borrowing the batmobile and the subsequent destruction of the famous Warner Bros. water tower. Interjected with scenes that depict the general bustle of film production, studio tours and corporate board meetings, *Back in Action* relies much less on the playing out of child-hood fantasy than on a series of reflexive relationships established across the history and terrain of the motion picture business.

In its hyperconscious style, *Back in Action* belongs to a particular genre form which Jim Collins suggests coalesced in the late 1980s in response to the expanding 'semiotic array' of cultural life. Specifically, Collins suggests that the accelerated rate of technological innovation in the eighties and nineties – specifically, VCR, cable, computers, and latterly DVD – established a new attitude towards the archive that has levelled effects on the art of (cinematic) storytelling. With a vast reservoir of texts and images now subject to 'perpetually reconfigurable random access', Collins points to a roster of films that engage the sophistication of media culture by playing out narrative action at two levels, 'one which revolves around character adventure and another which concerns the film's own adventures as it delves into the array, into the accumulated layers of popular culture stored within the screen memories of individual viewers' (Collins 1995: 137). In key respects, Looney Tunes animation has long been characterized by the 'ironic eclecticism' that Collins equates with the hybrid and reflexive tendency of contemporary cinema, up to and including the commercial reflexivity of *Space Jam*. However, technological developments such as the penetration of VCR ownership in the late 1980s and, similarly, that of DVD ownership in the early 2000s have augmented the scope of popular screen memory, providing a cultural backdrop for the register and address of animated features such as *Who Framed Roger Rabbit?* and *Looney Tunes: Back in Action*.[9] If the former draws on the history of studio animation and hard-boiled detective films, set within a moment where classic cartoons and studio pictures were becoming readily available through cable and video, the latter frames a cartoon adventure through, and in relation to, the hyperactive circulation of Hollywood's past. Although the domestication of home-viewing technologies should not be seen as a determining context in either case, it is perhaps not inci-dental that both films were released during high-points of video and DVD take-up; *Back in Action* can be seen as responsive, like its forebear *Roger Rabbit*, to an emergent cultural and commercial film sensibility based on the reconstitution of studio libraries and archives.

This highlights the degree to which new market conditions, particularly the boon given to restoring and repackaging film archives by the likes of video and DVD, may at times serve to enliven as much as purge or liquidate particular images and representational histories. In the case of *Back in Action*, this can be seen in the film's textual debt to 'classic' Looney Tunes animation. However, it is also signalled in the film's extra-textual economy, the DVD release of *Back in Action* including prominent trailers for 'remastered and restored' cartoons drawn from the 'Warner Bros. vaults'.[10] Kevin Sandler notes that, in the late 1990s, classic characters and new updated versions began to be compartmentalized into historical and contemporary 'clusters' on channels such as the Cartoon Network (Sandler 1998: 22). If, as he suggests, Warner Bros. animation stood at a crossroads at the end of the nineties, 'torn between dedication and corporatization', *Back in Action* sought to reconcile the Looney Tunes brand in and between these competing imperatives.

Rather than conflate the aesthetics of synergy in *Space Jam* and *Back in Action*, I have so far stressed the need to account for contextual and rhetorical differences in the way they 'speak' the economics of branding. Responding to the perception of *Space Jam* as a pure marketing event, *Back in Action* is especially quick to lampoon the marketing credos of the contemporary movie business. When the humourless 'VP of Comedy' (Jennifer Elfman) announces to Bugs Bunny that 'I was brought in to leverage your synergy', explaining that her function is to 'reposition your brand identity', the film derives its humour from popular knowledge about the entertainment business. Affording a degree of self-mockery to the promotional 'leveraging' widely associated with *Space Jam*, *Back in Action* seeks to clear space for itself as a franchise sequel. As I have discussed, this can be set in relation to the decline of the studio's store business, and the tactical decision amidst inconsistent box office returns on animated features such as *The Quest for Camelot* (1998), *The Iron Giant* (1999) and *Osmosis Jones* (2001) to exploit the 'classic' Looney Tunes and Hanna-Barbera character libraries across new delivery channels enabled by digitization.

The Looney Tunes films point to the need for precision in accounting for shifts in industrial-textual practice. However, they also reveal discursive continuities that ask questions about what might be called the 'politics of commercial obviousness'. Significantly, both films draw attention to the instrumental role of trademarks in the contemporary film industry, expressing the corporate reality made apparent by Steve Ross in the early nineties: 'we are not just in the movie business, we are in the intellectual property business' (cited in Epstein 2006: 219). In each film, the business of branding becomes a form of textual excess. When Daffy Duck states in *Space Jam* 'We are the exclusive property and trademark of Warner Bros. Inc.', lifting his tail to reveal the WB logo, the economics of the film is made plainly visible. If this makes sport of the intellectual property battles fought in the mid-nineties between fans of Warner Bros. animation and the legal department of Time Warner,[11] *Back in Action* draws on the criticism beginning to coalesce in the late 1990s around corporate branding, lampooning studio marketing orthodoxies but also the villainy of a global corporation (ACME) that would have amongst its board of directors a 'VP of Child Labour'. While *Space Jam* is figured in relation to a sports star whose identity and sneakers were synonymous with brand culture in the 1990s, *Back in Action* responds to a cultural moment where the hidden histories and labour dynamics of this culture, in particular questions of sweatshop exploitation and corporate ethical responsibility, had become a source of growing public disquiet.

These representational manoeuvres can be seen as legitimating strategies. Deflecting the systemic critique of global capitalism onto rogue individuals, both films set the quirky, profit-driven, but not iniquitous world of Warner Bros. against tyrannical corporate despots and lunatics. Ideologically, this vision of 'good' and 'bad' capitalism helps service what Beryl Langer calls 'the more intractable and enduring legitimation problems' of the children's culture industry in producing and selling branded goods (Langer 2004: 264). While *Space Jam* and *Back in Action* both allude to the global business operations of film studios, toy companies and fast food merchants – all involved in subcontracting the production of toys and merchandise to export processing zones in the Far East – the films posit a moral difference between the 'wacky' capitalism of the Looney Tunes, delivering beloved American brands to cheering global audiences, and the 'wacko' capitalism of alien or unhinged corporate bullies, threatening the free market through shady business practices and designs upon world domination. At some level, the Looney Tunes films can be seen as a paean to 'market populism', a new consensus that Thomas Frank suggests developed in the 1990s accepting 'the logic of the market as the functional equivalent of democracy' (Frank 2000: 57). On these terms, the Looney Tunes films champion American popular entertainment as a global right, connecting the brands of Warner Bros., Looney Tunes, Jordan and the National Basketball Association to ideas of popular cultural enfranchisement. In being enthralled to the planetary performance of American brands, the Looney Tunes films are rooted in the culture of neo-liberalism (Comaroff and Comaroff 2001). However, they legitimate themselves through forms of corporate irony that leave them knowing but 'open' in an ideological and commercial sense, bearing out Robert Allen's point that 'ambivalence and indeterminacy are the distinguishing formal qualities of texts that are subject to protean refashioning as commodities' (Allen 1999: 125).

This ambivalence has been notably expressed in forms of self-reflexivity about the movie business itself. Beginning with *Batman* in 1989, franchise films have been prone to reflect on the hype-based and logo-driven culture of which they are a part.[12] Charles Acland connects this to 'developments associated with the circulation of industry transparency' in the 1990s and 2000s (Acland 2003: 78). In this case, the regularity of self-reflexive movies about Hollywood life tap a certain 'vernacular understanding' of the film industry developed in the last two decades by such as the weekly reporting of box office statistics, the growing newsworthiness of film within popular entertainment and business journalism, and the tendency of DVDs to present data and information about the production and marketing of movies. If industry transparency can be seen as a dimension of the episteme of popular entertainment in contemporary culture, this has developed in broad accordance with what Constance Balides terms the 'extension of economics as an authoritative discourse across the social fabric' (Balides 2000: 141). Taking *Jurassic Park* (1993) as her cue, Balides argues that economic rationalizations are no longer hidden but have become 'hypervisible' within social and cultural life.[13] In a discursive juncture where economics has become productive of subjectivity and social meaning – a dominant paradigm for human activity in the West – commercial self-reflexivity is symptomatic, she contends, of a regime where the 'lustre of capital itself' is an attraction in a post-Fordist economy' (ibid.: 160). As with the iconographic T. rex logo that helped launch the *Jurassic Park* franchise, and that featured prominently in the movie, branding has acquired specificity not simply as a marketing mechanism but also in becoming its own source of generative identity and spectacle. On these terms, the Looney Tunes movies offer a striking example of the way that motion pictures are increasingly produced *as* economic phenomena, marked in the way they orchestrate meanings, address spectators and invite cultural uses (ibid.: 141).

To understand the commodity logic of total entertainment is, at one level, to think about the particularity of film as spectacle and 'attraction' in contemporary visual culture. In their presentational and participatory style of address, branded media properties (notably franchise movies) are often likened to early cinema in the way that 'energy moves outwards towards an acknowledged spectator rather than inward towards character-based situations essential to classical narrative' (Gunning 1990: 59). Whether or not a film is directly exhibitionistic on these terms, as can be said of the Looney Tunes features, franchise movies invariably lead the viewer away from the text to surrounding frames of commercial and media consumption. As Aida Hozic writes, 'The blurring of the boundaries between different forms of entertainment, the transformation of film into consumer products, the merging of make-believe and real life – these are no longer accidental and playful fragments of postmodern media culture but the economic preconditions of the continued existence of the global entertainment sector' (Hozic 2000: 217). While Hozic is wary of the 'ominous media enterprises lurking in the background' of a 'world where there is little but attractions left', it has been my argument that conglomerates are obliged to recalibrate the aesthetics of synergy to affect or authenticate brands in accordance with changing market conditions and ancillary priorities. *Space Jam* and *Back in Action* are what John Caldwell might call 'company confessions' or 'legitimating mechanisms' in this respect; they act as 'mediated forms of rationality' that seek to normalize industrial change, including transitions in the frameworks of consumption used to sell branded media content (Caldwell 2006: 124). If economic and textual systems of meaning are productive in relation to one another, the Looney Tunes films quite literally animate the vicissitudes of branding in the contemporary motion picture business. They express the 'commercial obviousness' involved in the production of franchised entertainment and articulate shifts in Warner Bros.' attempt to perpetuate and maintain a reliable system of consumerism. Having analysed the textual economy of brand animation, linked to specific ancillary imperatives, I want in the next chapter to consider a different facet of brand spectacle: the event-in-itself of blockbuster marketing. Instead of the politics of commercial obviousness, I turn in this case to questions of corporate obfuscation, moving from revived bats and recharged rabbits to the concurrent lauding of hobbits and wizards.

Chapter 6

The sustained event
Branding fantasies and the corporate blockbuster

At the same time that the franchise events of *Lord of the Rings* (2001–3) and *Harry Potter* (2001–present) were extending their global presence across the cultural land-scape, their mutual owner, AOL Time Warner, was constructing its own monu-ment to corporate grandeur and gigantism. Between 1998 and 2003, work continued on new headquarters in New York, a flagship home at Columbus Circle on the edge of Central Park. Combining AOL Time Warner's corporate offices and broadcasting facilities with a five-star hotel, shopping arcade, luxury apart-ments and a major jazz venue, Columbus Circle cost $1.7 billion and was designed to showcase the size and ambition of the world's largest media conglomerate. 'This is a great way to present yourself to the world', reported *Daily Variety* of the pitch sold to senior executives, 'this is branding, which is what the twenty-first century is all about' (cited in Lyons 2002: 1). Like the marquee blockbusters that would drive AOL Time Warner's major film divisions in the early 2000s, corporate power was linked to brand strategies that would cast a shadow over rival properties through material size and the sheer scale of investment.

As multimillion dollar project developments, both Columbus Circle and the franchise phenomena of *Lord of the Rings* and *Harry Potter* are indicative corporate ventures, combining staggering financial outlays on the creation of imposing fanta-sies with substantial revenue potential. They are also set squarely in the context of the $183 billion merger between America Online (AOL) and Time Warner, a corporate saga that unravelled between January 2000 and autumn 2003. Just as the merger between Time Warner and Turner Broadcasting fuelled the revival of the Looney Tunes franchise, the development of the fantasy blockbuster was index-linked to a subsequent, and more audacious, corporate marriage. Widely described as the prototype for a new kind of conglomerate, the AOL Time Warner deal married the new media potential of the Internet with old media wealth vested in cable systems and entertainment content. Anticipating a future of interactive consumer services, AOL chief executive Steve Case explained: 'The battle is shifting. It's going to be more and more about customer relation-ships, more than who's got the pipe, who's got the content' (cited in Gunther 2000: 33). This had implications for the film industry; it appeared that movies would be one of a number of content streams in AOL Time Warner's visionary digital tomorrow. However, as swiftly as the rhetoric of media convergence had gripped boardrooms and business discourse at the dawn of the new millennium, the promise of interactive consumer services was tarnished by the collapse of the dot-com boom and increasing federal interest in AOL by the Securities and Exchange Commission.

By 2002, AOL Time Warner's stock began to plummet in the face of mounting debt, accounting scandals, and the biggest annual loss in corporate history – an eye-watering $99 billion. Against a backdrop of fractious managerial relations, shareholder discontent, and the resignation of key AOL executives (including Richard Pittman and Steve Case), senior management took the decision in September 2003 to drop AOL from the corporate name. As stated by the new chief executive of Time Warner, Richard Parsons, 'We believe that our new name better reflects the portfolio of our valuable businesses and ends any confusion between our corporate name and the America Online brand name for our investors, partners and the public' (Naughton 2003). Recalibrating its corporate priorities, Time Warner downplayed the language of media convergence that initially framed the merger, reaffirming the value of 'the world-class franchises … [that] are the driving force behind our financial results' (Time Warner 2003: 3). As a means of finessing the AOL Time Warner debacle, and affirming the conglomerate's multi-divisional strengths, filmed entertainment became a source of prospective corporate renewal. Simone Murray frames this more broadly, suggesting that 'as consumer behaviour of recent years has demonstrated that technological format matters less than content loyalty in directing consumer habits, the commercial priority amongst global media players has gravitated from a desire to control *access* to a desire to control high-profile *content*' (Murray 2005: 418).

This was no doubt welcome news for New Line and Warner Bros. Ever since Time Warner merged with Turner Broadcasting in 1996, New Line's status as a 'major independent' (Wyatt 1998) had been threatened with the risk of being sold, shut down or absorbed within Warner Bros. Only by securing international distribution agreements and a financial credit line of $750 million from an international group of banks did New Line maintain its operational independence in the late 1990s. Independent financing assuaged Time Warner in trying to reduce its $18 billion debt load. Meanwhile, it enabled the parent company to maintain separate product streams within its filmed entertainment division. Specializing in niche franchise serials like *Nightmare on Elm Street* (1985–8) and *Teenage Mutant Ninja Turtles* (1990–3), New Line developed a varied annual release schedule in the late nineties that mixed two or three high-end productions ($50 million or more), a majority of mid-range films (between $20 and $50 million) and occasional films under $10 million released by Fine Line Features (Eller and Saylor 1999). In a market defined by the segmentation of audience tastes, New Line gave Time Warner breadth within its motion picture portfolio. Nevertheless, in one of the first acts of AOL Time Warner as a combined company, 125 New Line employees were laid off, almost 20 per cent of its staff. As a cost-cutting measure brought about by the exorbitant price of the merger, and linked to the studio's fragile position in the wider corporate infrastructure, New Line was, in the words of one employee, 'offered up as a sacrificial lamb' (Klein 2003: 251).[1]

This context is important in situating *Lord of the Rings* as a corporate franchise that would rescue New Line and, to some degree, the fortunes of Time Warner itself. Assuming Miramax's option for the live action rights to *Lord of the Rings* in 1998, New Line chairman Robert Shaye committed $130 million in production financing, rising across the trilogy to $281 million. This was a substantial risk. While a prized literary property, holding what Shaye described as 'incredible currency for an entertainment franchise' (Carver 1998a), New Line was widely perceived as 'betting the house' on the potential success of *Lord of the Rings*. With renewed discussion at AOL Time Warner of selling or absorbing New Line, a stellar box office performance was imperative. In particular, the marketing and merchandising strategy had to be realized as effectively as possible, not only to launch *Fellowship of the Ring* (2001) with all necessary hype, but to construct the trilogy as a sustained event that could replicate levels of expectation for successive December release dates in 2002 and 2003.

Although more secure in its industrial relationship with the parent company, Warner Bros. also banked on the success of its own 'sustained event' in the *Harry Potter* franchise. As discussed in chapter two, Warner Bros. underwent a period of transition in the late nineties, coinciding with the end of the regime of Robert Daly and Terry Semel. When domestic market share fell to 11 per cent in 1997 – lagging behind Sony (20.3 per cent), Disney (14.2 per cent) and Paramount (12.3 per cent) – Warner Bros. diagnosed the problem as one of promotion, firing its head of theatrical marketing. Pointing to skyrocketing production and distribution costs, and fearing the exhaustion of star-driven staples like *Batman* and *Lethal Weapon*, Warner Bros. initiated a streamlining process in 1998, striving to move away from event pictures and their breathtaking costs (Bart 1999). Terry Semel commented: 'We have not taken ourselves out of the big event-movie business. However, we don't need to do that very often. We don't need an event picture four or five times a year' (Cox 1998).

The merger between AOL and Time Warner changed this situation dramatically. Not only did it pre-empt a new executive regime at Warner Bros., heralding the rise of Alan Horn and Barry Meyer, AOL placed a mandate on a stable and continuous flow of multiplatform content. *Variety* characterized Warner Bros. as a newly charged 'movie machine' and 'franchise factory' (Harris and Hayes 2001). This involved a more encompassing, environmental approach to film as product line and brand. Simone Murray describes this strategy in the following terms:

> In twenty-first century mass-marketing, the art is to target affluent consumers willing to direct their informational, entertainment, and consumption practices increasingly within the 'walled garden' of a single conglomerate's content offerings. Such an idealized consumer avidly samples the diversified product range of the parent conglomerate, but does so specifically by consuming multiple products derived from essentially the same content reservoir.

Provided a match between consumer desire and brand can be achieved with sufficient accuracy and demographic breadth, the commercial returns are obvious: branded consumers pay multiple times for only marginally differentiated products.

(Murray 2002)

For Warner Bros., *Harry Potter* became the lynchpin of this 'walled garden' strategy; it became a core intellectual property leveraged across myriad exhibition and consumption windows, a media phenomenon renewable in its life cycle as a brand. Acquiring the movie rights to the first four Harry Potter books in 1998, with an option to buy the next three, *Variety* called *Harry Potter and the Philosopher's Stone* 'the apotheosis of a new genre – the corporate movie' (Bart 2001). Refashioning the blockbuster into a potential seven-part epic with enormous public presence and cross-promotional capacity, the *Harry Potter* brand was designed as a radiating source of corporate synergy.

If skyscrapers can be seen as a metaphor for the kinds of movie franchise that dominate the global media horizon, there was a certain corporate synchronicity in the simultaneous building of the towering AOL Time Warner headquarters in New York and the development of *Harry Potter* and *Lord of the Rings* as global franchise events. While Columbus Circle would become the spatial expression of a corporate will-to-power, a symptom of millennial merger mania, the brand architecture of *Lord of the Rings* and *Harry Potter* would stand differently, an inscribed rivalry obscuring their relation to the foundations of media consolidation. It is the indelible sense of competition between two pivotal cinematic brands of the new millennium that interests me in this chapter. If the Looney Tunes franchise made visible the brand economics of the film industry in the mid-1990s and early 2000s, Time Warner's fantasy franchises reveal a countervailing tendency, namely the deft masking of conglomerate holdings. These are not contradictory impulses. While the politics of commercial obviousness responds, as I have argued, to the circulation of industry transparency and the primacy of economic discourse in contemporary social life, the politics of corporate obfuscation anticipates potential public hostility to cartel power and its prospective threat to cultural and economic democracy. In different ways, these represent ideological symptoms of a capitalist formation defined by the holding discourse of market populism – call it neo-liberal capitalism if you wish.

In a rhetorical sense, the portrait of rivalry between *Lord of the Rings* and *Harry Potter* was largely born of journalistic convenience, review media habitually comparing the two fantasy brands and their respective stories, screens, revenue and appeal. And yet, a sense of product competition was also nurtured by New Line and Warner Bros. in their promotional tactics. Based around pre-sold fantasies and forged within a context of shared corporate ownership, the franchise events of *Lord of the Rings* and *Harry Potter* ask suggestive questions about branding and product differentiation in the early 2000s. At the same time, however, the two fantasy brands invite consideration of Time Warner's hold on media markets, the conglomerate's management wrangles barely disguising its stake in a billion dollar

franchise monopoly. Having analysed the textual production of branded entertainment, I want to concentrate more directly in this chapter on issues of film
marketing and distribution. This connects the discussion of branding to endemic
issues of publicity and promotion, but also throws into relief the fate of 'independent' studios like New Line in an industrial climate wedded to the success of the
corporate blockbuster.

Fantasy branding: marketing the modern blockbuster

The commercial success of *Batman* in 1989 is often seen as a turning point in
Hollywood's relation to marketing hype, giving rise to the promotional weather-
front that now routinely envelops the modern blockbuster. While marketing
budgets continued to soar in the nineties, rising from $10 million in 1990 to $31
million in 1999 (Klady 1999), commercial partners from toy, soft drink and fast
food empires were prepared to spend astronomical sums to secure their position
at the eye of marketing storms that would surround any potential blockbuster with
a strong youth and pre-teen demographic. This was epitomized by two films that
would become hype incarnate at the end of the nineties, *Godzilla* (1998) and *Star
Wars: Episode I: The Phantom Menace* (1999). While the former would provide lessons
in the perils of the hard sell, the duration and insistence of its marketing campaign
threatening to instil antipathy rather than anticipation, the latter would create its
own gravitational field in promotional terms. As Tom Shone colourfully writes,
'The hype for one blockbuster movie tends to blur into the hype for the next,
forming one long indiscriminate blur of Pepsi promotions and burger bonanzas,
but the hype for *The Phantom Menace* possessed its own peculiar inverse magnitude,
like that of a collapsing sun – so dense as to form a species of promotional black
hole' (Shone 2004: 276). With multimillion dollar partnerships forged with Pepsi,
Kentucky Fried Chicken and Taco Bell, and with Hasbro spending $650 million
for rights to extract the film's calculated 'toyetic' potential, *The Phantom Menace* was
the culminating franchise of the decade. It was certainly the most awaited. Once
the fervour of the film had subsided, however, and stock was taken of its relatively
poor merchandising performance, a more cautionary response developed toward
the value and management of cinematic hype. This was linked to the perceived
dangers of promotional saturation, the experience of over-shipped product
(Hasbro lost $150 million in under-sold *Phantom Menace* merchandise), and a more
hard-edged attitude amongst commercial partners and licensees to the inflationary costs of tie-in deals (Finnigan 2001b).

   These concerns barely changed the commercial fever surrounding Hollywood's
roster of event movies at the start of the new millennium. However, the evident
dangers of promotional excess led to particular calculations in the marketing
campaigns of *Lord of the Rings* and *Harry Potter* that are suggestive of attempts in the
early 2000s to manage film as brand. As media properties with a pre-constituted
event status, each fantasy/franchise had to negotiate some common challenges.

Firstly, marketing had to avoid alienating devoted readerships and fan communities committed to a beloved literary source. Marketing had to respond to concerns about fidelity and adaptation while also selling the genre of fantasy to less committed sections of the audience. Secondly, promotional strategy had to lay the groundwork for the co-ordinated development of the franchise. In each case, *Lord of the Rings* and *Harry Potter* were to be cast as long-term audience investments, movie sagas that would sustain their event status in and between instalments over a period of three or more years. This meant generating a form of hype that would create anticipation but that would not exhaust itself in the first round. Thirdly, marketing had to sufficiently differentiate itself from that of competing movie events, particularly from each other as fantasy sagas with rival patterns of release in November/December 2001 and 2002. While blockbuster marketing in the 1990s may have been inclined towards short-term saturation in seeking to 'buy our curiosity for the space of a single weekend' (Shone 2004: 274), the sustained events of *Lord of the Rings* and *Harry Potter* would demonstrate a growing tendency (also evident in *The Matrix*) to invite consumers to participate in the life of the franchise. The studio strategies involved in the process provide the basis for a telling case study in the recent history of movie marketing.

While *Harry Potter* was a closely supervised franchise-in-waiting, *Lord of the Rings* had a more precarious status. Made during a 15-month shoot in New Zealand to minimize costs (especially in assembling the cast and building sets), the success of the first instalment was crucial because it would inevitably affect the commercial and critical prospects of the remaining two films. Unlike *Harry Potter*, which was steered by the muscular international distribution and marketing apparatus of Warner Bros., *Lord of the Rings* was channelled through a network of international distributors. By selling international rights to the *Lord of the Rings* trilogy, New Line was able to raise 65 per cent of its production costs, signing output agreements with 18 companies, including Entertainment (UK), Nippon Herald (Japan), Village Roadshow (Australia/New Zealand), Metropolitan (France), Medusa (Italy) and Aurum (Spain). This also encouraged a flexible marketing strategy. In a veiled comparison with *Harry Potter*, *Variety* described marketing for *Lord of the Rings* as a 'guerrilla campaign fought by a loose network of local tribes with an unrivalled knowledge of the local terrain – and a hell of a lot more at personal stake than Warner's colonial officers' (Harris and Dawtrey 2001).

This trade language of insurgency chimed with the perception of New Line as a renegade player in the motion picture business, a view based on a number of factors: New Line's resistance to the majors' tendency of structuring release slates around summer and Christmas event pictures, instead releasing films throughout the year; the enlisting of young directors and a diverse talent base; the ability to keep budgets low (meaning below the majors' $59 million average); and the design of marketing campaigns using grassroots tactics and inventive television teasers. The figurative 'independence' of *Lord of the Rings* can be measured along these lines, specifically the recruitment of Peter Jackson as director, the unique shooting schedule, the complex distribution deals and the nurturing of grassroots fan communities. However, the trilogy was hardly marginal to the industrial structures of the dominant system; it was a mega-budget franchise that defrayed a large percentage of risk through co-financing deals with independent financiers and that returned the bulk of profits, potentially worth billions of dollars, to New Line.[2] Even *Variety*, keen to vaunt the studio's 'rebel rousing' status, had begun to acknowledge that 'some of New Line's films are starting to look a bit like the kind of product the company initially tried to avoid' (Lyons 2000). Unconcerned with constituency markets and gunning for the global holiday-season event, *Lord of the Rings* was the product of a studio staking its place within AOL Time Warner on the development of multiplex movies, following on from output such as *The Long Kiss Goodnight* (1996), *Last Man Standing* (1996) and *Lost in Space* (1998).

In 1998, Robert Shaye responded to what *Variety* called New Line's 'corporate studio approach' by commenting: 'We grew up playing in the streets but it's getting harder to avoid becoming an institution' (cited in Carver and Cox 1998). *Lord of the Rings* was, at once, a mark of New Line's flexible independence *and* growing institutionalization as a conglomerate-owned studio. This was especially evident in its marketing approach. While cultivating indigenous distributors and relying on the strength of localized market knowledge, New Line carefully co-ordinated global promotion, establishing guidelines for distributors and allocating a marketing budget of $145 million for the trilogy as a whole ($50 million each for the first and last film, $45 million for the second).[3] Ernest Mathijs suggests that 'never before have the attempts to manage the public presence of films been so elaborate' (Mathijs 2006: 9). If so, it is worth examining the nuances of New Line's marketing approach to better understand how the franchise was positioned.

The success of the initial campaign for *Fellowship of the Ring* turned on a particular breakdown of the trilogy's core audience. Russell Schwartz, a senior marketing executive at New Line, explained the studio's rationale in the following terms:

> From the beginning we divided up the audience into three groups. The first 25 per cent are fanatics who couldn't wait for the films to come out. The important thing there was to convince them that we were taking the project seriously and doing it right. Another 50 per cent were people who had heard of the books but hadn't read them. And the final 25 per cent were people who never heard of Tolkien and couldn't care less.
>
> (cited in Lyman 2001: 5)

Crosscutting this spectrum was a set of target niches. While the *Harry Potter* franchise focused on the family audience – the craze surrounding J. K. Rowling's novels creating a vast pre-sold audience made up of children and parents – the *Lord of the Rings*, with its PG-13 rating, looked to a core demographic of teen and adult males. With J. R. R. Tolkien's literary epic first published in the 1950s, it was deemed necessary to create familiarity with settings and characters to draw out the trilogy's action-centred fantasy appeal. Kristin Thompson suggests that the filmmakers of *Lord of the Rings* were confronted with two basic challenges: they had to make the fan base of the original books devotees of the film adaptation while simultaneously transforming 'a literary work primarily oriented towards adults into a movie for teenagers without that fact being obvious' (Thompson 2003: 47). While the trilogy had rich commercial potential, questions of positioning (appeal to audiences) and playability (the success of that appeal) were assiduously planned for and developed. In marketing terms, this relied on the orchestration of anticipation.

Rather than the brand blitzkrieg that characterized *Godzilla* or the promotional furore that consumed *The Phantom Menace*, marketing for the first instalment of *Lord of the Rings* was carefully paced. The initial trailer for *Fellowship of the Ring* was shown in January 2001, almost a year before the film's December release. Promissory in tone ('you will find adventure, or adventure will find you'), early trailers and TV spots mapped the release schedule, encompassing annual Christmas release dates until 2003. Packaged with New Line's Cuban-missile drama, *Thirteen Days*, the first trailer was designed to hit different audience subsets at a very early point; it pulled young audiences into a Cold War drama on the promise of 'first-see' footage and stimulated the interest of a captive adult audience through the trailer's epic quality.[4]

No singular concept was used to construct the brand identity of *Fellowship of the Ring*, or, indeed, the trilogy as a whole. In trailers and television spots, a variety of characters, images and narrative elements were recombined to maximize appeal for different audiences. While certain television spots (such as those made for MTV) played upon aspects of fantasy legend, emphasizing battle sequences, others highlighted the communal bonds of the fellowship, offering the film as missionary quest. Grandiosity informed the underlying rhetoric in each case. Of course, the use of trailers was hardly novel in creating anticipation (see Kernan 2004). Their circulation on the Internet, however, would represent a new tactical engagement with online communities, linked to pre-release publicity focused specifically on the activities of fans (Pullen 2006). Following Peter Jackson's 'question and answer' participation on the influential film update and spoiler site 'Ain't it Cool News', weeks after committing to *Lord of the Rings* in the summer of 1998, Internet publicity became a pivotal marketing tool. Accordingly, the official *Lord of the Rings* website was launched by New Line in May 1999, giving enormous lead-time for publicity. Releasing spoilers, interviews, downloadable screensavers, and behind-the-scenes videos, the site garnered over 500 million hits before the release of *Fellowship of the Ring*. When the first trailer was posted online on 7 April 2001, it drew over 1.7 million hits on the first day, the biggest one-day download of an Internet film promotion. Exploding the trend for online film marketing established with *The Blair Witch Project* (1999), the presence of *Lord of the Rings* on the Internet became a powerful means of cohering fan communities and building word-of-mouth awareness. In the lexicon of brand marketing, it established 'buzz' over 'hype', enabling the 'infectious chatter that spreads from consumer to consumer about something of genuine interest to them' (Lewis and Bridger 2001: 104).

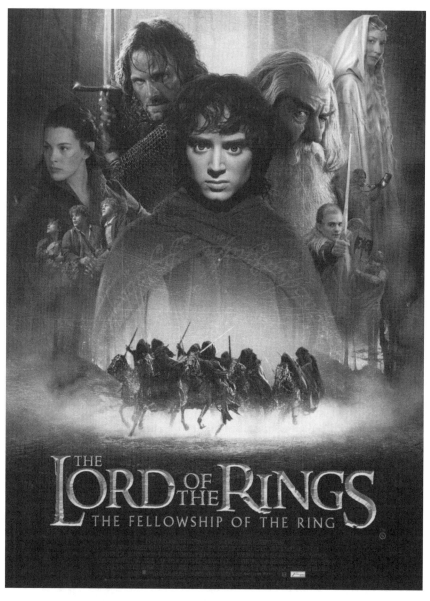

Figure 6.1 Ensemble poster for *The Fellowship of the Ring* (2001). Courtesy of New Line Cinema and the Ronald Grant Archive.

Just as significant as New Line's website in this respect was the unofficial web community that formed around the film, constituting what Bertha Chin and Jonathan Gray term 'pre-viewers for a pre-text' (Chin and Gray 2003). More than for any other preceding film franchise, the Internet became a key site of viewer congregation. Sometimes feeding websites information and courting amateur web editors with visits to the set, New Line carefully monitored this fan activity, seeking 'to capitalize on elaborate extant fan networks to distribute publicity more rapidly and cost effectively than could conceivably be achieved through traditional film marketing channels' (Murray 2004: 8) This asks questions of the extent to which fan activities may potentially shape the marketing (and even the filmmaking) process. For Simone Murray, companies like New Line selectively appropriated fan communities in publicizing *Lord of the Rings*, part of the attempt by corporate media to 'manoeuvre themselves into the paradoxical position of seeking to generate maximum emotional investment by consumers in a given content brand, but of needing to corral such emotional attachment into purely consumptive – as opposed to creative – channels' (Murray 2004: 10). In contrast, Matt Hills suggests that fan creativity 'partly succeeded in re-contextualizing the *Lord of the Rings* films within their own cult community's temporality of anticipation/dread, hence inciting New Line to reactively produce "official" pre-release information' (Hills 2006: 164). Whether New Line's marketing strategy was corralling or reactive in form, it relied, unusually, upon a notion of fan participation; the notional involvement of fan communities became a platform for the discourse of 'integrity' and 'fidelity' surrounding the franchise as brand.

The sense of being faithful to Tolkien's work, brokered through dialogue with fan communities, carried with it implications for the way that New Line handled the enormous commercial opportunities of *Lord of the Rings*. As with *Harry Potter*, care was taken to hold back a merchandising blitz, seeking to avoid the taint of commercialism that often comes with smash-and-grab approaches to product licensing. Instead, the sale of goods relating to *Lord of the Rings* was marshalled incrementally, generating upwards of $1 billion across the trilogy (Wasko and Shanadi 2006). With anywhere up to 300 licensees worldwide, channels of consumption were created in the form of videos, DVDs, games, toys, T-shirts, collectibles, trading cards, stamps, swords and music. While Hollywood's enchantment with fantasy in the early 2000s created fewer placement opportunities for consumer brands, partnership deals also remained important, a commercial bulwark against escalating production and marketing costs (Graser 2004). In the case of *Fellowship of the Ring*, lucrative tie-in deals (worth $11 million) were signed with Burger King, JVC, Barnes and Noble, and General Mills. According to Rolf Mittwegg, head of worldwide marketing at New Line, 'the commitment of the movie-going audience is needed for the first film ... we need audiences to buy in for all three' (cited in Nathan 2001). By fostering word-of-mouth interest over the course of 18 months, and developing full-scale blockbuster promotion in the months leading up to release, *Fellowship of the Ring* established public presence by using niche corridors and mass market highways, creating various levels of brand identification for audiences with different stakes, dispositions and curiosities in the franchise.

For New Line, brand marketing generated a promotional mix that brought fans into the creative process, relied on the incremental build of anticipation and engaged a licensing strategy of 'prudent aggression' (Harris and Dawtrey 2001). By contrast, for Warner Bros. and *Harry Potter*, it initially meant foreclosing unofficial Internet discussion, exploiting intrinsic media buzz, and striving to reign in the full possibilities of the commercial onslaught. Unlike New Line, which orchestrated its marketing campaign in conjunction with international distributors, Warner Bros. assumed complete control of the marketing and distribution of *Harry Potter and the Philosopher's Stone* (*Sorcerer's Stone* in the US release), even enlisting a brand management firm to develop a public relations strategy for the property. As with *Lord of the Rings*, Warner Bros. sought to avoid promotional and commercial overexposure that might jeopardize the long-term future of the franchise. Accordingly, Warner Bros. refrained from customary marketing ploys such as celebrity appearances and 'making-of' television shows. It also limited its domestic product licensees to 87 and chose a single promotional partner in that of Coca-Cola, albeit in a record deal worth $100 million (with clauses about the use of *Harry Potter* imagery and with emphasis on children's literacy programmes).

At some level, measures of restraint were concessions to J.K. Rowling, wary of ancillary merchandising that might diminish 'Harry's world'. However, it was also the result of corporate efforts to integrate cross-promotional strategies. *Harry Potter*'s 'brand manager' at Warner Bros., Diane Nelson, explained: 'This is the first brand where there's been a concerted focus at the inception of our planning to say we are going to coordinate divisionally and set guidelines to ensure we're protecting the brand's integrity for the long term' (cited in Eller 2001). As with New Line, marketing strategy sought to establish a base of consumer loyalty, preparing the way for the frequent, near annual, re-promotion of the *Harry Potter* brand throughout the coming decade. Central to this strategy was the idea that (child) consumers would grow with the franchise and its characters as sequels were produced, a principle of maturation that combined with the periodic re-release of the first film, geared to audiences previously too young to consume *Harry Potter* content (Murray 2002). Building a 'brand relationship' did not extend to fan participation, however, at least initially. Where New Line courted the online Tolkien fan base, Warner Bros. was quick to brandish proprietary rights against grassroots fan websites (often run by teenagers) with their own creative stake in the world of Hogwarts. Preparing for the launch of the official *Harry Potter* website in early 2001, Warner Bros. sent 'cease and desist' letters to 107 websites that incorporated characters, titles or key terms that were seen to infringe the studio's intellectual property warrants. This generated a storm of negative publicity, online protest campaigns mobilizing under the battle-cry of 'PotterWar' (Murray 2004). As a result, Warner Bros. developed a more collaborative relation with *Harry Potter* fans, emulating strategies deployed by New Line in striving to balance studio and fan 'ownership' of the text. This was a marketing issue in as much as studios began

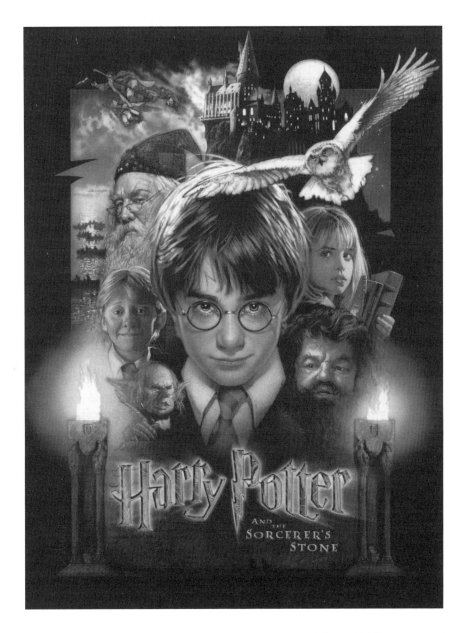

Figure 6.2 Ensemble poster for *Harry Potter and the Philosopher's Stone* (2001). Courtesy of Warner Bros., J. K. Rowling and the Ronald Grant Archive.

to realize the potential of fans to generate interest in their properties via the Internet. It was also a legal issue in that collaboration would also prospectively test the regimes of copyright and fair use mediating the relation between media fans and media producers, including fans *as* media producers (see Jenkins 2006: 169–205).

Fan disputes notwithstanding, the overall brand objective for Warner Bros. in managing *Harry Potter* was to create a long-term basis of corporate synergy. Internally, this meant orchestrating promotional efforts that capitalized on resources available at AOL Time Warner, but that were not bound by divisional clamour to exploit the boy wizard. While Warner Bros. made in-house deals to promote the *Harry Potter* films – showing online trailers through AOL's website, airing broadcast trailers on the WB network, holding sweepstakes on the Cartoon Network and Kids WB, selling the cable channel rights to HBO, producing the soundtrack through Warner Music's Atlantic Records – Warner Bros. also made deals with rival companies, including Viacom and Disney (Kirkpatrick 2002). New Line also capitalized on these relationships. The trailer for *Fellowship of the Ring* ran on the WB network, AOL plastered the brand across its website and Warner Bros. music released the soundtrack. However, the *Harry Potter* brand lay at the very centre of AOL Time Warner's corporate infrastructure, embodying its most fervent ambitions for synergy. In key respects, *Harry Potter* was distinguished from *Lord of the Rings* through its positioning as a 'calculated' rather than 'cult' franchise.

These two terms are discursive, rather than heuristic, categories and were significant in mobilizing a number of associational terms in the strong comparative strain that came to surround the two franchise events. Durable oppositions between 'independent' and 'mainstream,' 'cult' and 'mass', 'art' and 'entertainment' often structured the extra-textual discourses framing the blockbusting status of each fantasy brand. Much could be written of the conflicts that arise from these terms. As Matt Hills suggests, the idea of *Lord of the Rings* as a 'cult blockbuster' created particular fan conflicts around the potential valuation/devaluation of the trilogy, promising to elevate the genre of fantasy but also threatening to expose the trilogy's cult credentials to a mass audience (Hills 2006). As one fan commented, 'If the movie fails, I'll have a sense of relief. It's selfish, I know, but I have a snobbish attitude of, "Thank God, I can still enjoy my books"' (cited in Huffstutter 2001). Each franchise generated its own set of industrial and audience discourses. They were played out, however, within a framework of media and marketing hype energized, not to say tantalized, by the concurrence of *Harry Potter* and *Lord of the Rings*.

This invites consideration of the interpretive structures that develop around (franchise) films. For Martin Barker, this necessarily involves the 'ancillary prefigurative materials' that shape expectations of how movies are watched, including campaign books, press kits, teasers, posters, leaks, 'making-of' documentaries, interviews and other satellite materials that enable audiences to 'climb inside' a media text (Barker 2004). The prismatic case of the fantasy franchise is suggestive on these terms. While I do not claim exhaustive ancillary or discursive analysis of the first two instalments of *Lord of the Rings* and *Harry Potter*, I would draw attention to the comparative nature of their prefigurative development. Within news media ranging from the *Los Angeles Times* (McNamara 2001) to the *Wall Street Journal* (Lippman 2001) and in trade journals such as *Variety* (Groves and Dawtrey 2002) and *Brandweek* (Finnigan 2001a), a sense of product competition became a residual analytic trope. This incorporated statistical discussion of screens, revenues and estimated worldwide grosses, but also involved aesthetic determinants of value, the 'artistry' and 'moral heft' of *Fellowship* set against the more 'lightweight' *Philosopher's Stone*.[5] Meanwhile, the circulation of competing ancillary materials became integral to the discursive frameworks enveloping each fantasy, a sense of rivalry underpinning the mechanisms of hype surrounding the 'promises, interpretations and invitations-to-view offered on behalf of film' (Austin 2002: 30). While the first instalments of *Harry Potter* and *Lord of the Rings* were positioned to appeal to subtly different audiences, subsequent marketing strategies were in many ways fired by notions of a 'blockbuster bout' (Gibbons 2002), evidenced by the way that each sought to exploit rival territory.

In the case of *The Two Towers*, brand marketing capitalized on a groundswell of critical and commercial acclaim. One New Line executive responsible for promotional tie-ins commented: 'The first film was largely about getting broad-based awareness … now it's got to be about creating a one-to-one interaction with the consumer and creating a relationship with the partner' (cited in Rose 2002). In assuming the language of brand management, New Line emphasized the need to affirm the 'core values' of *Lord of the Rings*. In this case, positioning the second instalment was a matter of distilling the aesthetic credibility of the franchise. Not least, this meant reviewing tie-in deals, New Line ending its partnership with Burger King in favour of a two-year deal with Verizon Wireless. Instead of 'Frodo Fries', the new partnership would involve cross-promotion on network services geared to a young male audience. In choosing a communications partner, marketing for *The Two Towers* sought to consolidate its core audience – the high-spending, technology-proficient youth demographic – in ways that also sought to lose associations that could stigmatize the trilogy's bid for cultural (in particular Oscar) status.

Shoring up the aesthetic credentials of the franchise did not stop New Line from seeking out new commercial markets, notably that of the pre-teen audience. This was expressed in merchandising strategies designed to give the trilogy edge over *Harry Potter and the Chamber of Secrets*. While rated PG-13 for its 'scenes of violent combat and fantasy', the recruitment of pre-teens (essentially young boys) involved launching children's products such as pyjamas, slippers, duvet covers and toy figures. Rather than weaken the brand, these were seen as a means of ensuring the trilogy's cross-generational appeal. Jeremy Saul, licensing manager for the film's British merchandise, explained the strategy in the following terms:

> This time we have more aggressively pursued the kids' angle. It's part of our slightly different strategy to ensure our longevity … so while the first film was targeted at loyal fans, this time we have gone more for a younger audience of eight plus. The strategy was to keep it focused, so for the first film we wanted

to go for those who knew the book – older teens and adults. Now the characters are known we can market to younger boys.

(cited in Rumbelow and Lister 2002)

Targeting younger boys was combined with strategies that focused on the
female teen audience, New Line accentuating the heart-throb status of Viggo
Mortenson and Orlando Bloom in trailers, posters and making-of documentaries
broadcast on female-skewed platforms such as the WB network. With online
publicity continuing a drip-feed of spoilers and exclusive news, and with the DVD
launch of *Fellowship of the Ring* preceding the sequel's release, marketing strategies
sought to harden pre-existing audience investments while opening out new demographic niches.

Similar strategies were used by Warner Bros. in marketing *Chamber of Secrets*, in
this case developing a more foreboding atmosphere in the studio's promotional
material to attract older teenage niches. Posters saw characters looking older,
tougher and wielding swords. If, according to Warner Bros., 'the campaign is a bit
edgier, a bit darker', this was designed to meet *Lord of the Rings* in the challenge for
the youth audience (Cagle 2002). While maintaining key elements of its marketing
focus on pre-teens, hype surrounding *Chamber of Secrets* was quick to emphasize a
form of spectacle that not only gave reign to the freer reaches of Quidditch, but
that delivered what the British *Daily Mail* would go as far as to call a 'noirish threatening atmosphere in between the comical moments' (Tookey 2002). Each film
sought to exploit competitive market territory through expansion and cross-polli-
nation of its brand strategy. While *The Two Towers* became more calculated in
dealing with its proven appeal as a franchise, *Chamber of Secrets* played upon resonant, sellable images of fantasy cult, in some respects precipitating the move away
from 'mainstream' directors like Chris Columbus towards those associated with
'arthouse' traditions such as Alfonso Cuarón who directed *Harry Potter and the Pris-
oner of Azkaban* (2004).

Predictably, the second instalments of each fantasy franchise were drawn
together in review media. While critics hedged their bets in reviewing *Chamber of
Secrets* – described in cross-sections of the British press as a film of magic not
wonder, of clarity not subtlety – this paled against the general exuberance for *The
Two Towers*, what Philip French described in the *Observer* as 'a stunning visual epic
which eclipses Harry Potter in every way' (French 2002). Of course, these estimations reveal much about the aesthetic predispositions of the critical establishment,
but they also form part of the symbiotic discourse between critics, Wall Street
analysts and industry executives in maintaining the sport and story of brand rivalry
– as the *New York Times* was quick to herald: '*Harry Potter* to Battle *Lord of the Rings*,
Again' (Lyman 2002). The degree to which this discourse helped shape audience
expectation is an important question that has been taken up at length elsewhere
(see Barker and Mathijs, forthcoming). My point, in focusing on the comparative
nature of franchise development, is the rooted and widely reproduced sense of
rivalry surrounding *Harry Potter* and *Lord of the Rings* as content phenomena.

Such was the critical and commercial success of *The Two Towers* – at the time of writing, the 13th highest all-time domestic grossing film in the United States ($340 million) compared with *Chamber of Secrets* ranked 31st ($262 million) – that *Harry Potter* would not be released in close proximity to Middle Earth for a third time.[6] Of course, the blockbusting battle for audience share was by no means remarkable; it exemplifies what Barry Litman calls the 'extreme form of product competition' defining the motion picture industry. This is symptomatic of a failure to smooth the flow of product into the market, largely caused by the 'innate tendency of movie distributors to distrust each other concerning production schedules and budgets' (Litman 1998: 45). Intense product competition, illustrated by *Harry Potter* and *Lord of the Rings*, is an endemic feature of the film industry. However, the discourse of rivalry was particularly acute in this case. Although rivalry was denied in and between those at Warner Bros. and New Line, it became a powerful subtext in decisions about marketing strategy, release schedules, and in the tone of media coverage. What remains to be explored are the implications of brand rivalry when the brands themselves belong to the same corporate parent. One might ask in this respect how the differentiation of fantasy brands can be situated in a period of extraordinary concentration in corporate media ownership.

Branding fantasies: diversity and market domination

According to Naomi Klein, brand culture in the 1990s saw a 'strange combination of a sea of product coupled with losses in real choice' (Klein 2000: 159). This describes a situation where a shrinking number of corporate media owners are responsible for a specious number of branded commodities that, for all the appearance of difference, herald an untold market uniformity serving the interests of those in power. Within media critique, this concentration of ownership is often seen as inherently dangerous, stifling competition, homogenizing the production of news and popular culture, potentially factoring out social groups who cannot afford to consume, and ignoring social and political issues that cannot be rendered in 'sufficiently entertaining terms' (Schatz 1997: 110). Henry Giroux puts the matter starkly, suggesting that conglomerates such as Disney and Time Warner limit 'the vocabulary and imagery available for defining, defending, and reforming the state, civil society, and public culture as centers for critical learning and citizenship' (Giroux 1999: 2). Within such debates lie the place and status of Hollywood film. Routinely, the unholy grip of the corporate blockbuster is seen to have incorporated, or rendered asunder, marginal identities and filmmaking styles associated with independent or arthouse traditions. In particular, franchise filmmaking has become a frequent source of ire for those who find in its rise the death-knell of movie diversity.

For all the rhetorical seductiveness of arguments that rail against the blockbusting tendencies of corporate Hollywood, such viewpoints frequently fail to recognize the pleasures and complexities of popular entertainment and, just as significantly, misunderstand the workings of the contemporary film industry. In his account of the modern movie business, Edward Jay Epstein suggests that a powerful social logic (based around prestige, recognition and creative expression) operates in conjunction with Hollywood's governing economic logic. He writes: 'If studio executives made only films that maximized the amount of money in their clearinghouses, they would do so at the serious risk of losing their standing in that community and, with it, their connection to the people, events, honors, and opportunities that brought them to Hollywood in the first place' (Epstein 2006: 131). It is in this respect that studios acquired 'independent' arms and speciality units in the 1990s – Miramax, New Line, Sony Classics, Fox Searchlight, Paramount Classics, Warner Independent Pictures – not least to give them 'awards, media recognition, artistic bragging rights, and other noneconomic rewards' (ibid.: 342). It is not my intention to measure the industrial and creative stakes of Hollywood's embrace of American independent cinema in the nineties, a move driven by prestige, certainly, but also by the targeting of niche markets. My point is rather to suggest a more complicated relation to the current film system than is often assumed. As Simone Murray suggests, 'The market ubiquity of a limited number of successful franchises should not be mistaken for uniformity in the content marketplace as a whole. While the drive at managerial level is towards optimal brand extension, consumer fickleness and unpredictability work to ensure that only a small percentage of brands ever "take"' (Murray 2005: 431).

It is important to acknowledge the variable nature of corporate success within turbulent markets (De Vany 2004). And yet, it remains the case that *Lord of the Rings* and *Harry Potter* did 'take' in the content marketplace – almost simultaneously and for the same corporate parent. This asks questions of the relation of cultural artefacts to conglomerate power. While corporate ownership was never disguised in popular discourse surrounding the two franchise events, strategies of product differentiation fostered a serviceable picture of market competition and diversity. Rather than cut from the same cloth, *Lord of the Rings* and *Harry Potter* offered themselves up as alternatives within the spectrum of the high-budget blockbuster.

On certain terms, the films of each franchise *did* embody key differences in the production styles and product offerings of the motion picture industry. David Hesmondhalgh makes the point that within cultural industries, especially since the 1990s, loose control of creative input has enabled a greater degree of heterogeneity in the production of cultural and symbolic forms (Hesmondhalgh 2002). This is linked to increased flexibility within industrial organization and in the orchestration of consumer markets. The fact that *Lord of the Rings* was filmed in New Zealand by a 'cult' director, drew substantially upon independent technology workshops such as Weta, was financed and distributed through a network of interdependent firms and pioneered online publicity in its address to multiple niche audiences, in a sense illustrates the 'loose' transactional relations of the global film industry, generating (although not by definition) a cinematic trilogy different in style and purported substance to the paradigmatic studio franchise of *Harry Potter*.

And yet, as Hesmondhalgh suggests, loose control of creative input is matched with much tighter control of the key stages of reproduction and the rights of proprietary ownership. In the case of *Lord of the Rings* and *Harry Potter*, ownership was vested in New Line and Warner Bros. and, by turn, that of AOL Time Warner, a corporate parent hardly shy in its desire to concentrate market control. While media and industry discourse indulged the perception of rivalry between the two franchise fantasies, often nurtured by AOL Time Warner through its news and entertainment publications, shareholder reports focused on the integrated strength of corporate-owned brands, maximized for what the first annual report of the joint company called a 'moment of historic significance when the initial wave of Internet innovation is giving way to the next wave of consolidation and convergence' (AOL Time Warner 2000: 2). Amidst talk of the future of digital content streaming, *Lord of the Rings* and *Harry Potter* became tied to the branding fantasies of AOL Time Warner. Typically, the post-merger effect was to compel divisional units to demonstrate value through synergy. This fired the renewal of franchise features at both Warner Bros. and New Line, intensifying the volatile atmosphere that had been developing prior to the merger and that had encouraged financial and creative gambles by New Line on projects such as *Lord of the Rings*. The effect in industrial terms was to harden commitments to mega-budget filmmaking, a move that by no means nullified mid-budget pictures and specialized products but that did exert pressure on the figurative 'independence' of studios like New Line. Spurring aggressive cost-efficiency measures, the AOL Time Warner deal obliged New Line to confirm the revenue potential of 'independent' film, accelerating investment in projects with the blockbusting capacity to impress corporate shareholders. Put simply, New Line had to create a strategic fiscal argument for its own autonomy, bearing out the view of *Variety* editor, Peter Bart, that when it came to its film studios, 'the corporate titans were determined not to let Hollywood become an expensive philanthropy' (Bart 1999: 275).

Lord of the Rings represents a pivotal moment in the history of New Line as a 'major independent'. In 2002, it was the foundation of the studio's highest ever market share (9.8 per cent) and annual gross ($912 million domestically), creating revenue streams that would secure the studio's immediate future. In 2001, Richard Parsons had spoken of New Line returning to mid-budget films after *Lord of the Rings*, describing the modification of the company's 'positioning within the pantheon of movie companies, [taking] them closer to their core competency' (cited in Lyman 2001). However, for a conglomerate with heavy financial burdens, the success of *Lord of the Rings* by the trilogy's end (grossing $1,034 million, the third largest film franchise of all time after *Stars Wars* and James Bond) created uncertain precedents for New Line. For a studio built on relatively modest breakout and crossover hits, the trilogy threatened to mortgage New Line to repeating this success as a benchmark of corporate survival. It is perhaps suggestive in this respect that New Line optioned Philip Pullman's three-novel fantasy series *His Dark Materials* in 2002, the studio declaring with a mind to its future 'When *The Lord of the Rings* is over, hopefully we won't miss a beat' (cited in Thompson 2003: 61). This sense of hopefulness with regard to franchise momentum points towards a core issue within discussions of Hollywood hegemony, namely the degree to which the corporate blockbuster, like Frodo's ring, has become a bewitching, all-powerful force, a cinema 'to rule them all'.

There is no doubting the centrality of the blockbuster within the contemporary motion picture business. Questions are often asked, however, about the extent to which it has subsumed other kinds of filmmaking. While blockbusters are often set in opposition to categories of arthouse and indigenous film, the blockbuster has in fact no intrinsic cultural status that should preclude its relationship with 'independent' or 'regional' moviemaking. Here, we might think of how films such as *Pulp Fiction* (1994) or *Crouching Tiger, Hidden Dragon* (2000) combine ideas of 'minority' and 'mainstream' taste within their respective claim to be international blockbusters, identified less through definitive textual attributes than via industry and reception practices based on particular determinants of scale and size. Julian Stringer wryly notes: 'some movies are born blockbusters; some achieve blockbuster status; some have blockbuster status thrust upon them' (Stringer 2003: 10). It is important to remember that blockbusters are complex in form, variable in definition, and should not be dismissed in themselves as proving the triumph of commerce over art, spectacle over narrative, Hollywood popcorn movies over the rest. Clearly, however, the 'born blockbuster', in which Hollywood studios have a disproportionate stake, has significant implications for screen culture. This ranges from the staggering scale of their production budgets and the general turn towards genres that can translate well across regional and media markets (e.g. action, animation, fantasy) to the speed with which event movies appear and then are gone from theatrical screens, putting enormous stock on blizzards of hype geared towards opening weekends. The born blockbuster is hardly sinister, but neither is it benign. In formal and industrial terms, such blockbusters shape formations of taste while creating particular imperatives for controlling risk. Jon Lewis suggests that 'an effort to standardize and thus more accurately and more completely control product lines in the New Hollywood is at the root of the blockbuster mindset at the studios' (Lewis 2003: 66). While *Lord of the Rings* and *Harry Potter* demonstrate the flexible means by which corporate blockbusters are strategically differentiated, there is also a rationalizing tendency at work in each case, linked to adaptive industrial formulae about the variables necessary for market success.[7]

Lord of the Rings and *Harry Potter* were essentially made, and made in such a way, in order to maximize the promise of huge financial returns. Feeding the franchise strategies of big Hollywood companies, they had broad demographic appeal, lent themselves to a wide range of merchandising and tie-in deals, and were open to cultivation in the immediate and long-term future through audiences apt to purchase DVDs, videogames and other ancillary media. As a means of generating cross-platform content phenomena, the revival of fantasy was symptomatic of Hollywood's move in the late 1990s towards properties based less on major stars, with their exorbitant salaries, than on brand characters with limitless licensing potential. In this context, *Lord of the Rings* was an all-or-nothing gamble resulting from New Line's own precarious negotiation of a corporate system that maintained 'independent' interests so long as they remained profitable. While the trilogy, to borrow a phrase from Chuck Kleinhans, occupied the 'relatively freer areas of the margins and in-betweens of the conventional industry' (Kleinhans 1998: 313), it also brought New Line closer to the dominant Hollywood system. If hegemony describes how industrial and representational systems become normalized within specific historical junctures, *Lord of the Rings* was part of New Line's move in the late nineties towards the pre-sold, high-cost, effects-laden franchise, developed as a means of increasing the studio's stock price and staving off absorption into Warner Bros.[8]

The reason that New Line was not, in fact, sold or absorbed was linked to the studio's potential to generate flexible revenue streams. In one sense, this illustrates the means by which conglomerates like Time Warner seek to establish a portfolio of brand interests. However, the attendant sense of rivalry that can occur – such as that between *Lord of the Rings* as a New Line product and *Harry Potter* as a Warner Bros. product – also reveals the degree to which conglomerates often remain coyly reticent about the extent of their market control. Analysing the proclivity within annual reports, trade magazines and the popular press to frame divisional companies (Warner Bros., New Line, HBO, CNN, AOL) as independent entities rather than cogs in a conglomerate's larger holdings, Deborah Jaramillo writes: 'the crux of the problem is the saturation of the marketplace by conglomerates that seek to steer discourse in a direction that obscures ownership and questionable methods' (Jaramillo 2002: 73). While the merger between AOL and Time Warner exposed the 'questionable methods' by which companies controlling access to net and cable pipelines could own, in a regulatory moment, the content travelling through them, the case of *Lord of the Rings* and *Harry Potter* expressed something more specific. As sustained franchise events, they mobilized a discourse of product competition that often surrounds moments of market contraction.

The box office domination of *Lord of the Rings* and *Harry Potter* in 2001 and 2002 was symptomatic of the majors' ability to lock up screens with a small number of highly capitalized projects. As one New Line marketing executive would delight in commenting at the start of the corporate fantasy bonanza, 'AOL Time Warner will own Christmas this year' (cited in Dawtrey 2001). While market domination by a limited number of companies has long been the case within the motion picture industry, conglomeration has seen the hardening of corporate ties between powerful studios operationally figured as siblings. This has created new imperatives for brand strategies that create distinction amongst products while masking the concentrated forms of ownership (enabled by the dismantling of anti-trust laws) which have come to limit the distribution of unaffiliated cultural goods. *Lord of the Rings* and *Harry Potter* must be understood on their own terms, and in relation to specific production and reception contexts. Without wishing to collapse their place and appeal in the cultural terrain, they nevertheless substantiate Don Slater's point that 'marketing strategy is not – in the first instance – a matter of competition *within* market structures; rather it is a matter of competition *over* the structure of markets'

(Slater 2002: 68). In a promotional sense, *Lord of the Rings* and *Harry Potter* illustrate a broad corporate impulse to develop concentrated brand clusters that, in forging affective loyalties within a given product field, have the capacity to transform and control markets and competition.

To maintain perspective on the expanding reaches of corporate power, it is important to lay bare the materialist factors of product rivalry that sustain the hegemony of global media conglomerates. While dogged by problems with its corporate brand image during the release period of *Lord of the Rings* and *Harry Potter*, AOL Time Warner successfully rallied around the vast profit-making potential of cable networks and filmed entertainment, the success of its fantasy output leading *Variety* to comment that '*Harry Potter* and *Lord of the Rings* are so successful they are threatening to replace Bugs Bunny as the symbol of AOL Time Warner' (Bing and Dunkley 2002). While this may have been the case within shareholder reports, the discourse of 'blockbuster bouts' and 'franchise face-offs' helped create an implicit sense of rivalry between the two properties, *Harry Potter* and *Lord of the Rings* threatening to obscure the extent to which AOL Time Warner owned not just Christmas in 2001 and 2002 but all opportunities to consume within the 'walled garden' of its content offerings. Between Harry Potter and Frodo Baggins, AOL Time Warner established what might reasonably be seen as the principal *corporate* fantasy of our global media times – the development of megabrand phenomena that can drive synergy across media formats but that can also obscure the concentrated forms of ownership that rightly stir public unease about conglomerate power and its potential impact on frameworks of cultural consumption and political and creative entitlement.

Chapter 7

'The world is our audience'
Branding entertainment space

It has so far been my argument that the idea of 'the brand' relates in distinctive ways to the production and marketing of contemporary Hollywood cinema. More pointedly, I would suggest that the will-to-brand reveals key facets of the episteme of popular entertainment shaping current understanding of film as text and event. In the previous two chapters, I have described how branding creates a textual economy, and has given rise to promotional strategies that reflect a double movement within commercial film culture, towards studio excess and consumer display on the one hand, and towards calculated product differentiation and corporate non-disclosure on the other. These mediate two different principles of 'total entertainment', one based around the immersive and openly synergistic modalities of entertainment media and the other based around the extended, and never wholly transparent, concentration of media ownership. If the former gives rise to corporate orchestrations in the use and meaning of (film) commodities, the latter creates renewed impetus to disguise and deflect the contraction of markets. In examining these tendencies, I have drawn on the major franchise vehicles of animation and fantasy, exploring two discrete forms of brand spectacle in the process – commercially aestheticized film texts and internationally managed marketing campaigns.

Implicit in my discussion of branding is the relation of Hollywood and its franchise properties to the 'global cultural economy'. If, as Arjun Appadurai (1990) has theorized, texts and images now circulate in a newly heterogeneous and transnational public sphere, part of a complex series of flows that move between and across national boundaries, then both the synergy-driven example of the Looney Tunes and the synchronized marketing campaigns of *Lord of the Rings* and *Harry Potter* reveal much about the place of Hollywood within the global media system. While the Looney Tunes franchise served to animate the worldwide licensing of children's programming, toys and merchandise in the 1990s, linked to the penetration of US cartoon networks abroad and the creation of spatial fantasies such as studio stores and theme parks, Time Warner's franchise fantasies were positioned through international release strategies and promotional campaigns that drew out their appeal *as* global phenomena. In a textual and industrial sense, both franchise examples lend themselves to discussion about the globalization of film. They ask questions about the nature of internationally exportable products and genres, about the mix of international finance, marketing and labour that underpin high-budget studio movies, and about the commercial life of bankrolled blockbusters as they circulate, and are consumed, as global brands.

As core Time Warner properties, *Lord of the Rings*, *Harry Potter* and the Looney Tunes were developed as global cultural commodities. Not least, this reflects the increasing importance of international markets to Hollywood film companies and their corporate parents (Miller *et al.* 2001). It would be no exaggeration to say that the impact and significance of globalization has been at the forefront of Time Warner's corporate thinking and operational strategy ever since the merger that first brought the company into being. Indeed, the merger between Time and Warner in 1989 gave rise to a portentous motto that would signal the position and ambition of the newly formed conglomerate in the field of media convergence – 'the world is our audience'. This was indicative of Time Warner's attempt to develop a vision of global connectivity that figured the restructuring of national media industries, and the development of a global media market, as an emerging and borderless world order. Throughout the 1990s and 2000s, Time Warner's annual reports have returned doggedly to the finessing of mission statements, and to the larger scheme within which its portfolio of established and emerging brands might profitably function. That the conglomerate's activities are necessarily, and by definition, global has never been in question, however. The conception and dissemination of global media brands has become a core dimension of Time Warner's business strategy, actively constituting a 'world audience' that may potentially consume its vast repertoire of products/platforms and thereby feed its major revenue streams in content, subscriptions and advertising.

With the impetus towards vertical integration in the 1990s, theatrical exhibition was incorporated within this brand economy, part of the globalizing strategy of several giant media conglomerates that also owned film studios (Time Warner and Warner Theaters, Sony and Loews Cineplex, Viacom and UCI). As a means of shoring up film audiences, theatre building was seen variously as a method of developing under-screened markets, cementing global film distribution networks, and creating a marketing tool for the activity of cinemagoing that would prospectively energize the lucrative profit fields of video, DVD and pay television. According to Charles Acland, the construction of exhibition space in the 1990s was central to the internationalization of film culture, the rise of the megaplex becoming a focus for the activation of 'components of an industrial logic about popular and public entertainment, one that offers a certain controlled knowledge about and for cinemagoing audiences' (Acland 2003: 67). In this chapter, I want to draw on Acland's work to help consider the spatial formulation of branding within structures of the global and the everyday, especially as it bears on film exhibition. Having examined aspects of studio practice in relation to the production and marketing of Hollywood film, I want to round off my analysis by focusing on the locations where moviegoing takes place. This relates the discussion of branding, and by turn globalization, to the construction of entertainment venues that instil, to reiterate Acland's definition of the permanent marketing campaign, 'the promotion of a general interest and involvement with the newness of cinematic texts as an expression of contemporary living' (ibid.: 79).

In certain respects, the cinemagoing audience is far less important than the home audience within the strategic designs and profit expectations of global media industries. The domestication of digital technologies (computers, games consoles, DVD players, broadband networks) has served to reconstruct the home as a key delivery point for streamed media content. Together with new developments in home theatre technology, approximating the motion picture theatre, Barbara Klinger suggests that the contemporary home is now 'the most profitable and, arguably, the most experientially important sector of film exhibition' (Klinger 2006b: 241). If such is the case, we might ask why theatrical exhibition should concern us at all, a business that by some accounts is staring at its own imminent demise.[1] Firstly, movie theatres remain significant because public and domestic film consumption do not exist in a zero-sum competition. As critics such as Acland, Klinger and Mark Jancovich have shown, different social meanings are attached to the idea of 'going to the cinema' and 'staying in with a movie' (Jancovich *et al.* 2003: 9), and these help define each other as *entwined* sites and practices. Secondly, and as a result of the first, entertainment conglomerates have become fully aware of the activities associated with public film attendance, and have quickly come to 'understand the role of cinemas as a specific form of cultural engagement and as a key part in the life cycle of cultural commodities that extend beyond the cinema site itself' (Acland 2003: 146). In short, theatrical exhibition remains significant to the motion picture industry because it offers 'event status' to film; the space of the cinema provides both a gateway for the introduction of new film commodities and a means of connecting film with other kinds of public cultural consumption.

While exhibition has long been instrumental to the film business, a renewed significance was given to public cinemagoing in the mid-1980s, manifest in the rise of the multiplex. As a result of the deregulation policies of the Reagan Justice Department that enabled major studios to own exhibition circuits (for the first time since the Paramount decrees divorced production from exhibition in 1948), Hollywood engaged in a concerted theatre building programme, continuing throughout the nineties. In a period of growing uncertainty about the location of film consumption – both in terms of its potential venues (public/private) and its sources of generative income (domestic/international) – Hollywood sought to develop and modernize its exhibition systems. This focused especially on Hollywood's largest export markets and was typified by the evolution of Warner theatres in the United Kingdom. As one of the major companies bankrolling multiplex construction in Europe, Warner Bros. had opened four UK venues by 1990 (Pulleine 1990). This number increased substantially during the decade. Warner Bros. International Theaters (WBIT) entered a joint venture partnership with the Australian media company Village Roadshow in 1996 to operate theatres in Australia, Italy, Taiwan and the UK. This combined with agreements with other international exhibitors, including Mycal (Japan), Lusomundo (Portugal), and Lusomundo and Sogecable (Spain), to extend the Warner brand across regional territories. By 2002, Warner Village was operating 383 screens on 36 sites in the UK and over a thousand screens worldwide. This can be seen in the context of a period in which, as in other major markets such as Australia, New Zealand, France, Italy, Germany, Japan and Spain, the number of screens proliferated. In the UK alone, cinema screens almost doubled between 1988 and 1998, jumping from 1,242 to 2,454. This was enabled by the building of large multiscreen theatres, often multipurpose entertainment developments associated with the term 'megaplex' (see Eyles 1998; Hanson 2000).[2]

At its peak in 2003, Warner Village was the third largest operator of cinema screens in the UK, behind Odeon (owned by the consortium West LB, controlling 608 screens on 99 sites) and UGC (owned by Vivendi Universal, controlling 396 screens on 42 sites).[3] However, Warner was a leading operator of the upscale multiplex, symbolized in two flagship venues, one in London (Leicester Square) and the other in Birmingham (Star City). According to Millard Ochs, president of WBIT, these sites were emblematic of Warner's desire to create 'event destinations'. He commented: 'There are so many competing forces for people's leisure time these days that you have to make the experience of going to the cinema an event for people' ('Warner Village Rising Star' 2000). For Warner's premier London venue – used for gala openings since Warner Bros. purchased the site in 1938, the company's first cinema outside of North America – this meant refurbishing the cinema to give it a new air of luxury and elegance. This included a new art deco facade and a redesigned interior that incorporated large sepia photographs of the cinema's history and painted scenes of classic Warner Bros. movies. At Star City, which is a massive 30-screen megaplex that opened in 2000, architectural tropes of the theme park were employed: concession stands were designed as film-set caravans, distinct spaces were created such as the Prop Shop Café and giant images of Warner Bros. films and Looney Tunes characters were displayed throughout. While exceptional in scale, both venues symbolized what WBIT labelled its desire to 'bring cinema to life'. Using the grandeur of the larger megaplexes to help brand the Warner Village theatre circuit, these sites were purposely designed to highlight the *activity* of cinemagoing, 'heralding a return to "going to the movies" and not just going to see a specific film' ('Success by Design' 2000).

Despite rapid expansion in the UK, the Warner Village chain was sold to a private equity firm in May 2003 in a deal worth $402 million.[4] Having built up and realized the value of the British theatrical market, WBIT declared its intention to seed new markets in under-screened territories such as China and Russia. While the deal was also precipitated by AOL Time Warner's enormous debt burden, and by Village Roadshow's decision to sell assets as a means of boosting its filmmaking division, the divestment of Warner's theatrical stake in the UK market is suggestive of the promotional, rather than strictly pecuniary, function of theatrical film exhibition (at least for the Hollywood majors). As WBIT explained of its UK operations, the construction of multiplexes was 'not so much to generate profits as to encourage cinemagoing per se'. More specific to its concerns, cinema was seen as 'by far the most important marketing tool for the lucrative operations in home-video and pay TV' (Ilott 1993). It is on these terms that theatrical exhibition has assumed a concerted branding function within contemporary film culture, part of the attempt by Hollywood 'to seek out and shape an ideal standardized audience retooled for a global cinema environment' (Acland 2003: 234). In a strategic sense, the multiplex has served as a spatial and temporal staging point for the global orchestration of 'screen traffic', a process that Acland suggests is driven by the desire to augment a sense of coordination and simultaneity across locations: from the release dates of global movies such as *The Matrix* and *Harry Potter* to the regulation of the public spaces where films are consumed. However, as Acland also demonstrates, these processes within international cinema culture are neither even in flow nor determined in effect. The cinema complex, in particular, has been distinguished by variability in the dispersal of theatrical sites and in the identity (and favour) that entertainment venues assume in the cultures and cities where they are built. At one level, the case of Warner Village demonstrates the corporate flexibility involved in 'global' multiplexing, the majors responding to ever-changing business imperatives that can remove or replace brands across space and time. However, the presence of Warner Village in the UK also invites questions about the mediated nature of brand consumption as it impacts on patterns of city life and cultural practice. In terms of popular cinemagoing, the megaplex asks how 'the apparatus of the lived space of cinemas arranges a localized encounter with a transnational film culture' (ibid.: 239).

In the UK, the Warner Village chain became associated with a particular kind of theatrical experience, linked to multiplex features such as stadium seating, advanced projection systems, surround sound and expansive concession stand facilities. In functional terms, the brand value of Warner Village was developed through the standardization of comfortable and technologically enhanced environments for the consumption of (Hollywood) film. Theatrical branding is, however, more than a question of pure functionality; it can also be shaped by the brand strategies of the leisure and commercial developments within which multiplex cinemas emerge and operate. This chapter examines the place and experience of brand exhibition, focusing on the promotional and discursive situation of Warner Village in two specific local spaces, both of them major leisure developments in regional British cities: Gunwharf Quays, opened in February 2001 in the naval city of Portsmouth, and the Cornerhouse, opened in March 2001 in the Midlands city of Nottingham. Built by regional property developers, and each incorporating a multiscreen Warner Village as its 'anchor brand', these sites demonstrate how the global expansion of theatrical venues is linked to the customization of entertainment space for regional city identity. Located in 'ordinary' cities, as opposed to metropolitan centres where globalization processes assume more concrete forms, both examples provide the opportunity to analyse the local imperatives of entertainment branding and the everyday context of Warner's 'world audience'.

Regeneration, property development and the urban entertainment complex

As Thomas Guback has argued, one significant and largely overlooked feature of multiplex development since the mid-1980s is that exhibition companies invariably lease space from regional property developers rather than construct their own theatres (Guback 1987). The history of the multiplex is thus linked to the history of property development in specific national and regional contexts. In Britain, the multiplex was initially associated with mall-based and out-of-town developments and the construction of new consumption centres based on suburban size, convenience and transport access. During the 1990s, however, cinema increasingly moved back into the city. Generated by the recapitalization of inner-city real estate by the private sector, urban centres became important new investment areas, entailing spatial reorganization based around the spread of gentrifying neighbourhoods, expanding swathes of luxury housing, and new entertainment and consumption zones.

The development of the 'urban entertainment complex' (UEC) is linked to these changing patterns of capital flow and retail investment, as well as to transitions in planning policy that have re-emphasized city centres.[5] While akin to the multiplex in terms of its multiscreen exhibition facilities, the urban entertainment complex describes a more complete and synergistic convergence of space with other retail sectors, and is invariably situated in close proximity to commercial centres. In 1994, *Variety* recognized a new exhibition trend associated with the megaplex, in which 'every possible thing is contained under one roof, with free-standing theatres independent of malls that can operate as destinations in themselves by being coupled with entertainment centres encompassing everything from miniature golf and virtual reality games to "food courts" and toddler compounds' (Paul 1994: 498). With its integration of cinema, food and shopping, the urban entertainment complex maintains the mixed-use principle of the suburban mall, but incorporates cinema in a different way, as it becomes the organizing feature around which niche entertainment and consumer attractions are oriented, the overall experience of which can be promoted in terms of *lifestyle consumption*.

Mike Featherstone suggests that, as a discursive category, 'lifestyle' can be linked to the growth of 'expressive consumption norms' (Featherstone 1991: 83–94). Here, lifestyle is associated with new configurations of social identity and selfhood shaped in large part by cultural intermediaries.[6] As argued in chapter 1, branding has become central to current marketing orthodoxies, accentuating 'values and beliefs' in shaping lifestyles that are mediated through affluent consumption. Entertainment space has been influenced by the logic of this 'new branded world' (Klein 2000: 21). In significant ways, the urban entertainment complex has become a core component of the aesthetic discourse developing around the regeneration of city space, a discourse based on a city's ability, through branding, to 'appear secure, fun, upbeat and innovative' in the broad competition with other cities for capital investment (Christine Boyer 1994: 411).

According to Ian Taylor, Karen Evans and Penny Fraser, notions of lifestyle (and quality of life) have played a significant role in the transformations occurring in cities experiencing the demise of local manufacturing labour markets and the emergence of new infrastructures based on the reorganization of consumption. They argue that since the late 1980s 'a new centrally orchestrated public consciousness of local variation of performance has emerged against a backdrop of national and even global processes underlying the idea of competition and efficiency' in North America and Europe (Taylor *et al.* 1996: 24). The urban entertainment complex is an indicator of performance in this context, helping to calibrate the economic viability/visibility of local city cultures while patterning the lifestyle dispositions of a new middle class.

Both Gunwharf Quays and the Cornerhouse function in this manner in midsize English cities on the South Coast and in the East Midlands respectively. From the early 1990s, Portsmouth made largely successful attempts to reinvent itself after the demise of its once buoyant naval dockyard economy through the development of service industries and tourism. In a similar vein, following the collapse of regional mining industries in the 1980s, Nottingham began to augment its status as a consumer and retail centre, leading to the growth of bars and cafes servicing Nottingham's 50,000-strong student population and heightened image as a nightlife 'hot spot'. Identified as prestige leisure developments in each city, the urban entertainment complex would contribute to a discourse of local identification through the aesthetic and architectural branding of landmark sites in central city areas.

Gunwharf Quays is a mixed-use development recycling navy dockland occupied until 1986 by the torpedo and diving school HMS Vernon. Established as the main ordnance yard for the Navy in the seventeenth century, the site of HMS Vernon was traditionally used to load ships with gunpowder, cannon balls and weapons. In a climate where heritage value has inspired a multitude of urban restorations and commercial redevelopments, HMS Vernon combined historical atmosphere with a prime waterfront position overlooking Portsmouth's busy commercial harbour. In June 1997, a consortium made up of a UK property development firm (the Berkeley Group) and a South African management company (Lordland Holdings) was given planning permission by Portsmouth City Council to develop Gunwharf Quays into a £150 million retail and real estate venture.

Thematizing Portsmouth's naval heritage by restoring historic dockyard buildings and turning them into new consumption spaces, the Gunwharf development combined factory outlet shopping with restaurants, cafes, and entertainment venues in a 33-acre site incorporating sheltered arcades, waterfront promenades and a central square. It would also include the construction of a hotel and a large number of adjoining luxury apartments and townhouses. Gunwharf was the cornerstone of an ambitious council plan to develop Portsmouth's waterfront. This included a successful bid to the Millennium Commission, which was the government body charged with distributing money from the National Lottery for landmark projects that would 'achieve a lasting monument to the achievements and aspirations of the United Kingdom' ('Landmark Millennium Project' 1997). Choosing the renaissance of Portsmouth Harbour as one of twelve such projects, the Millennium Commission awarded £40 million to be spent, alongside private investment, on the development of new promenades, cross-harbour waterbus services, an armaments museum, and the signature development of Gunwharf Quays, including the landmark Spinnaker Tower (figure 7.1). The renaissance development aimed to create nothing short of a 'gateway to Britain'. From the outset, councillors and property entrepreneurs spoke of Gunwharf in terms of the city's heightened national and global competitiveness. 'When it is complete', said one Portsmouth city council leader, 'our harbour will rank alongside those of Vancouver, Stockholm and Sydney – a truly world-class destination' ('Portsmouth Reborne' 1995). In a similar vein, Secretary of State for National Heritage, Virginia Bottomley, called the development 'a quite magnificent and inspired initiative' (ibid.).

With less hyperbole, similar promotional rhetoric enveloped the Cornerhouse in the centre of Nottingham. Like Gunwharf, the Cornerhouse was the initiative of a local property developer (Forman Harding Holdings) seeking to redevelop a central city space in order to reinvigorate its investment potential. In this case, the recently vacated Nottingham Evening Post building, dating from 1870 and the historic location of the city's major newspaper, became the focus of major plans to create a £30 million office development. However, when UCI and other multiplex operators expressed interest in finding new locations in the city – with the

Figure 7.1 Spinnaker Tower and Gunwharf Quays, Portsmouth. Courtesy of Gunwharf Management Ltd.

perception that Nottingham was under-screened – the 200,000 square feet site was reframed as a potential leisure development, with plans drawn for a 20-screen cinema in a glass-fronted complex, also to include restaurants, wine bars, a health club and a nightclub. Sold to another regional property developer (Wilson Bowden), who built and then sold the Cornerhouse to BP Pension Fund in a £50 million deal, the development became a landmark project within the city. Reported enthusiastically by the *Nottingham Evening Post*, the Cornerhouse was trumpeted by developers as offering 'Nottingham a one-stop leisure venue not yet available outside of London ... unique because of the range of leisure under one roof' (Tressider 2000). According to David Hargreaves, the letting agent who first conceived and brokered the Cornerhouse as a leisure development, 'the scheme will be the jewel in Nottingham's crown'.

The ability of both Gunwharf Quays and the Cornerhouse to attract recognized brand names within their respective tenant bases was integral to the discourse of city vibrancy and investment potential. The mix of retail, entertainment and restaurant brands, including a wide combination of global brands and national chains, helped suggest a new regional importance that would bring Portsmouth and Nottingham into competition with major second-tier cities such as Manchester, Leeds and Birmingham. The anchor brand in each was that of Warner Village. Warner was the 'first big name to agree to go to Gunwharf', developing an 11-screen multiplex venue (Owen 1999). Likewise, Warner eagerly signed leasing agreements with the Cornerhouse after UCI pulled out, renting space for 25 years (at a cost of over £1 million a year) to build a 12-screen cinema. Securing a global multiplex operator was essential to the larger design of Gunwharf and the Cornerhouse as lifestyle consumption zones.[7] Although cinema, in itself, does not function as a major income generator within such developments, it invariably adds value by creating 'footfall', attracting a large public that creates flow in and between the mix of businesses at the site. While the Cornerhouse was promoted as 'a destination and circuit in its own right', Gunwharf emphasized reasons for return, proclaiming that 'there's *always* something different happening and no one visit is the same as another'. This luring and enclosure of consumer spending in many ways contradicted the claim that a 'knock-on' effect would inevitably spill into other parts of the city, benefiting the local economy as a whole. At the same time, it reinforced the need to brand space in ways that turned consumption from a geographically transferable activity into a spatially unique *experience*.

In asking questions about the nature of cinematic exhibition in a time of increasing globalization, one must consider how the experience of cinemagoing has been positioned in relation to questions of lifestyle and locality in particular city contexts. In assessing Warner Bros.' developing interests in exhibition across the world, one must explore how its presence is courted, mediated and often repackaged within local brand narratives of city regeneration and gentrified pleasure. While the discourse of 'Americanization' has been commonly associated with brand multiplexing in Western Europe (especially as it applies to mall-based developments), the urban entertainment complex has frequently been figured around an alternative discourse of *cosmopolitanism* in its patterning of cultural practice and consumer spending.

According to Ulf Hannerz, cosmopolitanism suggests 'an openness to divergent cultural experiences, a search for contrasts rather than uniformity' (Hannerz 1990: 239). This intellectual and aesthetic stance, as Hannerz describes it, has been swiftly mapped onto the selling of divergent *consumer* experiences within urban entertainment developments such as Gunwharf Quays and the Cornerhouse. Cosmopolitanism has become a commercial byword for the promotion of services, products and atmospheres that draw upon a notion of international variety, whether measured in terms of the food served, the wine poured, the clothes sold, the cappuccino frothed, or the films screened. Significantly, however, 'cosmopolitan' also carries with it connotations of social privilege, what John Tomlinson associates with 'the sense of a cultural elite with the means to rise above the petty concerns of the everyday' (Tomlinson 1999: 189). The customization of entertainment space plays with both notions; it reframes local experience in terms of new cultural diversity, at the same time that it plays with ideas of distinction and taste. Investigating the place of multiplex exhibition in brand-based fields of meaning, I wish to explore the means by which Warner Village has been taken up in the promotional aesthetic of local leisure experience.

Cinema, locality and lifestyle consumerism

I found myself part of Gunwharf's promotional discourse in December 2001, ten months after it opened. Exploring the new development with the express purpose of buying Christmas gifts, I was unaware that my photograph would shortly be used to promote Gunwharf as 'destination unmissable'. On six different occasions, the same photograph of satisfied Gunwharf visitors – me among them – appeared in the Portsmouth *News* and in various forms of publicity material. Unwittingly, I had become part of the crowd scene used to emblematize city vibrancy in the media stories surrounding Portsmouth's touted leisure development. I appeared in features ranging from the accessibility of the development by road and rail to the lure and importance of new city investment. As one headline in the business section of the *News* put it, 'Gunwharf wipes floor with rest'. Underneath the picture of satisfied shoppers, the article began, 'It's official – Gunwharf Quays is the perfect mix of facilities for shopping, entertainment, relaxing and dining' (Twich 2001).

In many respects, I was Gunwharf's target consumer: part of the 50 per cent of visitors who drove from outside the city, earned between £25,000 and £50,000, and who spent money in a variety of outlets during a two-hour visit. Gunwharf's financial success is premised on attracting large numbers from outside the local area. The profit expectation is based on a full car park with a two-hour turnaround in which every 'car should average a £100 spend' (*Estates Gazette* 1998: 83). As Mark Jancovich notes, this diminishes the importance of cinema in direct economic terms but gives it core significance in 'adding value' to the complex as a whole (Jancovich *et al.* 2003: 241–9). In the case of Gunwharf and the Cornerhouse, added value was linked to a promotional aesthetic that cast each development in terms of the lifestyle opportunities of an affluent or aspirant middle class.

This was principally forged through an association with designer goods or middle-market restaurants and bars in the tenant mix surrounding Warner Village. While appealing to family and youth markets through mass-market food outlets such as Burger King, Subway and Pizza Hut, the promotional aesthetic was based on gentrified pleasure and the creation of space for those with a clear amount of disposable time and income. With an events programme including temporary ice rinks, jazz musicians, street jugglers and carol singing, Gunwharf sought to foster social and spending habits through a promise of controlled ambience and event, the site assiduously patrolled by '28 customer service officers' and '100 closed circuit television cameras'. Much like Portsmouth's 'unmissable' destination, the Cornerhouse played bluntly with ideas of missing out with a rhetorical question linked to its own contrivance of atmosphere: 'shouldn't you get out more?' In both cases, the UEC called to audiences as specific kinds of consumer; each site offered itself up as a 'total entertainment' space for particular social factions. As leisure spectacles, Gunwharf and the Cornerhouse sold themselves as excitingly distinct from the private sphere but also promised security in tempering middle-class anxiety about possible engagements with an unfettered public. This bears out Charles Acland's point that 'in the end, the curating of cultural offerings and the industrial forces producing material sites and encounters are an articulation of lifestyle and ultimately of class' (Acland 2003: 202).

UEC developments are far from exclusive in terms of their target appeal, relying on the attraction of core youth and family markets as well as older, more affluent, consumers. They invariably legitimate themselves in city space through a notion of bourgeois city living, however, reconstituting public space through lifestyle consumerism and its particular logics of distinction. Leisure developments like Gunwharf Quays and the Cornerhouse rely on the promise and provision of lifestyle choices that demonstrate and enable (for the city and for individual consumers) participation in national and international systems of brand consumption. Frequently situated in central districts close to a city's major consumption zone, cosmopolitanism is a way of mediating brand space. Rather than signifying infiltration or threat through the takeover of commercial and public areas by faceless brands and hegemonic multinationals, cosmopolitanism validates external investment and influence as a productive cultural force, deflecting the powerful impetus towards consolidation that underscores capitalism's negotiation of homogeneity and difference in local and global markets. Megaplex developments are embroiled in these dynamics. While often signalling the demise of competing smaller cinemas – Gunwharf and the Cornerhouse precipitated the closure of the long-standing ABC and Odeon cinemas in Portsmouth and Nottingham respectively – large multiplex cinemas have been able to lever themselves into city space through an association with consumer glamour and the appearance of increased choice.

This gives rise to critical questions about the identity of the megaplex. While the urban entertainment complex has historical antecedents, traceable to the super-cinemas of the 1920s and their associated notions of luxury and glamour, the promotional and branding issues are specific. According to Gary Edgerton, while the early super-cinemas were based on the exhibition of dreams – elaborate, orna-mental and highly imaginative in design – the multiplex is based on a principle of efficiency and consumer compliance. He speaks of 'an unprecedented move toward homogeneity' where 'an AMC multiplex anywhere strikingly resembles a respective General Cinema complex, which both conjure up hints of recognition when comparing design, format, color scheme to the neighbourhood mall stores and fast food outlets' (Edgerton 2002: 156). From this perspective, identity for the contemporary motion picture theatre is hard to achieve beyond a certain mass cultural functionality. However, this does not account for the manner in which megaplex developments are frequently aligned with the branding of local leisure experience. As I have suggested, it is necessary to focus on the differential function of branding within the recycling of city space. Not least, this provides a means of analysing the promotional co-dependence that can frequently emerge between cities and media corporations in the desire to compete within contemporary consumer economies.

The urban entertainment complex depends on a brand matrix – a particular set of promotional and spatial relations that situate *high street brands* (Gap, Calvin Klein, Pizza Hut, TGI Friday, Marks and Spencer, etc.) around an *anchor brand* (Warner Village), under the umbrella of a *localizing meta-brand* (the name and structure of the complex as a whole). What I have called the 'promotional aesthetic' is vital to the adoption of such matrix-like developments in the context of local city culture and involves a combination of elements: an identifiable logo circulating in everyday media channels, the creation and management of news coverage and the architec-tural structure of the development itself. Warner Village was central to the promo-tional aesthetic of Gunwharf Quays and the Cornerhouse in each of these areas and provides a useful means of analysing the inter-relation of global and local branding imperatives. In such a relationship, regional developers acquire the commercial kudos and strategic importance of global brands like that of Warner Bros., while they in turn enjoy the benefits of customized marketing in central, and often sensitive, locations and city cultures.

Despite the pronouncements of renewed city prestige by entrepreneurs and city officials, both Gunwharf Quays and the Cornerhouse experienced resistance from local environmental and civic groups voicing concern about the poor quality of the respective projects in relation to issues of historic preservation, design quality, and the constitution of public space. In each case, the proposed development sites held a significant place in the city's historic memory. The Portsmouth Society, for example, labelled Gunwharf a 'third-rate waste of a world class opportunity' ('Gunwharf/HMS Vernon' 1997). The concern that historic buildings would be lost, and that unique waterfront views would be consumed by exclusive private housing, added to the general lament that factory outlet shopping and a new multiplex would leave an 'ugly white elephant' in a site of historic importance with civic, as well as commercial, development potential.[8] Meanwhile, Nottingham Civic Society orchestrated a petition designed to protect the Victorian facade of the Nottingham Evening Post building. Amidst complaints from elderly residents that the Cornerhouse would 'wipe out a part of the city's history' attempts were made to instil the structure with heritage value. Without being listed, however, the building was swiftly characterized by developers as an architectural remnant with limited use. While both UEC developments were viewed in different ways by different sections of the cities populations, there was little doubt that city space would be significantly remade in each case. In this context, branding became an important strategic concern. For both city boosters and business entrepreneurs, branding became a means of differentiating and imagining place-identity in ways that could positively situate the developments in local space.

As I have stated, Warner Village was central to the selling of Gunwharf Quays and the Cornerhouse and played its part in the brand strategy of each development. Multiplex cinemas anchor the UEC not only in the creation of footfall but also in the related business of generating 'buzz factor'. Writing about globalization's impact on the relationship between cinema and the city since the 1970s, Mark Shiel comments on the 'increasing tendency in disparate societies around the world for individuals to be struck more by, and for cultures to demonstrate, their sameness rather than their difference, rather than being arbitrary, to appear primarily American' (Shiel 2001: 11). This establishes an argument about homogenization and blandness: the production of 'non-places' (malls, multiplexes, hotels, airports) by global capitalism and the hegemonic exertions of US corporate power. There are, however, a number of difficulties with the idea of the homogeneous 'non-place'. Not only does it refuse the possibility that malls and multiplexes develop histories as they become integrated into the urban fabric of particular locales, it downplays the strategies of differentiation that may be undertaken by such 'non-places' through rebuilding, refurbishment, signage and marketing.[9] While the brand-based multiplex has often been associated with impersonality, lacking in local identity and symptomatic of a prevailing Americanization of cultural experience, place differentiation has become increasingly significant as cities compete for highly mobile capital investment. Multiplex developments are frequently taken up within these processes of differentiation, linked to spatial fantasies premised, rhetorically at least, on urban reform and community redevelopment.

The aura of Hollywood film infused the constitution of leisure experience at both Gunwharf Quays and the Cornerhouse. For Gunwharf, this began with the 'destination unmissable' tag, a slogan that semantically evoked the franchise release of the second film in the *Mission: Impossible* (2000) series, opening the year before that of the UEC. Within publicity for Gunwharf, the slogan was invariably accompanied by pictures of stylish 30-somethings – young couples enjoying the pleasures of the square ('the cosmopolitan heart'), waterfront ('an unrivalled social setting') and city quay ('ultimate style'). 'Destination unmissable' suggests the excitement and spectacle not simply of the movies on show, but of the style of life itself (figure 7.2). Together with staged pictures of Gunwharf's groomed and moneyed clientele, however, images of genuine shoppers were used within publicity material. In one glossy promotion, the well-circulated crowd scene mentioned at the beginning of this section was accompanied by a feature titled 'the berth of the nation', congratulating 'proud Portsmouth' on boasting 'one of the foremost retail and leisure developments in Europe'. In these examples, an implicit cinematic language is used to describe Gunwharf Quays within marketing that frames the 'experience' through a combination of high concept lifestyle imagery and low concept images of local use. In seeking to attract tourists, shoppers, diners, and moviegoers, a particular blurring of these roles is inscribed within Gunwharf's promotional address.

In contrast, the Cornerhouse sought to avoid calculated lifestyle images within its initial brand strategy. Instead, the developers employed the cartoonist Ralph Steadman (renowned in the 1980s for his biting anti-Thatcherite political and social cartoons) to create an individualized signature for the complex. Specifically, the Cornerhouse distinguished itself through a splash-paint logo and cartoon illustrations (of anthropomorphic animals laughing and socializing) displayed within the glass 'drum' of the building. Spending £250,000 on its marketing campaign, the Cornerhouse plastered its logo and 'shouldn't you get out more?' slogan onto buses, taxis, billboards, and at sponsored events ranging from school fêtes to maps of the city, developing its identity as a 'truly one-stop shop for enjoyment, a fun palace for all ages'. With emphasis on entertainment rather than tourism or shopping, Warner Village was encouraged to brand the Cornerhouse by putting up giant Looney Tunes characters within the building. That Warner Bros. declined may indicate the push and pull between the need for consistency in co-ordinating Warner's global brand identity and the accommodation of this identity within local space.[10] Distinguishing the Cornerhouse, however, was a clear appeal to an idea of social life anchored locally by the multiplex.

Indicative here is the James Bond weekend, organized in 2002 by the Cornerhouse's public relations firm, Audax. Just as Warner Bros. will lease space from regional property developers, they will also pay for local public relations expertise. Companies like Audax are responsible for creating and managing news around such developments. According to Fiona McKinley, who oversaw the Cornerhouse account, Audax's remit was to 'promote the Cornerhouse as a brand, as a destination, as a one-stop shop … something for everyone was an early key message' (McKinley 2002). The James Bond weekend is an example of the cross-promotional events designed to finesse the principle of entertainment synergy defining the megaplex as a site of public amusement. Coinciding with Christopher Lee's visit to the Cinema Store, one of this UEC's few retail outlets, Audax developed a cinematic theme, inviting tenants to serve Martinis and dress up as Bond characters. While bigger brands such as Warner Bros. may have a varied stance

Figure 7.2 'Destination unmissable': selling contemporary lifestyle. Courtesy of Gunwharf Management Ltd.

with regard to such PR stunts, preferring to centralize national and international brand strategy, inclusion within these events has become a necessary dimension of the negotiation of global/local brand image. For example, at Gunwharf the arrival of Prince Charles for a charity screening of *Die Another Day* (2002) – together with a Royal Navy spectacle of mock gunfire and a Bond-themed water rescue – helped establish Warner Village as a gala venue in the region rather than simply the latest American multiplex. This paid immediate dividends with wide media reporting and a headline that anchored the cinema to the city in determinate ways – 'from Portsmouth with love' (Collender 2002).[11]

Gunwharf Quays and the Cornerhouse pursued different promotional strategies in their first years of opening. While the emphasis at Gunwharf was 'decidedly upmarket', the Cornerhouse was based around a concept of 'getting out'. Both relied from the beginning, however, on the promise of lifestyle consumption and a principle of cosmopolitanism and social display. While Gunwharf advertised itself as '*the* place to be and to be seen in', the Cornerhouse described itself as 'the premier destination for the city and for people across the East Midlands'; the design of the building was instrumental to the promotional aesthetic in this respect. Both Gunwharf and the Cornerhouse provide an example of what M. Christine Boyer has termed 'architectural entertainments'. Boyer looks specifically at remnants of cities that have been 'recycled as gigantic image spectacles to enhance the act of consumption' (Boyer 1994: 423). She has a particular interest in heritage sites as tableaux of consumption, but she invites the question of how brand-based developments such as Gunwharf Quays and the Cornerhouse contrive and sell an *atmosphere* of consumption, facilitating, as Boyer describes it, a 'particular clientele delivered in the right frame of mind'. Once again, cinema plays a part in this process.

Gunwharf relies on a notion of maritime heritage. Together with the placing of gun shells, torpedoes and ship figureheads as ornamental sculptures, the boulevards and avenues where they are displayed play semantically with naval history.[12] Consumption is figured through an atmospheric staging of naval history and waterfront trade. While attractive to brand outlets with a maritime connection such as Crew Clothing Co., White Stuff, Speedo and Tog 24, the idea of wealthy yacht culture also provides a themed context for brands such as Gieves and Hawkes, Waterford Wedgwood and Ralph Lauren. With the restoration of naval buildings such as the Old Customs House (expediently turned into a 'traditional pub'), Gunwharf is what Boyer calls a 'historically constituted and compositionally structured place'; it employs seafaring heritage to create an atmosphere of maritime cosmopolitanism.

Situated in a dense city location, the Cornerhouse is based less on thematic spectacle than on the spectacle of physical presence (figure 7.3). This is created through a significant glass frontage and the use of neon lights to illuminate the building in bold shades of blue and green. In some respects, the Cornerhouse adopts the look of a cruise ship, with aqua trimming and portholes meeting the sandy colour of the brickwork. This is appropriate for conveying a sense of enclosed pleasure. It also

Figure 7.3 The Cornerhouse, Nottingham. Courtesy of The Cornerhouse.

provides a suitable context for the range of food and drink outlets – the international cuisine (from Japanese noodles and Portugese piripiri chicken to Indian curries and American steaks) generating a sense of culinary 'travel' and diversity. For the local council, the Cornerhouse was the flagship (metaphorically and in some sense aesthetically) of a vibrant leisure circuit, complementing the city's adjacent theatre and concert hall and fostering a 'cultural quarter' that, within the discourse of urban regeneration, would replace unruly youth behaviour with new models of bourgeois civility.

As the anchor brand, Warner Village helped contribute to the particular staging of atmosphere and cultural refinement at each UEC, significant in selling the complex to potential investors as well as to the city public. Before opening, the Warner Village at Gunwharf promised three 'gold class' cinemas, while the Cornerhouse spoke of luxury cinemas that would provide 'VIP treatment' involving 'waiters delivering gourmet food direct to leather reclining seats at two screens' (*Nottingham Evening Post* 1998). Targeting the 'cultured population' of each respective city, Warner Village hoped to attract an exclusive clientele prepared to pay £10 – twice the usual price for a ticket. Meanwhile, programming schedules were set to appeal to niche audiences by devoting two screens to 'foreign, arthouse and cult films'. A cosmopolitan ideal was reinforced by Warner Village in its proposed screening and programming schedule; it established each UEC as a place to expend cultural as well as economic capital. In advertising itself as a public cinema space, Warner Village developed the principles of cultural diversity and social privilege that framed the UEC as a whole. This did not bear significantly on the actual practice of film exhibition, however. Although the Cornerhouse reserved a small number of screens for Bollywood films, servicing the city's large Indian population, Mark Jancovich notes a swift reassertion of youth and families as the two key, and for the multiplex, traditional markets (Jancovich *et al.* 2003: 241–50). Perhaps unsurprisingly, the promise of foreign, arthouse and cult films – and of being able to watch these while eating sushi and drinking champagne – gave way quickly to the market power of Hollywood popcorn movies.

This hardly troubled Warner Village; its purpose as an exhibition venue was to act as a strategic landing pad for major studio movies. The more general assertion of mass-market taste and behaviour became a source of anxiety for the chairman of Berkeley Holdings (Gunwharf's owner), however, who expressed concern that 'instead of people flocking from out of town to the factory outlet stores, a significant number of visitors were locals just buying a drink and a burger' (Thomas 2002). These issues draw attention to the lived experience of the urban entertainment complex, including the taste formations and vectors of inclusion/exclusion that are worked out within the cultural and social spaces they create. Jancovich notes that while UEC developments often seek to cater to affluent consumers, there is evidence that this creates particular feelings of alienation from sections of the lower-middle and working classes who 'see these spaces as the playground of trendy middle-class consumers, and therefore reject city centres as a place of leisure' (Jancovich *et al.* 2003: 245). In the case of the Cornerhouse, this sense of alienation was further complicated along generational lines, the UEC becoming associated less with a 'cultural quarter' than with a youthful, and sometimes threatening, circuit of weekend nightlife. Patterns of local use had a bearing on promotional strategy. For the Cornerhouse, marketing began deliberately targeting the modish under-35 market, while for Gunwharf Quays, the tendency of locals to buy 'a drink and a burger' gave rise to a new focus on Spinnaker Tower, the imposing 550 ft viewing tower that opened in 2005; this facilitated a public relations strategy geared towards sightseeing visitors. Instead of the bourgeois promise of 'ultimate style', the attraction of Gunwharf Quays was increasingly developed in relation to a 'global icon' that 'will soon take a place in the nation's heart alongside the London Eye and the Eden Project' (Owen 2006: 3).

Both developments proved that, for all the promotional sheen used to attract and appeal to particular kinds of consumer, the possible consequences for experience and signification could never be guaranteed in advance. In each case, brand campaigns would recalibrate themselves around more discernibly youth-oriented or tourist markets. Within public relations strategies, however, the rhetorical tone would continue to celebrate the 'arrival' of international consumer culture, suggesting a connection to national and global processes that, in discursive terms, would also persist in shaping local press reporting in building up positive images of the city. From the luring of international brand outlets to the regional premiere of major blockbusters such as the latest James Bond movie, each UEC helped refine what Charles Acland calls a 'sensibility about the global', a mode of popular cosmopolitanism characterized by 'a structure of feeling about senses of allegiance and affiliation – about being in step – with imagined and synchronized populations' (Acland 2003: 237).

For all the profound transformations in cultural experience associated with globalization, and for which the UEC is arguably a part, John Tomlinson suggests 'they are not, typically, experienced as dramatic upheavals but are, on the contrary, rapidly assimilated to normality and grasped – however precariously – as "the way life is" rather than as a series of deviations from the way life ought to be' (Tomlinson 1999: 128) This brings together what Tomlinson calls the 'mundane' experience of globalization, and what Acland terms 'a local subjectivity lurching towards a felt internationalism' (Acland 2003: 243). It is within these multiple relations of force and sensibility that conglomerate power can be examined. Time Warner wrote in 1998: 'In a cluttered world where more media delivers more choices to audiences than ever before in history, customers increasingly turn to what's best, what's recognizable, what's familiar, what's trusted … the brands of Time Warner' (Time Warner 1998). On these terms, the example of film exhibition demonstrates the extension of the Warner brand name within global entertainment markets, but also the degree to which cinematic spaces, much like Time Warner's franchise properties, are subject to assimilation, adaptation and discursive reworking by particular communities of interest, be these local populations, fan groups, or other kinds of social and cultural agents. This supports Michael Storper's argument that consumerism sustains itself not by pushing itself upon people, but by 'becoming an intimate part of the frameworks of individuals, how they see themselves and define their interests' (Storper 2001: 105). From theatre building to the development of multimedia content, global media industries create a brand apparatus which, rather than designed to seduce or manipulate, is geared toward securing audience investment, participation and loyalty. If this can be seen as a means of stabilizing and regulating consumer behaviour, it invariably depends on a process where different accents can be given to global trends associated with the re-scaling of (enlarged and deepened) markets.

Rather than blankly impose the Hollywood blockbuster in rationalized theatrical settings, or exercise brand presence in a gesture of American will, Warner Village was taken up in the UK within the promotional aesthetic of local leisure experience. This is consistent with Time Warner's strategy of combining global reach with local touch. However, the examples of Gunwharf Quays and the Cornerhouse both illustrate the role that local cities play in the development and orchestration of brand space, attempting to demonstrate 'local variation of performance' via new infrastructures of consumption. While considerable attention has been given to the infiltration of superbrands (e.g. Nike, Disney, Starbucks, Microsoft, McDonald's) as a form of globalization critique, the requirement to live *through* brands and to create value through lifestyle experience, has been significantly reinforced by the rapid assimilation of consumerist orthodoxies within local contexts and specifically local redevelopment projects such as those described here.

Through regional initiatives of promotional imaging, news coverage and architectural design, cities have increasingly sought to brand artefacts and areas of symbolic value in order to lure capital investment. Attracting retail and leisure brands has taken on strategic importance in this regard. This is matched, however, by a particular impetus to locate these within brand narratives that belong to, and that can further promote, the region and the city. In terms of Warner's brand expansion, multiplex exhibition established space and meaning for itself in the centres of Portsmouth and Nottingham through the local politics of urban redevelopment. This relied upon, and engendered, a cosmopolitan consumption discourse rather than one based on Americanization. These may be equally complex and ambivalent in discursive terms, but cosmopolitanism has become a more significant feature of the attempt to instil difference and distinction within the contemporary articulation of place. David Harvey equates this with 'cultural homogenisation through diversification' (Harvey 1993: 22), describing the process of consolidation, amidst the language of difference, that remains central to hegemonic consumerism as it impacts on the spaces and discourses of modern life. While there is a need to resist instrumental notions of homogenization, this should not downplay issues of power and control that are vested in the rhetoric of lifestyle choice. If the attempt to instil difference often leads to a powerful replication of cultural and capital forms, the urban entertainment complex, with its local coding of consumer glamour, has become a strategic site through which Hollywood's global presence is spatially forged.

In its production of space and place, the megaplex carries the imprimatur of Hollywood's brand power within the new entertainment economy. This chapter suggests, however, that the situation and experience of the megaplex cannot be divorced from the local agents (local councillors, property developers, public relations firms) who seek to establish their own points of economic and cultural advantage through urban renewal, or from the indeterminate nature of people's lived encounters with emergent forms of public leisure space. Aida Hozic suggests that: 'the power of Hollywood within the American economy and the power of the American economy in the world have been highly dependent on the construction of new social and moral spaces and of new fantasies' (Hozic 2001: 13). The megaplex is an expression of Hollywood's organization of social space and architectural fantasy. It emerged as a nodal point in the industrial formation of the global audience in the 1990s, but was, and remains, bound in persistent negotiations over the meaning of location and everyday experience.

This last point provides a necessary and important coda to my consideration of the politics of branding. Part III has analysed the function of branding within the industrial operations of a major film studio, connecting the production, distribution and exhibition of film to particular contexts within the global media system, and to emblematic tendencies, or expressions, of brand meaning and power. Vertically integrated and relatively steadfast in its commitment to the movie franchise, the recent history of Warner Bros. offers up various, indicative forms of brand spectacle: synergistic film texts, sustained marketing campaigns, and themed exhibition and consumption venues. All, in their way, speak of the power of corporate media in the 'economies of signs of space'; they suggest a regime of value, and therefore a politics, based around the circulation and control of intellectual property, including the sites and environments where media content is consumed. In key respects, to analyse motion picture branding is to analyse the dominance of transnational media conglomerates such as Time Warner. In dissecting some of the contours of this power – the discourse of commercial obviousness, the tendency towards corporate obfuscation, the balance of cultural homogenization and diversity – my intention has been to examine specific *conjunctures* in the branding strategies of the movie business. Rather than assert a general and unambiguous theory of media hegemony, or equate branding simply with 'neo-liberal globalization', as some arguments are inclined, I have sought to examine the complex relationships established within and between Hollywood studios, media institutions, and the social and cultural world in which we live. Despite the ubiquity of the brand properties that are owned by major entertainment corporations and that shape the cultural terrain, such properties are neither produced nor consumed straightforwardly. The will-to-brand has developed in relation to volatile contexts of industrial pressure and need, and its effects will always ultimately be defined by the way that brand objects and commodities – be these organizations of content or space – are *made to mean* in the lived practices of everyday life, a fact not lost on the media executives and brand managers whose professional lives depend on the mercurial business of selling entertainment.

Conclusion

Total entertainment

This book has argued that branding provides a significant lens through which to consider transformations and developments in the status and selling of filmed entertainment. While the practice of branding is long established, emerging in the late nineteenth century as a strategy of differentiating goods and later becoming central to the discipline of marketing that took shape in the 1950s, branding was articulated in specific ways in the 1990s and 2000s. In industrial terms, this was linked to broad transitions in the marketing and media environment, the burgeoning synergies of the entertainment complex and the primacy given to intellectual property meeting particular concerns about the fragmentation of the audience and the perceived need to stabilize markets. In a promotional culture where traditional models of mass advertising met with a new impetus towards selling values, environments and experiences, the idea of the brand emerged as 'a key locus for the reconfiguring of contemporary processes of production' (Lury 2004: 17). This was especially marked in the movie business, the cultural work of branding and brand logos enabling the increasingly liquid commodity of film to flow across different texts, products, merchandise and media. Through case analysis of institutional strategies, logos, franchise properties and forms of consumption space – focusing on companies such as Disney, Paramount, Dolby, New Line and, in particular, Warner Bros. – I have sought to examine the will-to-brand in the contemporary motion picture business, considering, in the process, the implications of branding for the study of film as industrial commodity and affective entertainment.

In both a cultural and economic sense, branding has become central to the modern gestalt of 'total entertainment'. This term refers to industrial structures of corporate ownership as well as to particular textual and consumption practices that have developed at a juncture where entertainment content is inclined, and designed, to travel in mobile ways across media platforms and ancillary/territorial markets. If the function of branding is to pattern activities across time and space, the process of selling entertainment has come to rely, increasingly, on the principle of deepening audience involvement in immersive brand worlds. As a marketing conceit, the sense of 'entering a world' draws together my various case examples; it informs the transmedia architecture of *The Matrix*, provides a basis for the sensorial inhabiting of studio and trademark logos, frames and potentially strengthens loyalty to particular kinds of animated and fantasy universe, and gives a spatial coherence to themed entertainment and consumption sites. The concept of 'entering a world' is not in itself new in aesthetic or cultural terms; as Marie-Laure Ryan suggests, the concept of immersion is long established in the phenomenology of art experience, suggesting a corporeal experience that 'takes the projection of a virtual body, or even better, the participation of the actual one, to feel integrated in an art-world' (Ryan 2001: 21). She writes: 'the myths of total art express … the fascination of modern culture with ever more transparent, lifelike, and sensorially diversified media' (ibid.: 347), and this desire for immersion is echoed by Andre Bazin in his description of the 'myth of total cinema', the idea that cinema can faithfully re-create the world and achieve perfect verisimilitude. The gestalt of total entertainment essentially broadens and codifies the principle of world-building inscribed within the (re)presentation of sensory and textual habitats; it speaks of 'a world of new images, sounds, and specially fabricated sites' (Acland 2003: 79), developed through, and in relation to, the expanding environment and technological capacities of contemporary entertainment media.

For Richard Dyer, the widening of the entertainment environment carries with it a pointed ideological significance. With franchise-hungry conglomerates rapidly expanding the delivery channels for their vast array of branded media properties, and with 'entertainment value' built into an increasing range of cultural and social forms (from news reporting, political campaigning and museum display, to the managed occasions of sport, shopping and dining), entertainment has become a ubiquitous force within cultural and economic life. For Dyer, this ubiquity also speaks of an eclipse, precipitating the waning of the 'dynamic of escape' foundational to the ideology of entertainment. If entertainment once relied on a concept of separation from everyday reality, a world that could be escaped to as a treat and that classically dealt in glamour, utopia and the exotic, Dyer suggests that 'to the degree that everything becomes entertainment, entertainment itself ceases to be a category' (Dyer 2002: 177). By the terms of his argument, entertainment is something that audiences no longer escape to but has instead become an environment that consumers, specifically 'the comfortable overclass of Western society', are invited to live and play within.

Like other critical observers, Dyer claims that transitions have occurred in the past half-century that bear upon the practice and understanding of popular entertainment. Without discounting the complexity of modern leisure culture, Dyer reserves an implicit critical suspicion of the consumerist 'being in the world' that defines the horizon of contemporary entertainment. While he suggests that 'the waning of entertainment risks weakening the ability to be critical of the way things are by feeling how else they might be' (ibid.: 179), Lisa Kernan relates this point more directly to the commodification of amusement and desire. She writes: 'In an era in which popular culture figures the capacity for individual agency as increasingly delimited to the various realms of consumption, *being* "in a world …" replaces making one' (Kernan 2004: 215). Both critics raise questions about the degree to which contemporary entertainment represents a loss of will to consumer agendas – the immersion in brand worlds, whether those of Hollywood film, reality television, sporting events, or other kinds of self-sustaining universe, heralding a potential lack, or diminishing, of critical social agency and vision.

This sense of lack within the imagination of popular entertainment resonates with the wider critique of global corporate media, in particular the systems of branding and cultural marketing that lie at its core. In the last three decades, branding has become central to the regime of intellectual property that has given lifeblood to the cultural, or copyright, industries; the concept of 'the brand' provides a means of giving value and identity to entertainment commodities as they circulate in the time and space of a media environment controlled by corporate behemoths enthralled to the synergistic convergence of their business empires. By expanding their cultural rights and proprietary holdings, conglomerates such as Time Warner and Disney have sought to organize and co-ordinate the diversified and franchised media economy in which we live. Branding plays an important part in this process, differentiating products and services in ways that can foster cultural attachments and consumer loyalties but that can also then translate into forms of measurable (brand) equity.

There is no doubting the relation of branding to corporate media power; it is a specific market modality that helps constitute the 'event' of contemporary entertainment. This does not mean to say, however, that media conglomerates are able to fix the meanings of the brand worlds they create, or, indeed, prevent individuals from making or imagining productive social relations within these worlds. As work in cultural and fan studies has shown, social groups and consumption communities engage with commodified texts in active ways, using them as a potential resource for the construction of identity and collective allegiance. Not least, this frames what Rosemary Coombe terms 'the politics of producing derivative meanings', describing both 'how differences in the social fabric are expressed with commodified texts and how differences in meaning are inadvertently encouraged and overtly contained by regimes of intellectual property' (Coombe 1998: 15). In a critical sense, this points towards a form of cultural politics that allows for the dialogic, and participatory, nature of people's engagement with signifying and media practices. Strategically, it confronts the challenges surrounding corporate control over intellectual property rather than – as within key strains of political economy – elevates 'resistance' to global corporate media, and its franchise brands, as an end in itself (see also Jenkins 2006: 240–60).

It has not been my intention to focus on questions of media consumption. However, in examining the business of selling entertainment, I have sought to develop a form of analysis that moves against default theories of resistance, as well as critical laments about the current state of (brand-based) entertainment. To this end, I have focused on histories and industrial conjunctures that illuminate the contingent relations between production and consumption, specifically as this implicates, and bears upon, the practice, poetics and politics of branding. I would argue that by gaining a better understanding of the inherent unpredictability involved in the production and promotion of (cinematic) culture, it is possible to appreciate spaces of uncertainty, and therefore political and cultural opportunity, which present themselves in the media sphere. As Simone Murray suggests, to consider the flux that confronts the entertainment industry 'is not a fatalistic surrender to the inevitability of the oligopolized global media, but the use of that system's economic shortcomings to trace more precisely the contours of its political and cultural effects' (Murray 2005: 431). In the case of Hollywood, these short-comings are many and various. For conglomerate-owned studios, one might point to the burdens of escalating production, marketing and distribution costs, the inability to predict how a franchise will perform in the market (i.e. whether or not a movie property can become a sufficiently big enough phenomenon to offset its debt liabilities), and the tendency towards divisional infighting that can adversely affect the best laid plans of corporate synergy. These factors accompany the splin-tering of the mass audience and the development of new media technologies, both of which enable *and* threaten ways of doing business and controlling intellectual property. As I hope to have shown in my treatment of Warner Bros., focusing upon Hollywood's promotional culture of production does not mean ignoring the growing reality of media concentration. Nor does it mean downplaying the strate-gies of commercial obviousness, corporate obfuscation, and 'cultural homogeniza-tion through diversification' that have taken root in a discursive and material sense. We live in a period of economic enchantment and free-market belief. The will-to-brand distinguishes this moment. However, we must also recognize that, as a medium of exchange between companies and consumers, branding is also born of 'the very real complexities involved in making capital out of culture' (Hesmondhalgh 2002: 263). This necessitates a critical approach that avoids assuming in advance the malign status of marketing and the abject meaning of logos – that resists, in short, the temptation to transform branding into a *metaphor* of capitalist hurt or hubris.

Across its range of activities, the motion picture industry has shaped, and been shaped by, the brand imperatives that characterize global corporate strategies. In market terms, contemporary Hollywood is distinguished by the development of a new international division of cultural labour, by the movement of franchise prop-erties across textual and territorial borders, by the extension of transnational copy-right governance, and by the insinuation of commercial signification within hitherto protected space. (We might think, in this last case, of the way that major studios send lesson plans and teaching materials to schools as part of the marketing mix for upcoming movies skewed towards children.) The consolidation of Holly-wood's brand power has become a means of asserting its global hegemony. And yet it is important not to jump too quickly, or with too little hope, towards conclusions about the degraded state of our branded media world. For all that we may wish it otherwise, we live in a commodity-driven culture; brand objects and commercial signs are part of our everyday social reality. In making and selling its wares, Holly-wood is now, more than ever, a brand industry. Generalized complaints about the culture of marketing will only get us so far, however, in assessing the status and selling of film, especially its place in relation to the contemporary entertainment complex. Instead, patient analysis is required of the historically determined forms of knowledge and practice, meaning and feeling, pleasure and desire that serve to frame (and reformulate) the way that film is understood and experienced as object and commodity. In the global media age, where cinema is but one part of a broadly defined image industry, this means acknowledging the vicissitudes, as well as the more obvious victories, of the commercial film business as studios increasingly seek to renew their logos and rethink their brand capacities to meet an uncertain future.

Notes

Introduction: entertainment economies

1 Sponsoring individual letters for $28,000 each, Hefner claimed the Y, while Alice Cooper, Gene Autry and Andy Williams bought an O, L and W, respectively.

2 While Michael Storper suggests that flexible specialization has created new possibilities for inter-firm creativity and collaboration, emphasizing the rise of small independent production and service companies within a new 'entertainment industrial complex', Asu Aksoy and Kevin Robins are less sanguine, accepting the basis of industrial change but emphasizing the market domination of the major film companies in their assumed role as distribution gatekeepers (Storper 1989; Aksoy and Robins 1992).

3 The conclusion of Naomi Klein's *No Logo*, titled 'Consumerism Versus Citizenship', is suggestive here. Her critique of the attempt by multinational corporations 'to enclose our shared culture in sanitized and controlled brand cocoons' is in many ways compelling. However, it also romanticizes the principle of 'resistance' without accounting for the complex ways in which social groups negotiate their identities as consumers *and* citizens, whether via the possibilities of democratic representative politics (Heath and Potter 2005) or through cultural activity not always reducible to relations of antagonism (what Rosemary Coombe otherwise locates in forms of 'ironic appreciation, complicitous critique, affectionate annoyance, sympathetic intervention, and grudgingly respectful grievances' (1998: 271)). Politically, I am persuaded by the Gramscian approach to cultural critique offered by Coombe, Charles Acland, and others, stressing the need to produce 'a historical portrait of the dynamic relations between dominant and subordinate forms and practices, with the ultimate goal of knowing how to intervene, whether to disrupt, to target policy, to create alternative forms, or to act wisely from within existing institutions' (Acland 2003: 17).

4 Characteristic of the global nature of branded film production, both the Chanel advert (directed by Baz Luhrmann) and *The Matrix* (directed by Larry and Andy Wachowski) were shot at Fox Studios Australia. In terms of the 'media professional communities' involved, both works capitalized on regional digital expertise, as well as runaway cost efficiencies, to bring them to screen.

I The cultural economy of branding

1 With a rising tide of anti-Americanism reacting to the Bush administration's policies in Israel and Iraq, winning 'hearts and minds' became a diplomatic imperative in the political climate following 9/11. In response, Charlotte Beers used models drawn from the advertising industry, fielding consumer research in Jordan, Lebanon and other Middle Eastern countries, and devising a $10 million advertising campaign about Muslim life in the US to better present American values of diversity and tolerance. According to Beers, the rationale was to 'deliver

the intangible assets of the United States', to find and exploit the 'leverageable asset' and 'emotional underpinning' of brand America (cited in 'Building Brand America', 2000).

2 While I move between the terms 'advertising', 'marketing' and 'branding', I am ultimately concerned with branding as an outgrowth of marketing developments in the mid-to-late twentieth century, stemming from the targeted approach to publicity and consumer behaviour originating in the 1950s.

3 The problem with such arguments, as Liz McFall demonstrates, is that they belie the historical inextricability of cultural and economic spheres, generating a critical presentism that risks overstating the 'newness' of consumer culture and advertising's mediating role within it. Specifically, she demonstrates that qualities associated with contemporary branding – its saturation of cultural life and use of emotional strategies – can be applied to much earlier periods. While the interpenetration of 'art' and 'commerce' has become central to arguments about cultural/economic hybridity, for instance, she examines the way that advertising sought to blend styles and techniques with fine art, film and literature in the nineteenth century, often, and just as swiftly, tapping 'emotion' through different agency styles in the use of written and visual techniques (McFall 2004; Twitchell 1996).

4 This incorporates marketing theory 'which seeks to understand the emotional underpinning of consumer decision-making as a driving force behind viewing and purchasing decisions' (Jenkins 2006: 62).

5 Companies like Nike, Apple, Starbucks and The Body Shop were indicative brand ventures in this new marketing context. Rather than built around product-specific qualities, company image was in each case forged around designations of 'attitude' or 'belief', from the principle of sporting/cultural individualism to significations of upscale urban and/or ethical living. In the semiotics of brand culture, if you didn't 'Just Do It' you could always 'Think Different', organically moisturized and drinking a grande house blend in either case. (For a detailed discussion of Apple's 'Think Different' campaign, see Grainge 2000, 2002).

6 The Internet, in particular, was rich with promotional opportunity, annual expenditures on web advertising increasing from $1.9 billion in 1998 to $4.62 billion in 1999. While this was still modest compared with conventional advertising media – in 1998, broadcast television expenditures were $39.5 billion, newspapers $44.3 billion, direct mail $39.7 billion, and radio $14.6 billion – it represented an annual increase of 141 per cent. This compared with single- or double-figure percentage increases in all other sectors (Balnaves et al. 2001: 70). While the dot-com collapse in 2001 would see a downturn in Internet advertising revenue, online promotion has remained a nascent force.

7 The list used a brand valuation method developed by the consultancy firm Interbrand, analysing the current worth of a brand as set in terms of its future ownership/earnings. While 20 per cent of the bid prices of mergers and acquisitions in the 1980s were motivated by the value of brands, this figure stood at 70 per cent by the late 1990s (Arvidsson 2005: 239).

8 According to Karrh et al., 90 per cent of placements are still done on a barter basis, where the product or service is traded for exposure in the programme. However, some large deals have also been made such as the $5–7 million fees that Mokie and Lexus paid for interactive billboards to appear in *Minority Report* (Karrh et al. 2003).

9 Explaining the relation of FedEx to *Cast Away*, director Robert Zemeckis insisted that 'there was absolutely no product placement. We weren't paid by anybody to place products in the movie ... it just seemed to me that the whole integrity of the movie would be compromised if this was some phony transglobal letter delivery service'. This relies on Hollywood's default argument that placement adds to a sense of film realism. It belies the extensive resources given to the film by FedEx, however, and to the fact that some of its scenes – such as the package-eye view of a parcel's journey in a sequence that opens the film – echoed a 'Golden Package' series of commercials by FedEx that appeared a few years before (Friedman 2003).

10 The likes of Ridley Scott, Jean-Luc Godard, Federico Fellini, David Lynch, Woody Allen and Spike Lee have all made commercials.
11 While Nike made *Road to Paris* (2001), a one-hour documentary on the US cycling team's preparation for the Tour de France shown on CBS for the airtime fee of $250,000, *No Boundaries* (2001) saw Ford invest $6.5 million on a 13-part series featuring its vehicles, broadcast on the studio network the WB. More directly, *The Hire* inspired a television commercial by Mercedes (directed by Michael Mann and featuring Benicio del Toro) that disguised itself as a trailer for a non-existent movie called *Lucky Star*, surreptitiously guiding viewers towards an interactive web link for the new Mercedes SL sedan.
12 Baz Luhrmann notes: 'We're all engaged in the work of selling an audience something. In movies, it's an emotion, a belief, an observation – in advertising, a product or service. But the tools of the trade are the same and sometimes the art of advertising can even result in artistic greatness' ('Take Five' 2004). Similarly, David Fincher, whose production company Anonymous Content made *The Hire*, comments, 'There's this assumption that commercials are just close-ups of celebrities holding up products, but some of them are great art' (Swallow 2003: 27–33). While these statements reveal more than a hint of self-justification, both directors point to the false separation of art and advertising in the conception of their own work. More pragmatically, commercials give filmmakers opportunities to refine cinematic techniques through projects that are highly capitalized but relatively short in terms of labour and time.
13 In accordance with frameworks regulating promotional disclosure (overseen in Britain by the Advertising Standards Authority) the word 'advertisement' appeared at the bottom of the screen three times within the commercial's 180 second duration.

2 Media branding and the entertainment complex

1 By Epstein's definition, the 'clearinghouse concept' describes the way that studios determine the income and expenses assigned to individual films, and the money due to participants such as equity partners, co-producers, music publishers, stars, directors and writers. Studios have considerable power in this process, often using creative financial accounting and complicated royalty formulas to their own advantage. Epstein writes: 'As owner of the clearinghouse, and the provider of management services and financing, the studio takes a hefty cut of virtually all the money that flows in and out. This service fee amounts to 15 per cent of the total cost of each production for providing managerial "overhead"; 33 per cent of the revenue the film earns for its "distribution" facilities; and an annual charge of 10 per cent of the studio's budget outlays (until they are earned back) for "interest"' (Epstein 2006: 121). While studios may no longer own creative talent or the exclusive rights to film properties, they maintain power and wealth by gatekeeping the process (and the terms) by which film monies flow.
2 Mounting a legal defence in the early 1980s against an unauthorized television film of her life, Elizabeth Taylor proclaimed in court: 'I am my own industry. I am my own commodity'. Similarly, Arnold Schwarzenegger's holding company continued to protect his image rights after being elected Governor of California, warning toymakers that 'Schwarzenegger is an instantly recognizable global celebrity whose name and likeness are worth millions of dollars and are solely his property' (see Hozic 2000: 205, Epstein 2006: 299).
3 Acknowledging the 'de-' or 'non-' conglomerating tendencies of specific corporations in the 1980s (Gulf & Western and Warner Communications Inc. both divesting themselves of capital-intensive business interests to streamline their concerns around entertainment and leisure-time markets), my use of the term 'conglomerate' describes those entertainment behemoths that have vast and diversified stakes in the contemporary media environment. This follows common terminology used in trade publications such as *Variety*

and *Hollywood Reporter*. Although Disney was one of the few film studios to avoid merger and takeover bids in the 1980s, it may still be described as a media conglomerate for the vertical and horizontal breadth of its holdings.

4 Disney's financial showing weakened in the late 1990s, management wrangles between Eisner and Roy Disney compounding the poor performance of ABC, the loss of creative ground to animation rivals Pixar and DreamWorks, and the outright failure of ventures such as the Go: Network Internet portal (Blevins 2004). It was in this broad context that Eisner was deposed as Disney's Chief Executive, replaced by Robert Iger in 2006 (Stewart 2005).

5 Since the 1970s, the 'Fin-Syn' (Financial Interest and Syndication) rules prohibited the three major television networks (NBC, ABC, CBS) from owning or developing prime-time programming. It also limited their participation in syndication. If these measures were designed to prevent the networks from dominating the market through control of the airwaves, the repeal of Fin-Syn in September 1995 was part of the general deregulation of the broadcast industry, combining with the Telecommunications Act of 1996 to throw open television station ownership and programming limits (Holt 2003).

6 While niche channels such as MTV have long transformed their logos into 'videographic performing platforms', and premium channels like HBO have positioned themselves through programming/promotional strategies organized around a station moniker ('It's not TV, It's HBO'), major networks soon followed suit, NBC overhauling its corporate identity in the 1990s to brand itself as a competitor 'network family' (Caldwell 2006).

7 Demonstrating the multiple windows for filmed entertainment, the *Batman* franchise in the 1990s (comprising four films) generated $2 billion for Warner Bros. The revenue was split as follows: movies (34 per cent), home videos (29 per cent), licensing and merchandising (19 per cent), domestic television rights (10 per cent), foreign television rights (8 per cent) (Holson and Lyman 2002).

8 Church Gibson suggests that the mixed reception of *The Matrix: Reloaded* (2003) and *The Matrix: Revolutions* (2003) may relate in part to their lack of visual appeal, the grunge aesthetic of the bleak, post-apocalyptic enclave of Zion having a less seductive visual currency than the cool aesthetic of the first film.

9 Although the range of *Matrix* texts are self-sufficient, and can be viewed, played and understood independently, the franchise creates 'compelling environments that cannot be fully explored or exhausted within a single work or even a single medium' (Jenkins 2006: 114). For example, while the destruction of a power plant in *The Matrix: Reloaded* is briefly referenced in the film, it becomes a central scenario within the *Enter the Matrix* game. Similarly, marginal characters in the film trilogy take on a focal significance in the *Animatrix* series. While Jonathan Romney suggests that the elliptical qualities of the films gives them 'an unfinished feel at odds with the closure we expect from Hollywood sci-fi', critics like Henry Jenkins and Aylish Wood suggest that the presence of non-linear relations between textual elements creates new ideas about narrative chronology and origin, enabling consumers to make story connections on their own terms (Romney 2003; Wood 2005; Jenkins 2006).

10 By certain measurements of income, the videogame business soon outpaced film, the sale of games and consoles in the US earning $9.4 billion in 2001 compared with Hollywood's domestic box office of $8.35 billion (Clover 2004: 24).

11 In 2004, Warner Bros. released 'the ultimate Matrix collection', a five-disc DVD box-set including each film (with documentary featurettes and commentaries), the nine *Animatrix* stories, and a disc called 'The Matrix Experience', including all trailers, music videos and various features on the philosophical and technological 'inspirations' for the series. Like the multimedia versions of the story, the DVD offered up exploratory routes into the *Matrix* as text and spectacle.

3 Studio logos and the aesthetics of memory and hype

1 This inspired the growth of a small cottage industry of independent design companies, typified by the launch of Pittard Sullivan in 1987 that used advancements in digital technology to create integrated graphics packages for the entertainment industry, responsible for television title sequences such as Warner Bros.' *ER* and for specialized graphics in animated features like Disney's *The Little Mermaid* (1989) (See 'Imagemakers' 1997).

2 Transformations in logo design were undertaken either by in-house design units such as The Idea Place (Warner Bros.) or by one of the proliferating number of graphic design boutiques servicing the contemporary motion picture business.

3 Following Lisa Kernan, I would suggest that logos and trailers offer a means of analysing the 'implied audiences rhetorically inscribed in Hollywood promotional texts' (Kernan 2004: 15). Within contemporary promotion, this has moved towards conceptions such as the 'intermedia audience' and the 'active listener', as my respective consideration of Paramount and Dolby will suggest.

4 I am concentrating here on the logos designed for the presentation of feature films, although a full logo history would have to include the various permutations of the Warner Bros. logo designed for television, animation, music and home entertainment.

5 While MGM introduced a poster-style lion in 1966, Paramount moved towards a blue abstract rock face under Gulf & Western in 1968. Meanwhile, Columbia dispensed with its famous Lady in 1975 in place of a graphic torch symbol ('MGM Gets New Logo' 1966).

6 In the studio era, this was especially the case in films that drew upon the entertainment industry as a field of reference. For example, in *Road to Utopia* (1946) Bob Hope and Bing Crosby interrupt the film with show business 'shtick'. Playing on his star persona as a live performer, Hope admires the Alaskan landscape, exclaiming to his travel companion: 'Look at that mountain!' With little response from Crosby, Hope goes on to pronounce: 'It may be a mountain to you, but it's bread and butter to me', at which point the Paramount logo appears over the snow-covered peak (see Cohan 1997).

7 This anecdote is mentioned as part of the bonus commentary on the *Indiana Jones* DVD box-set, released by Paramount in 2003. Spielberg's idea for the opening sequence of *Raiders* required the location team 'to find a mountain that looked like Paramount's'. Without computer generated imaging to create or finesse a resemblance, producer Frank Marshall found a suitable mountain likeness in Hawaii, an example of the island's profligate ability to provide 'global Hollywood' with serviceable backdrops.

8 Lisa Kernan argues that the 'defacement' of studio logos within contemporary trailer sequences can be traced to Gus Van Sant's remake of *Psycho* (1998), the Universal logo freezing and burning at the edges. While acknowledging that logo defacement may have occurred in earlier trailers, she suggests that 'this is the first one to influence subsequent trailer practice' (Kernan 2004: 267). *Star Trek: Insurrection* can be placed alongside *Psycho* on these terms. Released in the same month as Van Sant's film (December 1998), it provides a parallel case of digital logo embellishment.

9 According to Barry Litman, uncertainty is caused by the inability on the part of studios to predict consumer tastes, the instability of market shares from one year to the next, and the frequent rotation of industry leadership among top firms (Litman 1998: 44–67).

10 Describing the phosphorous green image of the Warner Bros. studio lot that opens *The Matrix*, Joshua Clover suggests that the corporate logo, in this case, draws attention to the changing nature of the contemporary film business. With Hollywood movies increasingly defined by digital and runaway production, Clover writes: 'The branding image used to be a last promise of the real before the celluloid dream began: *Here's the actual place where movies are made*. Even the premiere audiences for *The Matrix* had seen the previews and posters knew what the colour signified: *There are no places any more. Just code*' (Clover 2004: 76). If the film's concern with digital/brand simulation has led *The Matrix* to be

read as a prognosis of big-budget Hollywood filmmaking, this arguably begins with the studio logo itself.

11 This would become especially necessary in positioning DreamWorks against Pixar in the late 1990s and early 2000s, both studios projecting their corporate logos to claim imaginative and proprietary turf in the emerging digital animation market. According to Pixar Chairman, Steve Jobs, writing in 1996, 'We believe there are only two significant brands in the film industry: "Disney" and "Steven Spielberg". We would like to establish "Pixar" as the third' (Pixar 1996). This would stimulate brand battles in the trailer marketing of pictures that mirrored each other thematically, including *A Bug's Life* (Pixar) and *Antz* (DreamWorks), both released in 1998, and later *Finding Nemo* (Pixar 2003) and *Shark Tale* (DreamWorks 2004). Thanks to Russell Garnett for this observation.

4 Dolby and the unheard history of technical trademarks

1 According to the taxonomy of different 'listening modes' offered by Michael Chion, Dolby's trailer can be seen to draw on a principle of 'reduced listening'. Rather than 'causal' or 'semantic' listening that depend, respectively, on the gathering of information about a sound's source, or the interpretation of sound as a code or language, reduced listening 'takes the sound – verbal, played on an instrument, noises, or whatever – as itself the object to be observed instead of as a vehicle for something else' (Chion 1994: 29).

2 The rationale of the Progress Report was made clear in the preface: 'People are talking about Dolby Stereo. Over the past year in particular, it has gained remarkable acceptance from film producers, directors, theatre owners, reviewers – and audiences. As a result, Dolby Laboratories has prepared a Progress Report, both to update you on what has been happening with Dolby Stereo, and to answer many of the questions being asked about it' (Dolby 1978).

3 From its earliest development, Dolby required movie soundtracks to be 'encoded' using a particular recording process and played back or 'decoded' on specifically designed equipment.

4 The brand name of THX does not describe a sound format but instead a theatre standardization system. As a trademark licensed to theatres and manufacturers, the THX certificate identifies compliance with performance parameters for the playback environment established by Lucasfilm Ltd.

5 According to the Lanham Act of 1946, which established the basis of contemporary trademark law, the licensor of a trademark is required to supervise the activities of its licensees to assure customers that whatever goodwill might have accumulated around a trademark is maintained (Merges 2000). It is estimated that licensing Dolby's noise reduction technology is worth 35 per cent of the company's revenues (Rothman 1992).

6 In short, Dolby must always be used as an adjective; its logo must always be in black, white, gold or silver and be recognizable as a third-party trademark; and it should always match the correct 'Stereo', 'Surround', 'Digital' format being used.

7 Similar to my own interests, Sobchack is concerned with the means by which Dolby trailers visibly articulate and imagine sound as an expressive tendency of contemporary cinema. Her argument is phenomenological in approach; she provides a detailed analysis of the 'sonority of being' that each trailer works to produce. On these terms, Sobchack provides an incisive textual reading of how 'sound *hears* and then *imagines* itself temporally sounding'. I seek to anchor these concerns industrially, to consider how the Dolby trailers relate to particular trademark strategies and to wider corporate attempts to structure the contemporary entertainment environment.

8 In particular, digital sound was increasingly promoted in theatrical lobbies and pre-film trailer sequences. This was part of wider concessions given to theatrical advertising, both in terms of Hollywood's permanent marketing campaign (in the form of expanded trailers for coming attractions and exhibitor logos) and by the measure of space and screen time given to product advertising.

9 Dolby Digital Surround EX added a third surround channel to digital film sound, reproduced by the speaker array at the back of the theatre. This enabled greater use of front-to-back and back-to-front transitions, especially useful for creating the effect of spaceships flying over the audience. DTS would also introduce a 6.1 format using a centre surround channel, launched as 'extended surround' or DTS-ES.

10 THX has used creative visual effects in specific trailer variations, all based around the brand initials. For example, the trailer 'T2' was made in collaboration with the production team of *Terminator 2: Judgment Day* (1991), electronic impulses surrounding the brand initials followed by a crushing metallic explosion.

11 In industrial terms, Dolby Digital was sold in ways that bore a marked similarity to the positioning of Dolby Stereo in the late 1970s. Emphasis was placed on the fact that Dolby Digital was a creative means not an end, that it could be used for more than special or dramatic effects, that it didn't make obsolete existing cinema installations, and that it could help filmmakers and exhibitors 'enhance that very special experience of going to the movies'.

12 As a measure of cost, the price of upgrading to Dolby Digital Surround EX stood at $2,500 in 1998, compared with DTS-ES at $1,875.

5 Licensing the library: of archives and animation

1 This included a new family entertainment label created by Warner Bros. in 1993, launched with *Dennis the Menace*. Seeking to challenge Disney for the family market, the label was distinguished by a product logo featuring Bugs Bunny leaning against the WB crest (Moerk 1993).

2 The library holdings for studios in May 1996 were as follows: Universal (3,101 films), Sony (2,327), Fox (2,077), Orion (1,986), MGM/UA (1,523), Warner Bros. (1,102), Paramount (908) and Disney (548) (Klady 1996).

3 The Looney Tunes films performed modestly or poorly by comparison with immediate animation rivals at the domestic box office. While *Space Jam* grossed $90 million in 1996, *Toy Story* took $192 million the year before. Meanwhile, *Looney Tunes: Back in Action* grossed $21 million in 2003 compared with *Shrek 2*'s $441 million the year after. Although Warner Bros. animation lagged behind Disney, Pixar and DreamWorks in terms of box office revenue, it maintained a strategic brand presence in the wider competition for family-focused ancillary businesses, ranging from theme parks to video/DVD sell-through.

4 Interestingly, Nike did not associate itself with *Space Jam* despite the film originating from two of its brand commercials. According to Naomi Klein, Nike boycotted the co-branding bonanza of the film because it resented Jordan becoming a commercialized brand of his own. She suggests that Nike's misgivings about *Space Jam*, which it criticized as a pure merchandising vehicle, represented 'a historic moment in the branding of culture, completely inverting the traditionally fraught relationship between art and commerce: a shoe company and an ad agency huffing and puffing that a Hollywood movie would sully the purity of their commercials' (Klein 2000: 58).

5 Jordan's impact on the American economy was estimated by *Fortune* in 1998 to be $10 billion, much of this benefiting the companies Jordan endorsed, in particular that of Nike (LaFeber 2002).

6 Bugs Bunny himself had labelled this a 'corporate takeover' in the early 1990s, appearing in two short cartoons – *Blooper Bunny* (1991) and *Invasion of the Bunny Snatchers* (1992) – that would parody the new affability given to the Looney Tunes under the Time Warner regime. These cartoons were initially suppressed by Time Warner or otherwise buried in crowded cartoon schedules (Sandler 1998: 16–17).

7 So important had the retail giant's shelf space become by the early 2000s – selling $5 billion worth of DVDs and videos in 2003 (Epstein 2006: 216) – that *Looney Tunes: Back in Action* featured Wal-Mart in a parody of product placement, lampooning its appearance in the film but also framing it as a retail paradise – 'nice of Wal-Mart to provide Wal-Mart beverages for us saying Wal-Mart so many times'.

8 Together with closing its studio stores, Warner Bros. signed agreements with the world's largest regional theme park company, Premier Parks, to take over the running of its Movie World operations in Germany and Spain in 1999. This saw Warner Bros. begin to relinquish its stake in the direct operational management of theme environments, becoming instead a brand licensor.

9 VCR ownership climbed from 2.4 per cent of US households in 1980 to 70 per cent in 1989, while DVD ownership exploded from 0 to 50 per cent between 1997 and 2004.

10 This does not suggest an untrammelled relation with the past. As Barbara Klinger suggests, our ability to re-experience the past through the purchase of video and DVD is mediated by 'the power that contemporary context has on perceptions of the object', including the prospect of technologically *enhancing* texts and representational histories (Klinger 2006b: 55–90).

11 This echoes the prohibitive tone of a number of 'cease and desist' letters sent to online fan sites in 1995 and 1996, a struggle that emerged over sexually explicit fan creations of Warner Bros. cartoons that precipitated a legal assault for trademark infringement when they appeared on the Internet (Mikulak 1998).

12 Tom Shone suggests that the battle between Batman and the Joker in Tim Burton's film is largely about the management of hype: 'It is a PR war for the soul of Gotham City, and it resembles less the battle between two superhero colossi, than it does a presidential race, with two candidates endlessly finessing their public personae' (Shone 2004: 194).

13 Balides takes up a Foucauldian position in making this argument, pointing toward a discourse of economics that 'increasingly presumes to tell the truth of people's behaviours by establishing the framework in which those behaviours make sense'. As she suggests, however, 'this truth is contingent and can be unmade, that is, as long as we know how it was made' (2000: 160).

6 The sustained event: branding fantasies and the corporate blockbuster

1 The New Line cutbacks were part of a broader company move that would lead to 3 per cent of AOL Time Warner's total staff (about 85,000 worldwide) losing their jobs (Klein 2003).

2 While New Line reaped all revenue from domestic release and 50 per cent from overseas release, *Lord of the Rings* did have significant implications for the independent financiers that signed agreements with New Line, including large minimum guarantees that would rise if the franchise became a worldwide success (Groves and Dawtrey 2002).

3 Global promotion was linked to the co-ordinated day-and-date release of *Fellowship of the Ring* in December 2001. The film opened simultaneously in over 10,000 theatres worldwide, the only exceptions being Italy and Japan where the film opened in January and March 2002, respectively. The former was to avoid a direct clash with *Harry Potter and the Philosopher's Stone,* and the latter was to raise visibility of the trilogy in a country where Tolkien's work was little known.

4 Significantly, the ardent fan base of *Lord of the Rings* gave rise to the trailers being heavily advertised in and of themselves, positioned as cinematic attractions throughout the theatrical, Internet and DVD life of the franchise.

5 *Philosopher's Stone* opened domestically on 16 November 2001 in 3,672 theatres, compared with *Fellowship* that opened on 19 December in 3,359 theatres. In terms of worldwide box-office gross, *Philosopher's Stone* made $976 million compared with *Fellowship* that made $870 million (Source: boxofficemojo/com/showdowns).

6 *Chamber of Secrets* opened domestically on 15 November 2002 in 3,682 theatres, compared with *The Two Towers* that opened on 18 December in 3,622 theatres. In terms of worldwide box-office gross, *Chamber of Secrets* made $877 million compared with *The Two Towers* that made $976 million. Therefore, while *The Two Towers* capitalized on the success of the first instalment, *Chamber of Secrets*, despite its phenomenal performance, did not perform as well, taking almost $100 million less than *Philosopher's Stone* (Source: boxofficemojo/com/showdowns).

7 It is in this respect that both franchise films were inclined to expand action scenes from the original books to position themselves for a core teenage audience and establish a basis for video games (Thompson 2003).

8 This was especially necessary considering that AOL Time Warner's early financial ills were blamed in certain quarters on expensive New Line flops like *Little Nicky* (2000) and *Town and Country* (2001).

7 'The world is our audience': branding entertainment space

1 The demise of theatrical exhibition is often related to the anticipation of digital distribution and, more concretely, to the shortened time-spans that blockbusters are run on the big screen. Indeed, declining theatrical runs and disadvantageous cost percentages for screening blockbusters lay behind the substantial losses incurred by America's four biggest theatre chains (Loews, Regal, Carmike, AMC) in the early 2000s, leading to a series of screen closures (Shone 2004: 290).

2 While the number of screens doubled in the nineties, the number of *sites* in the UK increased by only 14 per cent, rising from 655 to 748.

3 In terms of theatrical admissions, the United Kingdon saw sharp increases in the late 1990s, rising from 135 million in 1998 to 178 million in 2003 (the highest figure since 1971). Accordingly, gross box office takings rose from £500 million to £786 million between 1998 and 2003 (Hopkins 2003).

4 This gave rise to a new cinema chain in the UK called Vue, its owner SBC International Cinemas formed in 1998 by former Warner International and UCI executives.

5 In the United Kingdom, this is represented by changing government policy with regard to city centres, levied in Planning Permission Guidance Note 6 that requires planning authorities 'to determine planning applications in such a manner that the city centre must be considered before an out of town site'.

6 Drawing upon Bourdieu, Featherstone suggests that 'lifestyle' is linked to broad cultural developments where status groups are no longer fixed, where markets have become increasingly segmented, and where a new class has emerged (the 'new petite bourgeoisie') occupied centrally with the production and dissemination of consumer culture imagery and information. This class is particularly associated with those in advertising, marketing and public relations industries who seek to expand and legitimate their tastes and dispositions within the social field.

7 Both Gunwharf Quays and the Cornerhouse were designed by local architects. Typical of such developments, Warner Village was provided with an empty concrete shell in which to fit their equipment and specifications, with rent agreed on a scale related to the number of bars and units leased.

8 The sale of government-owned land created a political impetus for benefits to be returned to the community, especially when compared to the United States where defence sites are offered to the local community free before any sale.

9 For an analysis of Cineplex Odeon's strategies of differentiation in the 1980s as one of the pioneering North American multiplex operators, see Gomery 1990. For a broader consideration of differentiation as it relates to shopping malls in Britain, see Miller *et al.* 1998.

10 Looney Tunes characters have been used according to the situational context of theatrical venues. In regional terms, particular characters are often used according to ideas about national preference. In Germany, for example, Warner Bros. use the Tasmanian Devil with more frequency in theatrical brand displays, while in Japan the character of Tweetie Pie is deemed more popular. The main concern, however, is that WBIT creates 'a fairly consistent package' in terms of regional theatrical branding ('Warner Village Rising Star' 2000).

11 Sometimes, Warner Village undertook strategies of its own to allay national fears of multiplex encroachment. In Italy, for example, Warner Village organized a series of family- and child-based initiatives at its venues in Verona and Bari to incorporate the multiplex into local communities, designed to stave off the perception that Warner was, according to the head of marketing for Warner Village Italia, 'some big corporate entity coming into the area' (Goodfellow 1999).

12 Togo Avenue, Sirius Avenue and Caen Marché all evoke the international flow of peoples and cargos through the port's past and present. While Sirius was a ship in the first convoy of convict ships to sail from Portsmouth to Sydney, Admiral Togo was a Japanese naval officer who lived in Portsmouth in the early 1900s. Meanwhile, Caen Marché evokes Portsmouth's twin city in France (to which cross-channel ferries sail daily) and where, at Gunwharf, occasional markets of French produce and arts and crafts are held.

Bibliography

All unpaginated news and trade press articles were examined in clippings files at the Margaret Herrick Library, Los Angeles, and at Portsmouth and Nottingham Central Libraries.

(1999) '21st century chat room', *Advertising Age*, 20 September: 76.

Aaker, D. and Joachimsthaler, E. (1999) 'The lure of global branding', *Harvard Business Review*, 77(6): 137–43.

Acland, C. R. (2003) *Screen Traffic: Movies, Multiplexes, and Global Culture*, Durham: Duke University Press.

Adams, R. (2003) 'Selling the soft and fuzzy stuff', *Guardian*, 1 November: 34.

Aksoy, A. and Robins, K. (1992) 'Hollywood for the twenty first century: global competition for critical mass in image markets', *Cambridge Journal of Economics*, 16: 1–22.

Allen, I. (1983) 'Exhibs, public will soon eye Dolby Promos', *Variety*, 12 January: 19.

Allen, M. (1998) 'From *Bwana Devil* to *Batman Forever*: technology in contemporary Hollywood cinema', in S. Neale and M. Smith (eds) *Contemporary Hollywood Cinema*, London: Routledge.

—— (2003a) 'Talking about a revolution: the blockbuster as industrial advertisement', in J. Stringer (ed.) *Movie Blockbusters*, London: Routledge.

—— (2003b) *Contemporary US Cinema*, Harlow: Longman.

Allen, R. (1999) 'Home alone together: Hollywood and the "family film"', in M. Stokes and R. Maltby (eds) *Identifying Hollywood Audiences: Cultural Identity and the Movies*, London: British Film Institute.

Altman, R. (1992) 'The material heterogeneity of recorded sound', in R. Altman (ed.) *Sound Theory Sound Practice*, New York: Routledge.

Anderson, C. (1994) *Hollywood TV: The Studio System in the Fifties*, Austin: University of Texas Press.

AOL Time Warner (2000) *Annual Report*.

Appadurai, A. (1990) 'Disjuncture and difference in the global cultural economy', *Public Culture*, 2(2): 1–24.

Arvidsson, A. (2005) 'Brands: a critical perspective', *Journal of Consumer Culture*, 5(2): 235–58.

Austin, T. (2002) *Hollywood, Hype and Audiences: Selling and Watching Popular Film in the 1990s*, Manchester: Manchester University Press.

Bakker, G. (2005) 'Stars and stories: how films became branded products', in J. Sedgewick and M. Pokorny (eds) *An Economic History of Film*, London: Routledge.

Balides, C. (2000) 'Jurassic post-Fordism: tall tales of economics in the theme park', *Screen*, 41(2): 139–60.

Balnaves, M., Donald, J. and Hemelryk Donald, S. (2001) *The Global Media Atlas*, London: British Film Institute.

Barker, M. (2004) 'News, reviews, interviews and other ancillary materials – A critique and research proposal', *Scope: An Online Journal of Film Studies*. Available http://www.scope.nottingham.ac.uk/ (accessed 6 June 2004).

Barker, M. and Mathijs, E. (eds) (forthcoming) *Watching The Lord of the Rings: World Audiences for the Film Adaptation*, New York: Peter Lang.

Barry, A. (1993) 'Weight watchers', *New Yorker*, 16 August.

Bart, P. (1999) *The Gross: The Hits, the Flops – the Summer that Ate Hollywood*, New York: St Martin's Press.

—— (2001) 'What hath Rowling wrought?', *Variety*, 26 November: 5.

Batchelor, A. (1998) 'Brands as financial assets', in S. Hart and J. Murphy (eds) *Brands: The New Wealth Creators*, Basingstoke: Palgrave.

Baudrillard, J. (1988) 'The system of objects', in M. Poster (ed.) *Jean Baudrillard: Selected Writings*, Stanford: Stanford University Press.

Bing, J. and Dunkley, C. (2002) 'Kiddy litter rules H'wood', *Variety*, 8 January: 1.

Blevins, J. L. (2004) 'Battle of the online brands: Disney loses internet portal war', *Television & New Media*, 5(3): 247–71.

Boddy, W. (2002) 'New media as old media: television', in D. Harries (ed.) *The New Media Book*, London: British Film Institute.

—— (2004) 'Interactive television and advertising form in contemporary US television', in L. Spigel and J. Olsson (eds) *Television After TV: Essays on a Medium in Transition*, Duke: Durham University Press.

Bordwell, D., Staiger, J. and Thompson, K. (1985) *The Classical Hollywood Cinema: Film Style and Mode of Production to 1960*, London: Routledge.

Bowser, E. (1994) *The Transformation of Cinema, 1907–15*, Berkeley: University of California Press.

Boyer, M. Christine (1994) *The City of Collective Memory: Its Historical Imaginary and Architectural Entertainments*, Cambridge: MIT Press.

Bradshaw, P. (2004) 'Ad fab', *Guardian* (Review), 14 November: 14.

Brogliatti, B. (2003) 'Warner Bros. logos', E-mail (20 September).

Bruck, C. (1994) *The Master of the Game: Steve Ross and the Creation of Time Warner*, New York: Penguin.

Buckland, W. (2003) 'The role of the auteur in the age of the blockbuster', in J. Stringer (ed.) *Movie Blockbusters*, London: Routledge.

(2001) 'Building brand America', *Business Week*. Available online at http://www.businessweek.com (accessed 10 December 2003).

Bukatman, S. (1998) 'Zooming out: the end of offscreen space', in J. Lewis (ed.) *The New American Cinema*, Durham: Duke University Press.

Cagle, J. (2002) 'When Harry met Scary', *Time*, 11 November: 82.

Caldwell, J. T. (2004) 'Convergence television: aggregating form and repurposing content in the culture of conglomeration', in L. Spigel and J. Olsson (eds) *Television After TV*, Durham: Duke University Press.

—— (2006) 'Critical industrial practice: branding, repurposing, and the migratory patterns of industrial texts', *Television & New Media*, 7(2): 99–134.

Carney, C. and Misiroglu, G. (1996) *Space Jammin': Michael and Bugs Hit the Screen*, Nashville: Warner Bros. and Rutledge Hill Press.

Carver, B. (1998a) 'Alliance of rivals lord over Rings', *Variety*, 31 August: 1.

—— (1998b) 'New line school o'seas pic partners', *Variety*, 12 July: 7.

Carver, B. and Cox, D. (1998) 'New line: sibling revelry', *Variety*, 9 March: 61.

Chin, B. and Gray, J. (2003) '"One ring to rule them all": pre-viewers and pre-texts of the *Lord of the Rings* films', *Intensities: The Journal of Cult Media*. Available online at http://www.cultmedia.com/issue2 (accessed 20 January 2004).

Chion, M. (1994) *Audio-Vision: Sound on Screen*, trans. Claudia Gorbman, New York: Columbia University Press.

Christensen, J. (2003) 'The Time Warner conspiracy: *JFK, Batman*, and the manager theory of Hollywood', *Critical Inquiry*, 28(3): 591–617.

Church Gibson, P. (2005) 'Fashion, fetish and spectacle: *The Matrix* dresses up and down', in S. Gillis (ed.) *The Matrix Trilogy: Cyberpunk Reloaded*, London: Wallflower Press.

Cloud, J. (2002) 'Star Trek Inc.', *Time*, 23 December: 62–3.

Clover, J. (2004) *The Matrix*, London: British Film Institute.

Cohan, S. (1997) 'Almost like being at home: showbiz culture and Hollywood road trips in the 1940s and 1950s', in S. Cohen and I. R. Hark (eds) *The Road Movie Book*, London: Routledge.

Collender, G. (2002) 'From Portsmouth with love', *The News* (Portsmouth), 20 November: 3.

Collette, L. (1998) 'The wages of synergy: integration into broadcast networking by Warner Brothers, Disney, and Paramount', in B. Litman (ed.) *The Motion Picture Mega-Industry*, Boston: Allen and Bacon.

Collins, J. (1995) *Architectures of Excess: Cultural Life in the Information Age*, New York: Routledge.

—— (ed.) (2002) *High-Pop: Making Culture into Popular Entertainment*, Oxford: Blackwell.

Comaroff, J. and Comaroff, J. L. (2001) 'Millennial capitalism: first thoughts on a second coming', in J. Comaroff and J. L. Comaroff (eds) *Millennial Capitalism and the Culture of Neoliberalism*, Durham: Duke University Press.

Connor, J. D. (2000) '"The projections": allegories of industrial crisis in neoclassical Hollywood', *Representations*, 71: 48–70.

Cook, D. (2000) *Lost Illusions: American Cinema in the Shadow of Watergate and Vietnam, 1970–79*, Berkeley: University of California Press.

Coombe, R. (1998) *The Cultural Life of Intellectual Properties: Authorship, Appropriation and the Law*, Durham: Duke University Press.

Corrigan, T. (1998) 'Auteurs and the New Hollywood', in J. Lewis (ed.) *The New American Cinema*, Durham: Duke University Press.

Cox, D. (1998) 'WB tries to get the bugs out', *Variety*, 4 May: 1.

Crafton, D. (1998) 'The view from termite terrace: caricature and parody in Warner Bros. animation', in K. Sandler (ed.) *Reading the Rabbit: Explorations in Warner Bros. Animation*, New Brunswick: Rutgers University Press.

Crispin Miller, M. (1990) 'Advertising: end of story', in M. Crispin Miller (ed.) *Seeing Through Movies*, New York: Pantheon.

Cronin, A. (2000) *Advertising and Consumer Citizenship: Gender, Images and Rights*, London: Routledge.

Curtin, M. (1996) 'On edge: culture industries in the neo-network era', in R. Ohmann (ed.) *Making and Selling Culture*, Hanover: Wesleyan University Press.

Danan, M. (1995) 'Marketing the Hollywood blockbuster in France', *Journal of Popular Film and Television*, 23(2): 131–40.

Davilá, A. (2001) *Latinos, Inc: The Marketing and Making of a People*, Berkeley: University of California Press.

Davis, S. (2002) 'Brand asset management: how business can profit from the power of brand', *Journal of Consumer Marketing*, 19(4): 351–8.

Dawson, M. (2003) *The Consumer Trap: Big Business Marketing in American Life*, Champaign: University of Illinois Press.

Dawtrey, A. (2001) 'Will Lord ring new line bell?', *Variety*, 21 May: 1.

deCordova, R. (1994) 'The Mickey in Macy's window: childhood, consumerism, and Disney animation', in E. Smoodin (ed.) *Disney Discourse*, New York: Routledge.

Desser, D. and Jowett, G. (eds) (2000) *Hollywood Goes Shopping*, Minneapolis: Minnesota University Press.

De Vany, A. (2004) *Hollywood Economics: How Extreme Uncertainty Shapes the Film Industry*, London: Routledge.

Dick, B. (2001) *Engulfed: The Death of Paramount Pictures and the Birth of Corporate Hollywood*, Lexington: University Press of Kentucky.

Dolby (1978) 'Dolby stereo: A progress report', *Variety*, 16 August: 7.

Dolby (2000) 'Explore our World' (DVD). San Francisco: Dolby Laboratories.

Dolby (2003a) 'Licensing'. Available online at http://dolbysearch.dolby.com/lic/ (accessed 13 August 2004).

Dolby (2003b) 'Trademark'. Available online at http://dolbysearch.dolby.com/tm/ (accessed 13 August 2004).

Du Gay, P. and Pryke, M. (eds) (2002) *Cultural Economy*, London: Sage.

Dunkley, C. (2002) 'Paramount updates logo for 90th anniversary', *Daily Variety*, 1 March.

Dyer, R. (2002) *Only Entertainment* (2nd edition), London: Routledge.

Eckert, C. (1978) 'The Carole Lombard in Macy's window', *Quarterly Review of Film Studies*, 3(1): 1–21.

Edgerton, G. (2002) 'The multiplex: the modern American motion picture theater as message', in I. R. Hark (ed.) *Exhibition, The Film Reader*, London: Routledge.

Eisenberg, D. (2002) 'It's an ad, ad, ad, ad world', *Time*, 2 September: 38–41.

Eisner, M., with Schwartz, T. (1998) *Work in Progress*, New York: Hyperion.

Eller, C. (2001) 'Warner marketing "Potter" with care', *Los Angeles Times*, 5 November: C5.

Eller, C. and Saylor, M. (1999) 'New line cinema is still shopping the supermarket', *Los Angeles Times*, 23 April: C6.

Elsaesser, T. (2002) 'The blockbuster: everything connects, but not everything goes', in J. Lewis (ed.) *The End of Cinema as We Know It: American Film in the 1990s*, London: Pluto Press.

Epstein, E. J. (2006) *The Big Picture: Money and Power in Hollywood*, New York: Random House.

Estates Gazette (1998) 4 July.

Eyles, A. (1998) 'The last remaining sites for UK plexes', *Variety*, 15 June: 49.

Fahey, A. (1999) 'The odd couple', *Hollywood Reporter*, 7 June: 37.

Featherstone, M. (1991) *Consumer Culture and Postmodernism*, London: Sage.

Finnigan, D. (2001a) 'Harry and Rings vie for toy kingdoms', *Brandweek*, 19 February: 8.

—— (2001b) 'Hollywood gets humble', *Brandweek*, 11 June: 29.

Flint, J. (1995) 'Netlets bring new look to small screen', *Variety* (television), 11 December: 4, 14.

Frank, T. (2000) *One Market Under God: Extreme Capitalism, Market Populism, and the End of Economic Democracy*, New York: Anchor Books.

French, P. (2002) 'That's another fine myth ...', *Observer Review*, 15 December: 7.

Friedman, T. (2003) '*Cast Away* and the contradictions of product placement'. Available online at http://www.nc.gsu.edu/~jouejf/castaway (accessed 5 April 2004).

Frow, J. (2002) 'Signature and brand', in J. Collins (ed.) *High-Pop: Making Culture into Popular Entertainment*, Oxford: Blackwell.

Gaines, J. (1991) *Contested Culture: The Image, the Voice, and the Law*, Chapel Hill: University of North Carolina Press.

—— (2000) 'Dream/factory', in C. Gledhill and L. Williams (eds) *Reinventing Film Studies*, London: Arnold.

Gibbons, F. (2002) '*Lord of the Rings* set to win round two of blockbuster bout', *Guardian*, 12 December: 5.

Gillis, S. (ed.) (2005) *The Matrix Trilogy: Cyberpunk Reloaded*, London: Wallflower Press.

Giroux, H. (1995) 'Memory and pedagogy in the "Wonderful world of Disney"', in E. Bell, L. Haas and L. Sells (eds) *From Mouse to Mermaid: The Politics of Film, Gender and Culture*, Bloomington: Indiana University Press.

—— (1999) *The Mouse that Roared*, Lanham: Rowman & Littlefield.

Gitlin, T. (2002) *Media Unlimited: How the Torrent of Images and Sounds Overwhelms Our Lives*, New York: Henry Holt.

Gobé M. (2001) *Emotional Branding*, Oxford: Windsor.

Gomery, D. (1990) 'Building a movie theater giant: the rise of Cineplex Odeon', in T. Balio (ed.) *Hollywood in the Age of Television*, Boston: Unwin Hyman.

Goodfellow, M. (1999) 'When in Rome …', *Screen International*, 12 February: 11.

Grainge, P. (1999) 'Reclaiming heritage: colourization, culture wars and the politics of nostalgia', *Cultural Studies*, 13(4): 621–38.

—— (2000) 'Advertising the archive: nostalgia and the (post)national imaginary', *American Studies*, 41(2/3): 137–57.

—— (2002) *Monochrome Memories: Nostalgia and Style in Retro America*, Westport, CT: Praeger.

Graser, M. (2002) 'Land that brand!', *Daily Variety*, 15 November: 25.

—— (2004) 'Pic promos face perplexing plight', *Variety*, 4 April: 9.

Grove, M. (1996) 'WB is animated about catching up with Disney', *Hollywood Reporter*, 26 June.

—— (2003) 'All work is play for WB licensing guru', *Variety*, 9 June: B2.

Groves, D. and Dawtrey, A. (2002) 'Hogwarts and hobbits in global grab', *Variety*, 11 February: 1–2.

Guback, T. (1987) 'The evolution of the motion picture theater business in the 1980s', *The Journal of Communication*, 37(2): 60–77.

Gunning, T. (1990) 'The cinema of attractions: early film, its spectators and the avant-garde', in T. Elsaesser (ed.) *Early Cinema: Space, Frame, Narrative*, London: British Film Institute.

Gunther, M. (2000) 'These guys want it all', *Fortune*, 7 February: 29–33.

(1997) 'Gunwharf/HMS Vernon – the most important opportunity of our generation', *Portsmouth Society News*, January: 3.

Handy, B. (1996) '101 movie tie-ins', *Time*, 2 December: 78–80.

Hannerz, U. (1990) 'Cosmopolitans and locals in world culture', in M. Featherstone (ed.) *Global Culture*, London: Sage.

Hanson, S. (2000) 'Spoilt for choice? Multiplexes in the 90s', in R. Murphy (ed.) *British Cinema of the 90s*, London: Routledge.

Harris, D. and Dawtrey, A. (2001) 'Hobbit huzzah', *Variety*, 29 November: 25.

Harris, D. and Hayes, D. (2001) 'WB revs up movie machine', *Variety*, 7 May: 1.

Hart, S. and Murphy, J. (eds) (1998) *Brands: The New Wealth Creators*, Basingstoke: Palgrave.

Harvey, D. (1993) 'From space to place and back again: reflections on the condition of postmodernity', in J. Bird, B. Curtis, T. Putnam, G. Robertson and L. Tickner (eds) *Mapping the Futures: Local Cultures, Global Change*, London: Routledge.

Haug, W. (1986) *Critique of Commodity Aesthetics*, London: Polity Press.

Hay, J. (1997) 'Piecing together what remains of the cinematic city', in D. Clarke (ed.) *The Cinematic City*, New York: Routledge.

Hays, S. (2003) 'Entertainment advertising moves the needle'. Available online at http://www.imediaconnection.com (accessed 6 April 2004).

Hazelton, J. (1998) 'Eyes wide shut?', *Screen International*, 16 January: 18.

Heath, J. and Potter, A. (2005) *The Rebel Sell: Why the Culture Can't be Jammed*, Chichester: Capstone.

Hesmondhalgh, D. (2002) *The Cultural Industries*, London: Sage.

Hills, M. (2006) 'Realising the cult blockbuster: *The Lord of the Rings* Fandom and residual/emergent cult status in "the mainstream"', in E. Mathijs (ed.) *The Lord of the Rings: Popular Culture in Global Context*, London: Wallflower Press.

Hindes, A. (1998a) 'Universal finally says yes to Dolby format', *Variety*. Available online at http://www.variety.com/ (accessed 8 March 2004).

—— (1998b) 'Theaters surround Dolby ex', *Variety*. Available online at http://www.variety.com/ (accessed 8 March 2004).

—— (1998c) 'Dolby is digital leader', *Variety*. Available online at http://www.variety.com/ (accessed 8 March 2004).

Holson, L. (2006) 'Caught on film: a growing unease in Hollywood', *New York Times*. Available online at http://www.nytimes.com/2006/08/19/business/media (accessed 23 August 2006).

Holson, L. and Lyman, R. (2002) 'In Warner Brothers' strategy, a movie is now a product line', *New York Times*, 11 February: C1, 13.

Holt, J. (2001) 'In deregulation we trust: the synergy of politics and industry in Reagan-era Hollywood', *Film Quarterly*, 55(2): 22–30.

—— (2003) 'Vertical vision: deregulation, industrial economy and prime-time design', in M. Jancovich and J. Lyons (eds) *Quality Popular Television*, London: British Film Institute.

Hopkins, N. (2003) 'Bit players in the film world buys Warner Village', *The Times*, 14 May.

Horak, J. C. (2001) 'The Hollywood history business', in J. Lewis (ed.) *The End of Cinema as We Know it: American Film in the 1990s*, London: Pluto Press.

Hozic, A. (2000) 'Hollywood goes on sale: or, what do the violet eyes of Elizabeth Taylor have to do with the "cinema of attractions"?', in D. Desser and G. Jowett (eds) *Hollywood Goes Shopping*, Minneapolis: Minnesota University Press.

—— (2001) *Hollyworld: Space, Power, and Fantasy in the American Economy*, Ithaca: Cornell University Press.

Huffstutter, P. J. (2001) 'Overload of the rings?' *Los Angeles Times*, 13 December: A34.

Ilott, T. (1993) 'Multiplexing still perplexing', *Variety*, 4 January: 52.

(1997) 'Imagemakers', *Variety*, 2 June: 41–4.

Jancovich, M., Faire, L. and Stubbings, S. (2003) *The Place of the Audience: Cultural Geographies of Film Consumption*, London: British Film Institute.

Jaramillo, D. J. (2002) 'The family racket: AOL Time Warner, HBO, *The Sopranos*, and the construction of a quality brand', *Journal of Communication Inquiry*, 21(1): 59–75.

Jasper, B. (1998) 'A message from Dolby president', *Dolby News*, Fall: 1.

Jenkins, H. (1995) 'Historical poetics', in J. Hollows and M. Jancovich (eds) *Approaches to Popular Film*, Manchester: Manchester University Press.

—— (2004) 'The cultural logic of media convergence', *International Journal of Cultural Studies*, 7(1): 33–43.

—— (2006) *Convergence Culture*, New York: New York University Press.

Kapferer, J. N. (2001) *Reinventing the Brand*, London: Kogan Page.

Karrh, J. A., Brittain McKee, K. and Pardun, C. J. (2003) 'Practitioners' evolving views on product placement effectiveness', *Journal of Advertising Research*, 42(2): 138–50.

Keil, C. (2001) '"American Cinema" in the 1990s and beyond', in J. Lewis (ed.) *The End of Cinema as We Know it: American Film in the 1990s*, London: Pluto Press.

Kendrick, J. (2005) 'Aspect ratios and Joe Six-packs: home theater enthusiasts' battle to legitimize the DVD experience', *The Velvet Light Trap*, 52(Fall): 58–70.

Kernan, L. (2004) *Coming Attractions: Reading American Movie Trailers*, Austin: University of Texas Press.

Kim, H. (2002) 'Madison + Vine: Madison melds pitches and content', *Advertising Age*, 7 October: 1.

Kim, K. (1995) 'Spreading the net: the consolidation process of large transnational advertising agencies in the 1980s and early 1990s', *International Journal of Advertising*, 14(3): 195–217.

King, G. (2000) *Spectacular Narratives: Hollywood in the Age of the Blockbuster*, London: I.B. Tauris.

Kirkpatrick, D. (2002) 'A test of synergy', *New York Times*, 11 November: B1, 6.

Klady, L. (1996) 'Big boys anteing up to get library cards', *Variety*, 13 May: 13, 16.

—— (1999) 'Hollywood suffers severe shell shock', *Variety*, 11 March: 1.

Klein, A. (2003) *Stealing Time: Steve Case, Jerry Levin and the Collapse of AOL Time Warner*, New York: Simon and Schuster.

Klein, N. (2000) *No Logo: Taking Aim at the Brand Bullies*, London: Flamingo.

Kleinhans, C. (1998) 'Independent features: hopes and dreams', in J. Lewis (ed.) *The New American Cinema*, Durham: Duke University Press.

Klinger, B. (1998) 'The new media aristocrats: home theater and the domestic film experience', *The Velvet Light Trap*, 42: 4–19.

—— (2006a) 'What is cinema today? Home viewing, new technologies and DVD', in L. R. Williams and M. Hammond (eds) *Contemporary American Cinema*, London: McGraw-Hill.

—— (2006b) *Beyond the Multiplex: Cinema, New Technologies, and the Home*, Berkeley: University of California Press.

Krämer, P. (1998a) 'Would you take your child to see this film? The cultural and social work of the family-adventure movie', in S. Neale and M. Smith (eds) *Contemporary Hollywood Cinema*, London: Routledge.

—— (1998b) 'Post-classical Hollywood', in J. Hill and P. Church Gibson (eds) *The Oxford Guide to Film Studies*, Oxford: Oxford University Press.

—— (2006) 'Disney and family entertainment', in L. R. Williams and M. Hammond (eds) *Contemporary American Cinema*, London: McGraw-Hill.

Krueger, R. (1990) 'Cellar sales hit high returns', *Screen International*, 21 July: 7–8.

LaFeber, W. (2002) *Michael Jordan and the New Global Capitalism*, New York: W.W. Norton.

(1997) 'Landmark millennium project', *Portsmouth City Council News Brief*, 10 April.

Langer, B. (2004) 'The business of branded enchantment', *Journal of Consumer Culture*, 4(2): 251–77.

Lash, S. and Urry, J. (1994) *Economies of Signs and Space*, London: Sage.

Leadbetter, C. and Oakley, K. (1999) *The Independents: Britain's New Cultural Entrepreneurs*, London: Demos.

Leiss, W., Kline, S. and Jhally, S. (1986) *Social Communication in Advertising*, London: Routledge.

Lelyveld, N. (2002) 'Hollywood sign caught in secession tug of war', *Los Angeles Times*, 6 May: A1, A16.

Levin, G. (1995) 'Making a name for yourself', *Variety* (television), 11 December: 3, 22.

—— (1996) 'The branding of animation', *Variety*, 24 June: 86, 90.

Lewis, D. and Bridger, D. (2001) *The Soul of the New Consumer*, London: Nicholas Brealey.

Lewis, J. (1998) 'Money matters: Hollywood in the corporate era', in J. Lewis (ed.) *The New American Cinema*, Durham: Duke University Press.

—— (2003) 'Following the money in America's sunniest company town: some notes on the political economy of the Hollywood blockbuster', in J. Stringer (ed.) *Movie Blockbusters*, London: Routledge.

Lippman, J. (1996) 'Bugs, Michael team up in ultimate commercial movie', *Wall Street Journal*, 24 September: B1, B10.

—— (2001) 'Turning books into film franchises', *Wall Street Journal*, 16 November: 24.

Litman, B. (1998) *The Motion Picture Mega-Industry*, Boston: Allen and Bacon.

Littleton, C. and Kit, Z. (2002) 'Fraser in action with Warners on Looney revival', *Hollywood Reporter*, 11 June: 1, 64.

(2003) 'Looney 101' Warner Bros. Available online at http://www.warnerbros.com/looneytunesbackinaction/prodnotes.html (accessed 8 January 2005).

Lukk, T. (1997) *Movie Marketing: Opening the Picture and Giving it Legs*, Los Angeles: Silman-James Press.

Lury, C. (1993) *Cultural Rights*, London: Routledge.

—— (1996) *Consumer Culture*, Cambridge: Polity Press.

—— (2004) *Brands: The Logos of the Global Economy*, London: Routledge.

Lury, C. and Warde, A. (1997) 'Investments in the imaginary consumer', in M. Nava, A. Blake, I. MacRury and B. Richards (eds) *Buy This Book: Studies in Advertising and Consumption*, London: Routledge.

Lyman, R. (2001) 'Gambling on a film fantasy', *New York Times*, 12 December: E1, 5.

—— (2002) '*Harry Potter* to battle *Lord of the Rings*, again', *New York Times*, 21 October: E3.

Lyons, C. (2000) 'Rebels without a pause', *Variety*, 11 September: 48.

—— (2002) 'Central Park jazzed for AOL/TW home', *Daily Variety*, 30 May: 1–2.

Lyons, J. (2004) *Selling Seattle: Representing Contemporary Urban America*, London: Wallflower Press.

McChesney, R. (1999) *Rich Media, Poor Democracy*, Champaign: University of Illinois Press.

McClintock, P. (2005) 'Kids get muscled by marketers', *Variety*, 20 June: 8–9.

McFall, L. (2002) 'Advertising, persuasion and the culture/economy dualism', in P. Du Gay and M. Pryke (eds) *Cultural Economy*, London: Sage.

—— (2004) *Advertising: A Cultural Economy*, London: Sage.

McGuigan, J. (2004) *Rethinking Cultural Policy*, Maidenhead: Open University Press.

McKinley, F. (2002) Personal interview with author, 12 September.

McMurria, J. (2003) 'Long-format TV: globalisation and network branding in a multi-channel era', in M. Jancovich and J. Lyons (eds) *Quality Popular Television*, London: British Film Institute.

McNamara, M. (2001) 'Can fantasy take flight?', *Los Angeles Times*, 11 November: 32.

Mallory, M. (1996) 'Unified libraries', *Variety*, 1 October.

Maltby, R. (1998) 'Nobody knows anything: post-classical historiography and consolidated entertainment', in S. Neale and M. Smith (eds) *Contemporary Hollywood Cinema*, London: Routledge.

—— (2003) *Hollywood Cinema* (2nd edition), Oxford: Blackwell.

Marshall, P. D. (2002) 'The new intertextual commodity', in D. Harries (ed.) *The New Media Book*, London: British Film Institute.

Maslin, J. (1996) 'Icons meet: Bugs, Daffy and Jordan', *New York Times*, 15 November.

Mathijs, E. (2006) 'Popular culture in global context: The *Lord of the Rings* phenomenon', in E. Mathijs (ed.) *The Lord of the Rings: Popular Culture in Global Context*, London: Wallflower Press.

The Matrix Revisited (2004) *The Ultimate Matrix Collection*, DVD recording, Warner Bros.

Meehan, E. (1992) 'Holy commodity fetish, Batman!: the political economy of a commercial intertext', in R. E. Pearson and W. Uricchio (eds) *The Many Lives of the Batman: Critical Approaches to a Superhero and his Media*, New York: Routledge.

Mellencamp, P. (2001) 'The zen of masculinity – rituals of heroism in *The Matrix*', in J. Lewis (ed.) *The End of Cinema as We Know It: American Film in the 1990s*, London: Pluto Press.

Merges, R. P. (2000) 'One hundred years of solicitude: intellectual property law, 1900–2000', *California Law Review*, 88(6): 2187–240.

(1966) 'MGM gets new logo', *Variety*, 21 September.

Mikulak, W. (1996) 'The canonization of Warner Brothers cartoons, or how Bugs Bunny came to the Museum of Modern Art', *Journal of American Culture*, 19(1): 21–8.

—— (1998) 'Time Warner: who owns *Looney Tunes*?', in K. Sandler (ed.) *Reading the Rabbit: Explorations in Warner Bros. Animation*, New Brunswick: Rutgers University Press.

Miller, D., Jackson, P., Thrift, N., Holbrook, B. and Rowlands, M. (1998) *Shopping, Place and Identity*, London: Routledge.

Miller, T., Govil, N., McMurria, J. and Maxwell, R. (2001) *Global Hollywood*, London: British Film Institute.

Moerk, C. (1993) 'Family volume at WB', *Daily Variety*, 14 May: 3.

Moor, E. (2003) 'Branded spaces: the scope of new marketing', *Journal of Consumer Culture*, 3(1): 39–60.

Mottram, S. (1998) 'Branding the corporation', in S. Hart and J. Murphy (eds) *Brands: The New Wealth Creators*, Basingstoke: Palgrave.

Murphy, A. D. (1995) 'WB library home after 40 years', *Hollywood Reporter*, 25 September.

Murphy, J. (1998) 'What is branding?', in S. Hart and J. Murphy (eds) *Brands: The New Wealth Creators*, Basingstoke: Palgrave.

Murray, S. (2002) 'Harry Potter, Inc', *M/C: A Journal of Media and Culture*, 5(4). Available online at http://www.media-culture.org.au/mc/0203/recycling.php. (accessed 20 October 2006).

—— (2004) '"Celebrating the story the way it is": cultural studies, corporate media and the contested utility of fandom', *Continuum: Journal of Media and Cultural Studies*, 18(1): 7–25.

—— (2005) 'Brand loyalties: rethinking content within global corporate media', *Media, Culture & Society*, 27(3): 415–35.

Natale, R. (1995) 'Three companies wage battle for the hearts – and ears – of US moviegoers', *Los Angeles Times*, 5 September: D1.

Nathan, I. (2001) 'Please believe the hype', *The Times*, 6 December: 14.

Naughton, J. (2003) 'Time Warner name game won't heal old wounds', *Guardian* (Business Section), 21 September: 8.

Nava, M. (1997) 'Framing advertising: cultural analysis and the incrimination of visual texts', in M. Nava, A. Blake, I. MacRury and B. Richards (eds) *Buy This Book: Studies in Advertising and Consumption*, London: Routledge.

Neale, S. (2003) 'Hollywood blockbusters: historical dimensions', in J. Stringer (ed.) *Movie Blockbusters*, London: Routledge.

Nisch, K. (2002) 'JGA Inc: Warner Bros studio store'. Available online at http://www.visualstore.com (accessed 1 November 2003).

Nixon, S. (2002) 'Re-imagining the ad agency: the cultural connotations of economic forms', in P. Du Gay and M. Pryke (eds) *Cultural Economy*, London: Sage.

Nottingham Evening Post (1998), 20 November.

Nussenbaum, E. (2003) 'Coming to a theater near you: the moviemercial', *New York Times*, 21 September: B4.

—— (2004) 'Products slide into more TV shows', *New York Times*, 6 September: C1.

Olsen, Eric J. (1998) 'Fresh star sounds', *Variety*. Available online at http://www.variety.com/ (accessed 8 March 2004).

Owen, C. (1999) 'Big names sign up for Gunwharf shops', *The News* (Portsmouth), 13 September: 3.

—— (2006) 'Global icon that has given us £10 Million boost', *The News* (Portsmouth), 17 October: 3.

Paul, W. (1994) 'The K-Mart audience at the mall movies', *Film History*, 6: 487–501.

Perren, A. (2001) 'Sex, lies and marketing: Miramax and the development of the quality indie blockbuster', *Film Quarterly*, 55(2): 30–40.

Pine, J. and Gilmore, J. (1999) *The Experience Economy*, Boston: Harvard Business School Press.

Pixar (1996) *Annual Report*.

Pokorny, M. (2005) 'Hollywood and the risk environment of movie production in the 1990s', in J. Sedgewick and M. Pokorny (eds) *An Economic History of Film*, London: Routledge.

Pool, B. (1994) 'Security system erected to protect Hollywood sign', *Los Angeles Times*, 24 August: B1, B7.

(1995) 'Portsmouth reborne', *Public Service and Local Government* (24) November.

Pratley, G. (1968) 'Modern masterminds scorn of much-loved old film trademarks', *Variety*, 3 March.

Prince, S. (2000) *A New Pot of Gold: Hollywood under the Electronic Rainbow, 1980–89*, Berkeley: University of California Press.

Pulleine, T. (1990) 'Multiplexing: Basingstoke to Moscow', *Sight and Sound*, Winter: 5.

Pullen, K. (2006) '*The Lord of the Rings* online blockbuster fandom: pleasure and commerce', in E. Mathijs (ed.) *The Lord of the Rings: Popular Culture in Global Context*, London: Wallflower Press.

Quart, A. (2003) *Branded: The Buying and Selling of Teenagers*, New York: Perseus.

Ries, A. and Ries, L. (2002) *The Fall of Advertising and the Rise of PR*, New York: Harper Business.

Romney, J. (2003) 'Everywhere and nowhere', *Sight & Sound*, 13(7): 24–7.

Rose, M. M. (2002) 'NL rings in new strategy', *Hollywood Reporter*, 5 December: 1.

Ross, A. (1999) *The Celebration Chronicles: Life, Liberty and the Pursuit of Property Values in Disney's New Town*, New York: Ballantine Books.

Ross, S. (2000) 'The Hollywood flapper and the culture of media consumption', in D. Desser and G. Jowett (eds) *Hollywood Goes Shopping*, Minneapolis: Minnesota University Press.

Rothman, M. (1992) 'Dolby, Sony sound war noisy affair', *Variety*. Available online at http://www.variety.com/ (accessed 8 March 2004).

Rumbelow, H. and Lister, S. (2002) 'Rings sequel stuff of nightmares and boys pyjamas', *The Times*, 12 December: 3.

Ryan, M. (2001) *Narrative as Virtual Reality: Immersion and Interactivity in Literature and Electronic Media*, Baltimore: Johns Hopkins University Press.

Sandler, K. (1998) 'Introduction: *Looney Tunes* and merry metonyms', in K. Sandler (ed.) *Reading the Rabbit: Explorations in Warner Bros. Animation*, New Brunswick: Rutgers University Press.

Schatz, T. (1997) 'The return of the Hollywood studio system', in E. Barnouw (ed.) *Conglomerates and the Media*, New York: The New Press.

—— (1998) *The Genius of the System: Hollywood Filmmaking in the Studio Era*, London: Faber and Faber.

Schmitt, B. and Simonson, A. (1997) *Marketing Aesthetics: The Strategic Management of Branding, Identity and Image*, New York: Simon & Schuster.

Schreger, C. (1985) 'Altman, Dolby, and the second sound revolution', in E. Weis and J. Belton (eds) *Film Sound: Theory and Practice*, New York: Columbia University Press.

Schudson, M. (1986) *Advertising, the Uneasy Persuasion*, New York: Basic Books.

Sconce, J. (2004) 'What if?: charting television's new textual boundaries', in L. Spigel and J. Olsson (eds) *Television After TV: Essays on a Medium in Transition*, Durham: Duke University Press.

Seabrook, N. (2000) *Nobrow: The Culture of Marketing, The Marketing of Culture*, London: Methuen.

Sergi, G. (1998) 'A cry in the dark: the role of post-classical film sound', in S. Neale and M. Smith (eds) *Contemporary Hollywood Cinema*, London: Routledge.

—— (2001) 'The sonic playground: Hollywood cinema and its listeners', in M. Stokes and R. Maltby (eds) *Hollywood Spectatorship: Changing Perceptions of Cinema Audiences*, London: British Film Institute.

—— (2004) *The Dolby Era: Film Sound in Contemporary Hollywood*, Manchester: Manchester University Press.

Shankar, A. and Horton, B. (1999) 'Ambient media: advertising's new media opportunity', *International Journal of Advertising*, 18(3): 305–21.

Shergill, S. (1993) 'The changing US media and marketing environment: implications for media advertising expenditures in the 1990s', *International Journal of Advertising*, 12(2): 95–115.

Shiel, M. (2001) 'Cinema and the city in history and theory', in M. Shiel and T. Fitzmaurice (eds) *Cinema and the City*, Oxford: Blackwell.

Shone, T. (2004) *Blockbuster: How the Jaws and Jedi Generation Turned Hollywood into a Boom-town*, London: Scribner.

Simensky, L. (1998) 'Selling Bugs Bunny: Warner Bros. and character merchandising in the nineties', in K. Sandler (ed.) *Reading the Rabbit: Explorations in Warner Bros. Animation*, New Brunswick: Rutgers University Press.

Slater, D. (1997) *Consumer Culture and Modernity*, London: Polity Press.

—— (2002) 'Capturing markets from the economists', in P. Du Gay and M. Pryke (eds) *Cultural Economy*, London: Sage.

Slide, A. (1992) *Nitrate Won't Wait: A History of Film Preservation in the United States*, Jefferson, NC: McFarland.

Smith, D. (2005) 'Star Wars empire strikes gold', *Observer*, 15 May: 3.

Smith, M. (1998) 'On the philosophy of Hollywood history', in S. Neale and M. Smith (eds) *Contemporary Hollywood Cinema*, London: Routledge.

Sobchack, V. (2004) *Carnal Thoughts: Embodiment and Moving Image Culture*, Berkeley: University of California Press.

—— (2005) 'When the ear dreams: Dolby digital and the imagination of sound', *Film Quarterly*, 58(4): 2–15.

Solomon, M. and Englis, B. (1994) 'Reality engineering: blurring the boundaries between commercial signification and popular culture', *Journal of Current Issues and Research Advertising*, 16(2): 1–17.

Springer, C. (2005) 'Playing it cool in *The Matrix*', in S. Gillis (ed.) *The Matrix Trilogy: Cyberpunk Reloaded*, London: Wallflower Press.

Staiger, J. (1990) 'Announcing wares, winning patrons, voicing ideals: thinking about the history and theory of film advertising', *Cinema Journal*, 29(3): 3–31.

Stenger, J. (1997) 'Consuming the planet: Planet Hollywood, stars, and the global consumer culture', *The Velvet Light Trap*, 40: 42–55.

—— (2001) 'Return to Oz: the Hollywood redevelopment project, or film history as urban renewal', in M. Shiel and T. Fitzmaurice (eds) *Cinema and the City*, Oxford: Blackwell.

Stewart, J. B. (2005) *Disney War: The Battle for the Magic Kingdom*, London: Simon & Schuster.

Stole, I. L. (2001) 'Advertising', in R. Maxwell (ed.) *Culture Works*, Minneapolis: University of Minnesota Press.

Storper, M. (1989) 'The transition to flexible specialization in the US Film Industry: external economies, the division of labour, and the crossing of industrial divides', *Cambridge Journal of Economics*, 13: 273–305.

—— (2001) 'Lived effects of the contemporary economy: globalization, inequality and consumer society,' in J. Comaroff and J. L. Comaroff (eds) *Millennial Capitalism and the Culture of Neoliberalism*, Durham: Duke University Press.

Streitfeld, D. (2002) 'The cultural anarchist vs. the Hollywood police states', *Los Angeles Times Magazine*, 22 September: 10–14.

Stringer, J. (ed.) (2003) *Movie Blockbusters*, London: Routledge.

(2000) 'Success by design', *Screen International* (promotional feature), 17 November: 7.

Swallow, J. (2003) *Dark Eye: The Films of David Fincher*, London: Reynolds & Hearn.

(2004) 'Take five', *American Vogue*, September: 717–21, 825, 826.

Taylor, I., Evans, K. and Fraser, P. (1996) *A Tale of Two Cities: Global Change, Local Feeling and Everyday Life in the North of England*, London: Routledge.

Teinowitz, I. (2001) 'Affairs of state: looking for love through branding', *Advertising Age*, 9 April: 8.

(1975) 'The lady may be gone', *Hollywood Reporter* (advertisement), 1 October.

Thomas, P. (2002) 'Gunwharf is not a flop, insists boss', *The News* (Portsmouth), 17 September: 11.

Thompson, K. (2003) 'Fantasy, franchises, and Frodo Baggins: *The Lord of the Rings* and Modern Hollywood', *The Velvet Light Trap*, 52: 45–63.

THX (2003) 'Press release'. Available online at http://www.thx.com/news (accessed 7 October 2004).

Time Warner (1989) *Annual Report*.

Time Warner (1995) *Annual Report*.

Time Warner (1996) *Annual Report*.

Time Warner (1997) *Annual Report*.

Time Warner (1998) *Annual Report*.

Time Warner (2003) *Factbook*.

Tomlinson, J. (1999) *Globalization and Culture*, Cambridge: Polity Press.

Tookey, C. (2002) 'At last, the secret', *Daily Mail*, 15 November: 52.

Tressider, R. (2000) '£50m change to city's face', *Nottingham Evening Post*, 21 February: 1.

Turcotte, S. (1995) '"Gimme a bud!" the feature film product placement industry', unpublished MA thesis. Available online at http://advertising.utexas.edu/research/papers/Turcotte/Toc.html (accessed 15 March 2004).

Twich, E. (2001) 'Gunwharf wipes the floor with rest', *The News* (Portsmouth), 7 December.

Twitchell, J. (1996) *Adcult USA: The Triumph of Advertising in American Culture*, New York: Columbia University Press.

Valenti, J. (1998) 'Collapse of the common wisdom', speech delivered at ShoWest conference. Available http://www.mpaa.org (accessed 10 January 2003).

Wang, S. (2003) 'Recontextualizing copyright: piracy, Hollywood, the state, and globalization', *Cinema Journal*, 43(1): 25–43.

Warner Bros. (1996) 'Welcome to the museum', grand opening guide.

(2000) 'Warner Village rising star', *Screen International* (promotional feature), 28 July: 14–15.

Wasko, J. (1994) *Hollywood in the Information Age*, Cambridge: Polity Press.

—— (2001) *Understanding Disney*, Cambridge: Polity Press.

—— (2003) *How Hollywood Works*, London: Sage.

Wasko, J. and Shanadi, G. (2006) 'More than just rings: merchandise for them all', in E. Mathijs (ed.) *The Lord of the Rings: Popular Culture in Global Context*, London: Wallflower Press.

Wayne, M. (2003) 'Post-Fordism, monopoly capitalism, and Hollywood's media industrial complex', *International Journal of Cultural Studies*, 6(1): 82–103.

Wernick, A. (1991) *Promotional Culture: Advertising, Ideology and Symbolic Expression*, London: Sage.

(1993) 'What's in a logo?', *Los Angeles Times Magazine*, 12 September.

Willmott, M. (2001) *Citizen Brands: Putting Society at the Heart of Your Business*, New York: John Wiley.

Winkler, A. (1999) *Warp-Speed Branding: The Impact of Technology on Marketing*, New York: John Wiley.

Wolf, M. J. (1999) *The Entertainment Economy*, New York: Penguin Books.

Wood, A. (2005) 'Vectorial dynamics: transtextuality and complexity in the matrix', in S. Gillis (ed.) *The Matrix Trilogy: Cyberpunk Reloaded*, London: Wallflower Press.

Wyatt, J. (1994) *High Concept: Movies and Marketing in Hollywood*, Austin: University of Texas Press.

—— (1998) 'The formation of the major independent: Miramax, New Line and the New Hollywood', in S. Neale and M. Smith (eds) *Contemporary Hollywood Cinema*, London: Routledge.

Index